Standing in the Intersection

Standing in the Intersection: Feminist Voices, Feminist Practices in Communication Studies

Edited by Karma R. Chávez and Cindy L. Griffin

Foreword by Marsha Houston

SUNY PRESS

Cover art entitled Hybrid Intersectionality (Self-Portrait)
By Alana Boltwood, 2011
Acrylic and paper on canvass

This painting is part of a series of artworks combining
the sociological concept of "intersectionality" with the
intersection of sets in mathematics. See the full series at
http://meta-geometer.com/other-geometries/intersectionality

Published by
State University of New York Press, Albany

© 2012 State University of New York

For information, contact State University of New York Press, Albany, NY
www.sunypress.edu

Production by Diane Ganeles
Marketing by Anne M. Valentine

Library of Congress Cataloging-in-Publication Data

Standing in the intersection : feminist voices, feminist practices in
communication studies / edited by Karma R. Chávez and Cindy L. Griffin.
    p. cm.
  Includes bibliographical references and index.
  ISBN 978-1-4384-4490-1 (pbk. : alk. paper) — ISBN 978-1-4384-4489-5
(hardcover : alk. paper)
  1. Feminism. 2. Feminist theory. 3. Women—Communication.
  4. Rhetoric—Social aspects. I. Chávez, Karma R. II. Griffin, Cindy L.
  HQ1155.S86 2012
  305.42—dc23   2012003670

  10 9 8 7 6 5 4 3 2 1

Contents

Acknowledgments

This project emerged through our many conversations that transpired during and after coediting a special issue of *Women's Studies in Communication* on power feminism. Throughout that journey, we felt a need to continue to strengthen conversations in feminism and communication and build upon the excellent work that some, though not many, of our colleagues were doing from an intersectional perspective. In the midst of these conversations we realized the 20th anniversary of a special issue of *Women's Studies in Communication* (1988), "What Distinguishes/Ought to Distinguish Feminist Scholarship in Communication Studies?" had arrived. In that issue, feminists, including Lois Self, Karlyn Kohrs Campbell, Celeste Condit, Sonja Foss, Karen Foss, Marlene Fine, Jan Muto, Julia Wood, Marsha Houston, Carole Spitzack, and Kathryn Carter, offered their thoughts regarding the state of feminist scholarship and their visions for where it might be headed. We are grateful to these feminists for initiating that conversation, and we used that question, and their ideas, as our impetus for our brainstorming and thinking about how we might contribute to feminist intersectional scholarship.

We decided to reintroduce that question at two different panels in 2009, one sponsored by the Organization for Research on Women and Communication at the Western States Communication Association Conference and the other sponsored by the Feminist and Women's Studies Division, and also featured as a Five Years Out Spotlight Panel at the National Communication Association Convention. The following scholars took part in those two panels: Bernadette Calafell, Carole Spitzack Daruna, Marlene Fine, Karen Foss, Sonja Foss, Michelle Holling, Jan Muto, and Shanara Reid-Brinkley (WSCA); and Brenda J. Allen, Celeste Condit, Cerise Glenn, Radha Hegde (who was unable to attend at the last minute), Shane

vii

Moreman, Sara McKinnon, and Julia Wood (NCA). These panels, the insights and arguments the scholars offered, and our reflection on the question of the state and place of feminist scholarship helped to frame our thinking on the issues in this book, and we are grateful to all the participants for their willingness to share their ideas, question one another, and consider carefully the ways feminist scholarship is linked to intersectional ideas and practices.

At the 2009 NCA Convention, we also held a preconference seminar, and this is where most of the essays in this collection began. We are grateful to the following participants: Janell Bauer, Olga Idriss Davis, Maisha Fields Vogel, Shiv Ganesh, Cerise Glenn, Leslie Hahner, Sara Hayden, Michelle Kelsey (who was unable to attend at the last minute), Sara McKinnon, Lynn O'Brien Hallstein, Denise Oles-Acevedo, T. M. Linda Scholz, Christine Scodari, Danielle Stern, Carly Woods, and Kate Zittlow Rogness. The conversations, questions, agreements, and disagreements offered during that seminar helped us think in new ways about intersectional scholarship and feminisms. We appreciate the honesty of these scholars, their careful work, and their insistence on integrity and innovation in their feminist scholarship.

We also are very appreciative of the helpful feedback we received on our introduction from Marsha Houston, Aimee Carrillo Rowe, and Sara McKinnon. Lester Olson and Shanara Reid-Brinkley pointed us to existing scholarship we had not been aware of, and for that we are very grateful. At SUNY Press, we are thankful that Nancy Ellegate originally agreed to take on this project, and we are incredibly grateful for the amazing work of our editor, Beth Bouloukos, who assumed control of the project and efficiently moved it through this process.

We thank Belle Edson for initially introducing us. Of course, our scholarship is strengthened and nurtured by our partners, Sara McKinnon and Michael Harte, and our numerous, faithful, and entertaining animal companions; for them we are extraordinarily thankful. Finally, to Trouble and Bruiser, it's been a great ride.

Foreword

Difficult Dialogues:
Intersectionality as Lived Experience[1]

Marsha Houston

At a National Communication Association (NCA) meeting during the 1990s, an Asian American woman colleague greeted me warmly and said, "Marsha, you figure in a lot of people's mythologies! I've just come from a panel where someone was discussing you." Although the personal reference was a bit disconcerting—since *I* and not *my work* was the subject of discussion—because my colleague and I had known each other a while and her comment was accompanied by an ironic smile, I didn't need to ask who had said what. On more than one occasion, I had asked a question, presented a paper, or provided a response to a panel at the NCA or other communication association meetings that were intended to promote understanding of women's diversity, but that others (particularly white others) interpreted as accusing them of being "racist."

For example, in the mid-1980s I attended an NCA Women's Caucus panel on "diversity" in feminist communication research. All the presenters were white women; among them were lesbian scholars who spoke as insiders about communication and lesbian identities. I wondered why there were no scholars of color speaking as insiders about our communicative lives. When the question and answer period opened, I turned to my mentor and dissertation advisor who was sitting next to me and whispered something like, "How can they truly explore *diversity* when all of them are white?" "Well," she replied, "ask them." I did; and this initiated a conversation that enmeshed me in the mythologies of certain feminist communication scholars for many years.

In the introduction to this volume, Griffin and Chávez effectively summarize a history of published feminist and related scholarship

that has advanced intersectional understandings of human communication. They detail some of the ways those efforts have been
impeded, reframed, expanded, and complexified. But there is a history of efforts to center ideologies of difference, diversity, and intersectionality in feminist communication research that is seldom
apparent in published scholarship. That history is indicated in the
encounter at the NCA panel that I described above; it is a back story
of sometimes uncomfortable but often illuminating conversations
among innumerable feminist scholars from diverse backgrounds
that incited or inspired research that advanced intersectional perspectives. It is also a story of feminist scholars from marginalized
groups, mostly women of color and lesbian women, who struggled
to claim, assert, embrace, and celebrate their intersecting identities
in face-to-face interactions as well as in print. Finally, the back story
of efforts to make intersectional perspectives central to feminist
communication research is about scholars from socially dominant
groups (e.g., white, middle-class, heterosexual, and/or able-bodied),
some of whom encouraged or employed such perspectives, while
many others too often ignored and denied their social privilege, its
influences on their scholarship, and their power to silence the work
of scholars without such privilege.

In the mid-1990s, a white feminist was asked why her special
issue of a communication journal focused on feminist rhetorical scholarship included no articles by or about women of color.
I was told that her response was, "Let *them* do *their own* special
issue!" Despite the roadblocks that she and other feminist scholars
had encountered in getting feminist voices heard in communication journals, this scholar's response suggested that all researchers
and research approaches were accorded easy and equal access to our
journals. I once pointed out to a white feminist scholar that the
question she had just asked about my work was one I often heard
from white women. This encounter became a controlling vignette
in an essay that she later published in which I was excoriated for
calling attention to her race in responding to her question; after
all, she considered herself able to "transcend" race. Yet as Chávez
and Griffin remind us, there are no interracial encounters between
women that are not simultaneously informed by each woman's
race, with its attendant histories, privileges, or oppressions, as well
as by gender. Too often, feminist communication scholars writing
in the last three decades of the 20th century such as the two individuals mentioned above, had a command of theory, but no sense
of how theoretical concepts related to feminist praxis and communicative performance; to use Griffin and Chávez's metaphor, they

had no conception of "theory in flesh," of intersectionality as lived experience.

The conversations I have recounted give some indication of the extent to which concepts related to intersectionality (e.g., diversity, multiple identity, multiple oppression, white privilege) were resisted, ignored, or marginalized in the first four decades of feminist communication research. That resistance is apparent in the majority of published work in which elite, heterosexual, white women's communicative performances are universalized or in which monolithic conceptual frameworks focused solely on gender are employed.

When I completed my doctoral program in 1982, I was unprepared for resistance to intersectionality by feminist scholars. I was mentored at the University of Massachusetts by Fern Johnson, a white feminist scholar who directed my dissertation on Black women's talk.[2] Because much of her own work explored language diversity, she realized that the lived communicative experiences of Black women could not be effectively explored within monolithic conceptual frameworks. Chávez and Griffin trace the origins of intersectionality as a concept in U.S. feminist scholarship to Black women active in the second wave of feminism, which began in the 1970s. I would suggest that its roots are even older, traceable to 19th-century Black women rhetors, such as Maria Stewart, a free woman of color in Boston who was the first American woman to speak in public and leave a record of her speeches. In her "Lecture Delivered at Franklin Hall" (1832), Stewart calls attention to differences between the material conditions of Black and white women that led to differences in their self-definitions:

> O, ye fairer sisters, whose hands are never soiled, whose nerves and muscles are never strained . . . [h]ad it been our lot to have been nursed in the lap of affluence and ease, and to have basked beneath the smiles and sunshine of fortune, should we not have naturally supposed that we were never made to toil?[3]

Patricia Hill Collins argues that some version of what we now call intersectionality always has been a core element of Black women's epistemology.[4]

In 1990, a small group of feminist communication scholars, most of them white, chose to confront some of the challenging issues entailed in intersectionality at the Eighth National Conference on Research in Gender and Communication, for which I served as convener. The conference focused on ethnic-cultural differences among women using the theme "Difficult Dialogues: Gateways and Barriers to Women's Communication Across Cultures." Among the forty-one participants were many pioneers in feminist communication research, including Karen Foss, Sonja Foss, Victoria Leto-DeFrancisco, Roseanne Mandzuik, and Julia Wood. Keynote panelists bell hooks, Elizabeth Spelman, María Lugones, Cheris Kramarae, Dorthy Pennington, Navita Cummings James, and Victoria Chen challenged participants who saw themselves as silenced or oppressed because of their gender to interrogate how white, middle-class privilege implicated them in disadvantaging women without such privilege. In writing about the conference in the journal *Women and Language*, I summarized responses to one of its key questions, "How can feminist scholars ethically examine difference?":

> What emerged . . .was an analogy of relationships among diverse groups of women as alliances. . . . Alliances are based upon mutual trust; each ally builds and sustains that trust by not co-opting, appropriating or cannibalizing the other's history, knowledge, creative products, or skills. . . . Because they regard each other as equals, allies never presume to speak *for* one another.[5]

The "Difficult Dialogues" conference did not end the struggle to foreground intersectional issues in feminist communication research. It was a small meeting, and many feminist scholars were unaware of it. Continued marginalization of intersectional approaches during the following two decades has occasioned this book. I would suggest, however, that through work published by several conference participants and their graduate students after 1990, the conference influenced ongoing scholarly conversations about how women's complex, multifaceted identities are formed, performed, and transformed through communication.

This book aims to move intersectionality to the center of feminist communication research. Writing in the fifth decade of feminist communication scholarship, Chávez, Griffin, and their contributors speak with more nuanced voices and to a more open and sophisticated audience than those of us who first struggled to introduce intersectional issues in our field. The varied theoretical perspectives and research approaches presented in this work are potential catalysts for feminist research programs that can illumine human communication in the full range of its complexities. If, however, scholars use the concepts and approaches presented in this book merely to enhance the number of their publications, the book will not accomplish its transformational goal. For intersectionality to become central to feminist communication scholarship, feminist scholars must develop honest understandings of their own intersecting identities and the influences of their intersectionalities on all facets of their communicative lives. For example, feminist scholars who gain access to publication outlets might use that privilege to act as allies to those whose ideas or approaches are marginalized by or excluded from such outlets, perhaps by encouraging their submissions or including them in special issues. I benefited from such allies throughout my career; the first was the pioneering feminist scholar Cheris Kramarae who invited my contribution to an anthology that she coedited.[6]

If a new generation of scholars embraces intersectional perspectives as personal as well as scholarly outlooks, then the future of feminist communication research will be substantively different from its past, and every back story entailed in that research, each feminist researcher's lived experience, will be affirming and empowering. This is the transformative potential entailed in this book, and I look forward to seeing it realized.

NOTES

1. The author thanks Profs. Janice Hamlet and Karla Scott for their comments on earlier drafts of this essay. The phrase "difficult dialogues" is taken from Johnnella Butler's discussion of resistance to diversifying academic curricula: Johnnella Butler, "Difficult Dialogues," *Women's Review of Books* 6, no. 5 (1989): 16.

2. Marsha Houston Stanback (now Houston), "Code-Switching in Black Women's Speech," doctoral dissertation, University of Massachusetts, 1982.

3. Maria W. Stewart, "Speech Delivered at Franklin Hall (1832)," accessed February 20, 2011, www.blackpast.org/q=1832-maria-w-stewart-why -sit-ye-here-and-die.

4. Patricia Hill Collins, *Black Feminist Thought: Knowledge, Consciousness and the Politics of Empowerment*, 2nd ed. (New York: Routledge, 2000), 257–262.

5. Marsha Houston, "Difficult Dialogues: Report on the 1990 Conference on Research on Gender and Communication," *Women and Language* 22 (1990): 32; emphasis added.

6. Marsha Houston Stanback (now Houston), "Language and Black Woman's Place: Evidence from the Black Middle Class," in *For Alma Mater: Theory and Practice in Feminist Scholarship*, ed. Paula Treichler, Cheris Kramarae, and Beth Stafford (Urbana: University of Illinois Press, 1985), 177–193.

Introduction

Standing at the Intersections of Feminisms, Intersectionality, and Communication Studies

Cindy L. Griffin and Karma R. Chávez

Despite the widespread belief that intersectionality has
arrived, I think that it is important to stop and recognize
that this way of looking at and living within the world
constitutes a new area of inquiry that is still in its infancy.
—Patricia Hill Collins[1]

For decades, feminist scholars in communication studies have
urged, pushed, and even invited the field of communication to
consider the problems inherent in some of its foundational assumptions, values, theories, and methods.[2] As feminist scholars generally
have challenged disciplinary norms, critical race, queer, and postco-
lonial feminists continually critiqued feminist scholarship itself for
its assumptions and values, especially as they pertain to thinking of
gender in isolation from other systems of power such as race, class,
nation, and sexuality.[3] These challenges to the foundations of our
discipline, and to feminism, remain necessary: they represent some
of our discipline's most important conversations, dilemmas, and
struggles. The challenges, and the responses to them, ask scholars to
clarify and alter the values and norms of our profession, and they reflect the ever-contested nature of communication scholarship. Both
authors of this introduction have stimulated some of those challenges, participated in them, received them, and listened to others
engage them, and we are continually reminded that many of our
discipline's most venerated assumptions about how communication
and rhetoric work, and how they are at work in the world, reflect a

particular set of ethics, values, preferences, and assumptions about our world and the roles of humans in it. We have a canon, a foundation, and a long-standing tradition of communication research, but these have for too long been built around and informed by singular, monolithic, and homogenous views of identity and subjectivity. As a handful of persistent voices have continued to argue, those views are not, nor have they ever been, sustainable or even productive for communication and rhetorical scholarship. Indeed, as Lisa A. Flores suggests, when individuals live in the borders, they "find themselves with a foot in both worlds." The result is "the sense of being neither" exclusively one identity nor another.[4] Although our extensive body of scholarship tells us a great deal about some people, some places, and some positions of power, it neglects (and even refuses) to tell us much about many other people, and places, with complex identities, subjectivities, and relationships to power. Nearly two decades ago, Marsha Houston wrote specifically about feminist communication theory, articulating that it "has not yet adequately accounted for the different worldviews, different life-changes, and differential treatment of women from nondominant U.S. social groups."[5] And a decade later, in the introduction to their path-breaking collection, *Centering Ourselves*, Houston and Olga Idriss Davis remarked, "placing the traditions of African American women *at the center* of our analyses . . . produces an angle of vision on Black women's communication that is rare."[6] Despite the intellectual labor of feminist communication scholars who challenge both the discipline at large and feminist scholarship specifically, today, such a dearth persists.

Through our own individual experiences in the academy, and through our experiences as colleagues, friends, and allies in that same system, we have become increasingly committed to understanding the ways identities and subjectivities can be theorized productively through feminist lenses. Our commitment as feminist scholars of communication and rhetoric is to create new frameworks for understanding the rich and complex facets of identity and subjectivity and to explore the overt and covert uses and manifestations of power and privilege. Our goal is to build upon and help lay a foundation for productive conversations around power, identities, and subjectivities that have been erased, ignored, and under- and inappropriately theorized. Without these conversations, and this theorizing, we argue that communication scholarship moves ever closer to irrelevance. To turn away from exploring them is to deny the complexity of our lives and the communicative exchanges we live by and in; indeed, it is to deny the intersectional and interlocking

conditions of our world. This book, then, responds to these ongoing and pressing intellectual concerns and maintains that theories
of "intersectionality" are vital to the continued viability of feminist communication scholarship. We further maintain that feminist communication scholars have much to contribute to ongoing
conversations about intersectionality. *Standing in the Intersection*
attends to the contours of intersectional thought, theoretically and
methodologically, in order to evidence what rigorous engagement
between feminist communication studies, particularly feminist rhetorical studies, and intersectionality can look like.

This introduction will explore the definitions of and metaphors
for intersectionality and what those definitions and metaphors tell
us about intersectional scholarship and the difficult work scholars
must do. We then provide an overview of key moments in the past
fifty years of communication and rhetorical scholarship—moments
that represent foundational attempts to attend to race, gender, class,
or sexuality—in order to call attention to the ways these first attempts to address identities other than the heterosexual, white,
middle-class male, moved our thinking about intersectionality
forward, stalled that thinking, or perhaps offered some of both. Finally, we turn this discussion toward suggesting what intersectional
scholarship might look like in the work of scholars interested in
studying symbolic exchanges and some of the difficulties inherent to intersectional approaches. With these sections, we hope to
stimulate the thinking of those interested in intersectional work in
communication and rhetorical studies, and beyond, to tease out the
nuances and difficulties of that work and to contribute to the lively
and productive conversations that are just now reaching the pages of
our scholarship regarding intersectionality.

INTERSECTIONALITY:
CONSIDERATIONS, DEFINITIONS, METAPHORS

During the midst of multiple, interwoven struggles for liberation
catalyzed in the middle of the 20th century in the United States,
U.S. third world feminists began to theorize the "multiple displace-
ments" that shaped U.S. women of color identities.[7] These feminists
of color, working-class feminists, and lesbians articulated the "interlocking" nature, as well as the "double" or "multiple jeopardy"[8]
of having several oppressed identities.[9] From writings and speeches
such as these, Black[10] feminist legal scholar Kimberlé Crenshaw
named and derived a theory of intersectionality. Crenshaw's early
work articulated the ways in which the experiences of women of

color, poor, and immigrant women are subsumed and erased in legal practices, political decisions, and social norms. This erasure occurs, according to Crenshaw, because in fundamental ways, all women are assumed to be white, and all Blacks are assumed to be men within arenas such as law, politics, and media representation.[11] Crenshaw explains how an inability to think outside of singular axes of identity has detrimental effects for women of color. Through examining how both feminist and antiracist identity discourse elide the problem of difference, and how race and gender (as well as class and sexuality) interact in the lives of women of color, Crenshaw evidences the need to prioritize the multiple factors that constitute the lives of women of color, as opposed to attending only to issues of gender or race. For example, focusing only on a single axis of identity, such as gender, when constructing policies and offering services designed to help rape survivors ignores the many resources that may not be available to women of color due to race, class, and culture. Because all women can become victims of rape, it might seem as if any policy or service provision designed to help women as a general category should be sufficient; however, race, gender, and class interact to construe different experiences for women of color and poor women as compared to white and middle-class women. White, middle-class women, for instance, are more likely to be financially secure than working-class women of color. White, middle-class women rarely are oppressed because of their race, thus their needs after a rape may be very different when compared to working-class women of color, who may have needs that extend beyond recovering from the violent act (e.g., finding and affording safe shelter, accessing health care, confronting institutionalized racism, and gaining assistance with language barriers, are a few of the differences in possible needs). If service providers are equipped only to help white middle-class women recover from a rape and do not account for the other social and economic conditions that may be present for poor women and women of color, this service effectively favors the needs of white or middle-class women. This absence of attention to the needs of poor and working-class women of color is but one example that speaks to the necessity of thinking more complexly about identity politics and difference in order to adequately theorize and account for the lives of poor women and women of color.

To be sure, as Lester C. Olson notes in this volume, the idea of intersectionality as Crenshaw conceives it bears its own erasures, particularly of sexuality and class, since Crenshaw primarily emphasizes race and gender. Still, the term possesses significant staying power and traction for both concretely describing how interlocking oppressions manifest in relation to various structures, and in providing a metaphorical resource with which to engage in theory construction, as many of the authors in this collection do. As Olson also notes in an earlier published work on Audre Lorde, no metaphor for describing the condition of being multiply oppressed is perfectly adequate.[12] The premises put forth in Crenshaw's theory of intersectionality have been articulated variously as "interlocking oppressions,"[13] "theory in the flesh,"[14] avoiding "pop-bead metaphysics" or "additive identity politics,"[15] "seriality,"[16] "intermeshing oppressions" and "curdling vs. separation,"[17] "matrix of domination,"[18] and "coalitional subjectivity,"[19] with each metaphor or perspective offering something slightly different. These articulations have, indeed, helped scholars work with intersectional theories, yet, as feminist scholars from various disciplines attempted to name, describe, and access women's multifaceted identities, points of contention emerged. We suggest that these points of contention speak not only to the complexities of intersectional identities, politics, and theories but also to the role of and utility for intersectional theories and practices for feminist communication studies. Although intersectionality remains the most flexible and useful term for our purposes, we realize that in deciding upon this term as opposed to other options, we enact our own erasures. This is a risk that we believe is worth taking in order to advance the kind of work we have included in this collection. We hope readers will allow us some flexibility and understanding given the limits of language to always adequately convey meaning. What follows is a review of some of the most poignant of these metaphors, descriptions, and contentions.

Interlocking Oppressions

Writing in the 1970s, the Combahee River Collective, a radical collective of Black lesbian feminists, articulates its politics as follows: "we are actively committed to struggling against racial, sexual, heterosexual, and class oppression and see as our particular task the development of integrated analysis and practice based upon the fact that the major systems of oppression are interlocking."[20] An example of what Moraga and Anzaldúa later termed a "theory in the flesh," members of the Collective utilize their multiply-oppressed identities to derive a theory of identity and a feminist politics. As the now familiar story goes, during the second wave of the U.S. feminist movement, many white, heterosexual, middle-class feminists talked only of oppression against a seemingly unified category of women—white, heterosexual, middle-class women. Women of color, third world women, working-class and poor women, and lesbians challenged this politics as myopic, racist, homophobic, classist, and imperialistic. Born of Black women's identities, the Combahee River Collective's "A Black Feminist Statement" is one of the (if not the) foundational statements that names and advocates an intersectional approach to feminism. The authors note that there is no "racial" or "sexual" oppression; rather, a "racial-sexual oppression" always occurs because *both* racism *and* sexism *exist*. Thinking in terms of racial-sexual oppression, the Combahee River Collective argues, necessitates recognition of, and explanation for, the configurations of racial privilege (or oppression) and sexual oppression (or privilege), which are central to intersectionality.

Theory in the Flesh

In 1981, Cherríe Moraga and Gloria Anzaldúa published *This Bridge Called My Back: Writings by Radical Women of Color*. This anthology gave birth to the label "theory in the flesh" and helped scholars begin to articulate theories of intersectionality that address class inequities, racism, sexism, and heterosexism. Moraga explains:

> When I lifted the lid to my lesbianism, a profound connection with my mother reawakened in me. It wasn't until I acknowledged and confronted my own lesbianism in the flesh, that my heartfelt identification with and empathy for my mother's oppression—due to being poor, uneducated, and Chicana—was realized. My lesbianism is the avenue through which I have learned the most about silence and oppression, and it continues to be the most tactile reminder to me that we are not free human beings.[21]

Moraga suggests that "silence is like starvation" and that from one starvation "other starvations can be recognized, if one is willing to take the risk of making the connection."[22] Intersectionality, as a theory in the flesh, then, recognizes that "looking like a white girl ain't so great," since women can be beaten "on the street for being a dyke." And, if "my sister's being beaten because she's Black, it's pretty much the same principle. . . . In this country, lesbianism is a poverty—as is being brown, as is being a woman, as is being just plain poor." Moraga, and the other writers in *This Bridge*, urge feminists to move beyond dealing with oppression on a purely theoretical basis: "The danger lies in ranking the oppression. *The danger lies in failing to acknowledge the specificity of the oppression.*"

Theorizing from and in the flesh, in sum, involves working with emotion and from the heart, "grappling with the source of our own oppression" because, "without naming the enemy within ourselves and outside of us, no authentic, non-hierarchical connection among oppressed groups can take place."[23] As an important piece of intersectional history, this theory requires that scholars identify, and give voice to, the interconnected nature of being silenced, in multiple ways, and the lived (bodily) manifestations of those silencings.

Pop-Bead Metaphysics

It is no secret that many white, middle-class, heterosexual feminists largely ignored queer, working-class or poor women of color's insistence that a singular focus on gender oppression was highly problematic. Recognizing that this ignorance erased the many privileges that such women held on account of race, class, and sexual orientation, some privileged feminists did work with queer, working-class women of color as allies, in order to help convey the necessity of understanding interlocking oppressions *and* privileges.[24] Describing her concern for what she sees as a metaphysical "sleight of hand," Elizabeth Spelman, in *Inessential Woman*, suggests that she cannot talk about the "woman" part of herself without also talking about the "white" part of herself: identity is not analogous to a Tootsie Roll or a necklace made of pop beads. Citing Beverly Smith, Spelman argues for the impossibility of this pop-bead metaphysics because "Women don't lead their lives like, 'Well this part is race, and this is class, and this part has to do with women's identities' so it's confusing."[25] Contrary to this additive, pop-bead sleight of hand, there never are situations in which one woman's whiteness and another woman's Blackness or brownness do not profoundly affect or inform what it means to be a woman.

For Spelman, attempts at this type of conceptual tidiness—the claim that there is some category "woman" and some category "man," distinct from a separate category "white" and yet another "Black"—only results in linguistic and epistemic failure. An additive, pop-bead mentality can only lead to the erasure of profound historical and contemporary inequities, oppressions, privileges, and opportunities. In order to even talk about the identities of "woman," "of color," or "white," and whether there are similarities or differences, Spelman claims we must first ask "Who is doing the investigating? Whose views are heard and accepted? Why? What criteria are used for similarity and difference? Finally, and most important, what is said to follow from the exposed similarity or difference?

Have those under investigation been asked what they think?"[26] For
Spelman, the authors of *This Bridge*, and the Combahee River Collective, theories of intersectionality, then, must make use of "conceptual messiness," rather than tidiness, and epistemic fluidity,
rather than separation.

Curdling versus Separation

As evidenced by Spelman, theories of intersectionality are often
centrally concerned with the politics of coalition and alliance building. This concern means that feminists must also think complexly
about oppressions and identity outside the specific context of feminist movements and in relation to feminist goals and the experiences
of women and queer people in other movement contexts. Feminist
concerns thus intersect with alliance building among and within
movements such as those for racial, class, or sexual liberation. In
gesturing toward the difficulty of both building alliance and adopting an intersectional approach within nationalistic politics, María
Lugones uses the specific case of Latino/a nationalisms and notions
of home therein in order to uncover how logics of oppression work
to prevent an intersectional analysis and the possibility of coalition
building. To demonstrate these logics, Lugones begins with a discussion of "curdling-separation" as a "metaphor for both impurity and
resistance."[27] When something curdles, rather than completely separating, the parts actually "coalesce toward" one another. The parts
are interlocked and intermeshed, rather than distinct. On the other
hand, splitting or separating something "impure," into its "pure"
elements, is an act of power, a colonial logic. Separation/purity are
conceptually at odds with intersectional thinking and coalition. As
a logic of curdling, Lugones offers the notion of "*mestizaje*," which
she defines as "*in the middle of either/or, ambiguity, and thinking
of acts that belong in lives lived in mestizo ways*," and explains,
"*Mestizaje* defies control through simultaneously asserting the impure, curdled multiple state and rejecting fragmentation into pure
parts."[28] *Mestizaje* involves "breaching and abandoning dichotomies," resisting notions of purity, of control over possibilities, and
of domination.

Curdling implies multiplicity rather than fragmentation. It
operates through a logic of complexity, heterogeneity, and one in
which "each person is multiple, nonfragmented, embodied." Curdling calls attention to interlocking and intermeshing oppressions
and stands opposed to "split-separation," which is the logic of the
oppressor. "According to [split-separation,] the logic of purity, the

social world is both unified and fragmented, homogenous, hierarchi-cally ordered."[29] Lugones sees that both logics exist simultaneously, but the curdling metaphor offers a useful conceptual framework for understanding intersectionality, while the metaphor of separation is conceptually useful for understanding the operation of oppression.

Though split-separation and fragmentation are logics of white domination and colonial oppression, within oppressed communities, people of color often resort to homespaces (nations) as resources of resistance. Within these homespaces, however, the split-separation logic of the oppressor often reigns. Those Lugones describes as the "culturally homeless" are subject to "authenticity tests" that chal-lenge whether they truly "belong" to the home. Some, often queers and women, who challenge sexism are considered "fakes." As Lu-gones explains, one's "body, its color, features, its movement, and the culture expressed in its movements and clothes, [are] all up for mistrust and inspection. One's voice, the accent in one's voice, the culture in one's speech, deeds, ways inspected, over and over by those one would like to call one's own."[30] When the split-separation paradigm reigns within oppressed communities, it tries to purify the oppressed group and erase or negate those who would pollute the pu-rity. In this way, those who belong are "transparent," which means that these individuals understand a group's ways, needs, and inter-ests as their own. Other individuals, however, who are "thick," are aware of their otherness to the group.[31] As "transparents," individu-als within groups fail to recognize their own differences from other individuals within that group. When groups assume "solidness" of the group, which means solidness of the transparents, they deny the possibilities of building coalitions and of curdling, or engaging in an intersectional understanding of the group, because the needs of the "thicks" aren't seen or considered valid. And in some cases, when those thicks are "culturally homeless," they are considered inau-thentic and thus split off from the purity of the group.

Transparency is also part of the power of what Spelman has deemed "boomerang perception," whereby whites see people of color as the same as, and different from, the self at the same time.[32] Within boomerang perception, the person of color is only an image, as in both a reflection and an imitation, in the eyes of whites, and this perception always comes back to whiteness as origin. As Spel-man argues: "'I look at you and come right back to myself.'"[33] A similar logic operates within "homespaces" between individuals possessing the logic of transparents and their perceptions of individ-uals who are thicks, those "relegated to the margins in the politics of intragroup contestation,"[34] specifically those who are queer. And this test of authenticity/purity is a manifestation of internalizing the colonial gaze. Lugones writes:

> The idea of nation brings the logic of the colonizer inside Latino life. The logic of modernity that "unifies" the disparate elements that face the colonizer oppositionally prevents them from creating disruptions of traditions in their encounters with domination. A unified front is itself a commitment to a logic of self-destruction: nationalism leaves colonialism undisturbed when it places different Latino practices, values, traditions and limits outside of critique and recreations. . . . Nationalism leaves colonialism undisturbed when it affirms a line of connection between the colonizer and the colonized in their weddedness to heterosexuality. [35]

As a form of nationalistic identification, it is worth questioning under what conditions the identification is created, and who is left outside of the nation's borders. Nearly every nationalistic movement in U.S. history has explicitly or implicitly denounced queer sexualities and genders in order to preserve patriarchy and ensure women's role in the reproduction of that nation. The logic of purity, maintaining a proper gender/sexuality for all members of the nation, and clear gender roles for men and for women, is a colonial logic, and one that ignores the intermeshing of oppressions. Assuming that belonging is only transparent, Lugones argues, forecloses genuine possibilities for coalition and alliance building and, we argue, for understanding the complex role communication plays in maintaining hegemonic structures and practices.

Coalitional Subjectivity and Differential Belonging

Within the field of communication studies, Aimee Carrillo Rowe successfully utilizes and extends feminist intersectional theories to help scholars understand the possibilities for, and failure of, feminist alliances. Her work moves scholars toward theorizing intersectionality because, as seen above, the failure to consider oppression and privilege as interlocking or intermeshing often prevents alliances. Moreover, Carrillo Rowe's notions both emerge from, and provide a mechanism for, understanding identity and power as intermeshing. Carrillo Rowe extends Chela Sandoval's notion of "differential consciousness," which refers to the mode of consciousness utilized by third world feminists who must shift "between and among" different positions "like the clutch of an automobile, the mechanism that permits the driver to select, engage, and disengage gears in a system for the transmission of power."[36] Carrillo Rowe offers "differential belonging," which is "a politics of relation,"[37] that contends who we love and relate to is political. Building feminist alliances across racial (and other) difference helps people to create what Carrillo Rowe names "coalitional subjectivities." One achieves a coalitional subjectivity when she sees her oppression and privilege as inextricably bound to others and when she cannot envision her existence and politics as separate from others' existence and politics. Developing a coalitional subjectivity can only occur when alliances and belongings are built across power lines so that privileged and oppressed people learn to long to belong to one another and to learn from one another about the nature of power and the possibility for social change. These concepts advance theories of intersectionality because the multiply displaced location from which Sandoval and Carrillo Rowe write is that which authorizes the differential movement.

Coalitional subjectivity, power lines, and differential belonging insist that scholars theorize the intersections of belonging as dynamic and shifting. The point of what Carrillo Rowe calls transracial belonging is to understand these multiplicities and how they can, do, and must shift for feminist politics. The transracial feminist alliances across power lines that Carrillo Rowe theorizes illuminate the necessity of developing a feminist coalitional subjectivity that accounts for the multiplicity of identity, positionality, *and* relationality in order to build effective alliances. Carrillo Rowe sheds light upon historical reasons why some white feminists have had difficulty accepting intersectionality and the importance of interlocking oppressions. Since intersections have been articulated as issues of oppression, talking about intersectionality seems to exclude white women. However, theorizing transracial belonging emphasizes the intersections between feminist allies, evidences the dynamic nature of oppression *and* privilege, and through transracial belonging, white, straight, middle-class feminists can develop a subjectivity that does and must account for interlocking oppression and privilege.

Intersectional Metaphors:
Multiplicity, Power, Privilege, and Politics

These powerful and different metaphors for and theories of what we are organizing under the name, intersectionality, help point to the myriad ways feminist scholars have conceptualized the question of multiplicity in relation to power, oppression, and privilege. As we have shown here, some of these approaches focus on having multiply oppressed identities, others emphasize the logics of oppression and critique singular approaches to identity, and still others examine the important interplay between privilege and oppression within individual subjects. Though the approaches here differ in both obvious and nuanced ways, what they share and call attention to is a commitment to challenging simplistic thinking in terms of only one axis of identity, form of oppression, or manifestation of power. These differences in approach are also important because they identify the various routes one might take in theorizing the complexity of intersectionality and help scholars highlight the political agendas and practices within these routes. Placing these approaches in conversation, as we have done here, provides feminists with an array of resources from which to theorize how oppression and resistance work without having to rely on pure or singular theories, and with our political, social, and emotional frameworks clearly in focus.

Though exceptions exist, much of the early work of our discipline that wrestles with questions of the politics of identity and subjectivity considers identities as singular, pure, and separate from one another. Important complexities have been lost as we have tried to narrow experiences and identities into singular and homogenous nouns or monolithic, all-encompassing adjectives. In the next section, we offer a brief exploration of early communication scholarship on identity, and then gesture toward a vision of what intersectional scholarship does and might look like in the future.[38]

APPROACHES TO COMMUNICATION SCHOLARSHIP: BEYOND A POP-BEAD EPISTEMOLOGY

In one of her many essays on difference, Houston opens with the following observation: "Ever since Sojourner Truth asked her famous question, 'Ain't I a woman?' during a speech at an 1851 women's rights meeting, feminist women from nondominant social groups (Folb 1985) have openly challenged the exclusion of their experiences from the public discourse about women."[39] Despite this seemingly evident point, for the most part, the earliest essays in communication journals that acknowledged nondominant perspectives come from a pop-bead metaphysical perspective, an attempt at conceptual neatness, and ignore the interlocking impacts of gender and race, sexuality, and class.[40] We demonstrate this by examining early communication scholarship on race, we then move to discuss

LGBTQ issues, we briefly address class and disability before ending on feminist and gender scholarship.

Examining early scholarship that took up the issue of "race" reveals the pop-bead perspective. Franklyn S. Haiman's, "The Rhetoric of the Streets: Some Legal and Ethical Considerations"; Herbert W. Simons, "Patterns of Persuasion in the Civil Rights Struggle"; Parke G. Burgess, "The Rhetoric of Black Power: A Moral Demand?" and Mary G. McEdwards, "Agitative Rhetoric: Its Na-ture and Effect" are among the first essays in our communication journals that attempt an explanation of civil rights discourses and a centering of Black perspectives.[41] Although these are foundational and honest attempts to understand civil rights rhetoric within the traditional neo-Aristotelian paradigm, each takes an approach that argues that there is "white" and "Black," "white" has power, while "Black" does not, and "Black" is making a good deal of "noise" that makes "white" uncomfortable and uncertain.

Philip C. Wander's "The Savage Child: The Image of the Negro in the ProSlavery Movement" prompted scholars to begin to exam-ine not just the individual "'beads" but their relationship to power in more nuanced ways.[42] In this essay, Wander names the bead "rac-ism" and asks communication scholars to consider what it is, and how it works, on its own terms. Wander is joined by Francis S. Dub-ner's "Nonverbal Aspects of Black English" and Jack L. Whitehead and Leslie Miller's "Correspondence between Evaluations of Chil-dren's Speech and Speech Anticipated upon the Basis of Stereotype," scholars who begin to attempt to identify and explain the relation-ship of power and racism to Black individuals.[43] Other scholars begin to take up these questions of race, power, and racism, includ-ing Jack L. Daniel's "Black Folk and Speech Education"[44]; W. A. D. Riach's "'Telling It Like It Is': An Examination of Black Theatre as Rhetoric"[45]; Arthur L. Smith's "Some Characteristics of the Black Religious Audience"[46]; Lloyd D. Powers's "Chicano Rhetoric: Some Basic Concepts"[47]; Michael Victor Sedano's, "Chicanismo: A Rhetor-ical Analysis of Themes and Images of Selected Poetry from the Chi-cano Movement"[48]; and Alberto Gonzalez's "Mexican 'Otherness' in the Rhetoric of Mexican Americans."[49] Daniel makes a logical and impassioned argument for the importance of speech education to Black people. Riach argues that Black discourse is "real," while white discourse is "escapist," a Western aesthetic that has run its course, and that it is now impossible to construct anything mean-ingful within its decaying structure. Powers, Sedano, and Gonzalez disrupt the logic that individuals can be "studied" from outside and argue instead that any legitimate understanding of the discourse of a group necessitates understanding the norms, practices, beliefs, angst, talents, and inner workings of that community.[50] Early scholarship on racial identities, though often engaging with questions of power and racism, generally approached race as isolated from most other facets of identity and power.

Significantly, few essays address gay and lesbian communication prior to the edited collection *Gayspeak*.[51] These essays include Julia P. Stanley's "Homosexual Slang"; James W. Chesebro, John F. Cragan, and Patricia McCullough's "The Small Group Technique of the Radical Revolutionary"; Joseph Hayes's "Gayspeak"; and Barry Brummett's "A Pentadic Analysis of Ideologies in Two Gay Rights Controversies."[52] These essays each approach gay people and gay rhetoric as monolithic and male, and distinct from other minority groups, though Hayes does question whether the characteristics of gay speech are also impacted by factors such as race and class. Other essays on gay and lesbian people are scarce within the communication discipline until 2004, and, for the most part, it is only after this time that bisexual, transgender, or queer perspectives are introduced to the discipline.[53] Discussions of disability, outside of a few scant articles on speech impediments, only recently entered scholarly conversations in communication.[54]

Although related fields of sociology, linguistics, and political science regularly talked of social class, communication scholars rarely addressed social class. This scholarship, however, offers some of the most significant nods in the direction of intersectional analysis. Frederick Williams and Rita C. Naremore's essay "On the Functional Analysis of Social Class Differences in Modes of Speech," which, though published in a communication journal, largely takes a sociolinguistic approach to the research.[55] Still, the essay accounts for race and sex in relation to social class as relevant variables. Jack Daniel's essay, "The Poor," argues that the poor are "aliens in an affluent society," and understanding the problem of communication across the poor/affluent divide should be approached as a cross-cultural dilemma.[56] Importantly, Daniel also mentions the intersection between race and class, as he notes that a number of people in the poor class are also members of minority groups, though this fact does not feature in the analysis he offers. The early work of Gerry Philipsen, including, "Speaking 'Like a Man' in Teamsterville: Culture Patterns of Role Enactment in an Urban Neighborhood" and "Places for Speaking in Teamsterville," offers interesting intersectional discussions of how location, class, gender, and race manifest in how people speak to one another and develop social roles.[57] Although these early essays on class approach intersectionality, few such essays exist.[58]

We suggest that the power dynamics at play here are several: nonintersectional scholarship helps preserve a specific understanding of who can speak and how that person or those people should speak. Nonintersectional approaches also sanction speaking about Others as a legitimate practice (Spelman's question "have those under investigation been asked what they think?" is important here). Nonintersectional approaches embrace Lugones's description of fragmentation, which divides aspects of a self into discrete and clearly defined categories and posits that those aspects be theorized in monolithic ways. Generally, race, as a label, applies to those who are not white, sex or gender to those who are not male, sexuality to those who are not straight, and the like. Scholarship is produced in ways that erase or minimize the damages inflicted (structurally or personally) by those with power and privilege. And, finally, the communication of those with power and privilege need not be called into question.

Not surprisingly, early feminist communication studies disrupted the monolithic view of "male" but followed a similar trajectory to that of scholarship on "race" and "sexuality" as singular or isolated categories. Although foundational to bringing "women" into the conversation, essays such as Brenda Robinson Hancock's "Affirmation by Negation in the Women's Liberation Movement"; Karlyn Kohrs Campbell's "The Rhetoric of Women's Liberation: An Oxymoron"; and Cheris Kramer's (now Kramarae's), "Women's Speech: Separate but Unequal?" reinscribe the category of "woman" as occupied by a monolithic group of white, middle-class, heterosexual females.[59] And, while several essays on African American women bring Black women into the analysis in a pop-bead fashion, it is not until Houston's "What Makes Scholarship About Black Women and Communication Feminist Communication Scholarship?"; "Feminist Theory and Black Women's Talk"; and "The Politics of Difference: Race, Class, and Women's Communication" that theories and ideas of intersectionality really come into play.[60] Since Houston's essays and her persistent work within the field to call attention to the necessity of an intersectional approach to scholarship, several feminist communication scholars have introduced intersectional perspectives or called for their importance. Brenda J. Allen, Karen Aschraft, Bernadette Marie Calafell, Aimee Carrillo Rowe, Karma R. Chávez, Carrie Crenshaw, Olga Idriss Davis, Lisa A. Flores, Michelle A. Holling, Sara L. McKinnon, Aysel Morin, Shane T. Moreman, Dawn Marie McIntosh, Lester C. Olson, Patricia S. Parker, Karla D. Scott, and others[61] have dealt with the conceptual messiness, the slipperiness of identities (ascribed or avowed),

the embodied experiences of oppressions and their material implications, and what standing at those intersections means not only for
individuals but for communication theories and scholarship.[62] Such
approaches are especially needed in communication studies, which
is historically a field that produces theories designed to maintain and
enhance the status quo. Even in those examples of communication
theories designed to rupture or challenge the establishment, many
of our discipline's familiar norms and logics are often repeated—
identities are cast as unified and as transparent rather than thick, for
example, while singular aspects of oppression and one-directional
analyses of power are offered so that we learn of pop-bead episte-
mologies and metaphysics rather than curdling and coalitional ones.
Still, without these foundational approaches to feminist intersectional communication scholarship, we would not be as informed as
we are, or as able to offer this volume of intersectional work.

These key works are significant, and their messages, important,
yet we believe that, in large part, the call to intersectionality has
not had a widespread impact on the field. This, in part, stems from
the way communication, subjectivity, and identity have been approached in rhetorical and social-scientific scholarship. For example, even our most complicated communication models, such as the
transactional model, assume stable subjects who communicate in
a particular communicative environment. These models often fail
to take up questions of power and difference between communicators and also in how communicators are constituted as individuals.
Moreover, as Stanley Deetz and others have argued, communication
is often theorized as the transmission of information and not the
creation of reality.[63] Such a conception of communication suggests
fixed identities and a stable role for communication as a mediator,
and not a creator, of subjectivity, identity, and reality.

Social-scientific approaches to communication also have long
invited marking identities such as race, class, or gender as unique
variables that can be tested independently and in relation to one another. Even though interpretive and critical scholars, including feminists, have denounced the reductionism implied by thinking these
facets of identity as unique variables, such simplicity continues to
pervade communication scholarship more generally by emphasizing
only one "dimension" of identity and neglecting others: as if race
isn't always classed, always gendered, always sexualized, always differently abled, and produced in and by (trans)national contexts. The
rhetorical tradition is equally notorious for such reductionism as a
brief glance at the field beyond what we offer here suggests a focus
on "feminine style,"[64] "Black Nationalism,"[65] "gay liberation,"[66]

"Chicano rhetoric,"[67] "Japanese Culture,"[68] and the "American Indian Movement."[69] The overemphasis on identity-based rhetoric and social movements, while important in suggesting that marginalized voices are central to rhetorical study and challenging the status quo, is equally responsible for promoting a singular perspective on identity and, hence, reproducing normative logics for understanding subjectivities, identities, and communicative behavior. In the next section, we question what these moments of thinking about diverse groups outside of white, property-owning men could look like if they were to incorporate an intersectional analysis.

ALL OF US ARE INTERSECTIONAL
AND SOME OF US ARE BRAVE[70]

As scholars study any form of communication, an intersectional approach offers several foundational principles that could and should guide research. These foundations are naming, power, and epistemic frameworks. To begin, when scholars select a communicative moment or series of moments to study, they might reflect on who is being named, what name is being given or offered, who has the power to do so, and what privileges exist that sanction this naming. Additionally, as Sara L. McKinnon's chapter in this collection demonstrates through her analysis of audiencing in the immigration courtroom, scholars should reflect on how that naming circumscribes or opens up what is possible and "real" as well as what can be known or understood. Scholars could consider what abuses and uses of power inform that naming and how they, as scholars, are connected to that naming. As scholars confront discourses deemed unsettling or angry or even irrational, they might consider what epistemic frameworks are at play, what valuable ways of knowing are embedded in those discourses, and how that adds to our body of knowledge about communication. So, for example, as we explore civil rights discourses, in the broadest or most focused sense of civil rights and discourse, intersectional scholars might attend not only to the confusing and disparate group of individuals who are calling themselves "a group," but also to the diversity that exists in the group and who is left out of "the group" (Lugones's "transparents," and "thicks," for example). Leslie A. Hahner's chapter raises precisely such questions in her examination of how "feminist" gets constituted during "feminist coming out day." Scholars also might productively attend to how those inside and outside the discourse of civil rights are positioned in the larger culture, what kinds of requests for rights are being made, who is making those requests and of whom, and who decides that the thing being requested is, in fact, "a right" (whose epistemology is being privileged, for example). They might also take up how those who are being denied rights are being talked about; the myriad ways those rights are withheld; and the logics that enable the withholding of rights (questions of power and its distribution, for example). Finally, scholars could consider "theories in the flesh" in terms of how those who are oppressed and those who are doing/enabling the oppressing experience, express, and understand that oppression. Were scholars to apply these questions to discourses such as "Black power," "women's rights," "immigration," "gay marriage," "transgender politics," or "disability," we suggest, an understanding of communication, and how it functions, would expand considerably.

Additionally, as scholars explore unsettling discourses, whether they are positioned within the unsettled discourse or outside of it, an intersectional approach could help them articulate the ways that politics, social norms, and personal histories lay the foundation for that discourse, which is what Carly Woods's chapter on Barbara Jordan in this volume attempts to do. As Shanara Rose Reid-Brinkley shows in her chapter critiquing the narrowness of *feminine style*, scholars could begin to embrace conceptual messiness and give voice to the nuances of identities, the ways that identities can be both stable and organic, and the roles that communication plays in that stability and fluidity. So, for example, as scholars explore single communicators, historical or contemporary texts, and even the collective actions of rhetors, an intersectional approach would prompt them to attend to the many aspects of power and privilege—their presence and absence—and how communication fostered, created, organized, helped maneuver through, silenced, and gave voice to that presence or absence. Much like Jennifer Keohane's chapter in this volume questions how communist belonging was constructed during the 1940s, and in the same vein as the past scholarship of Houston, intersectional scholars could attend to which identities are said to "belong"—in an organization, public space, or nation— why, and how what is said comes to be "true." Scholars could consider which identities are said to have a "right" to marry and why and how that saying comes to be "legal." Scholars might address which identities must negotiate second or third "homes" within a society, culture, or nation, and why and how that negotiation is or is not accomplished. Scholars might even question which identities are safe on our streets, in our cars, in public, and in our homes, why that safety is present, or not, the discourses that sustain this safety or lack of it, and why *safety, home, legal, right, true,* and *belong* are even states of being that can be granted and withdrawn.

Finally, integrating an intersectional approach to the study of communication requires that scholars recognize that each individual stands and swims in the intersections of race/gender/sex/sexuality/ability/economic means and more. No individual is outside this paradigm, however much our scholarship has tried to deny this or to suggest that only some are "intersectional bodies." So, for example, intersectionality requires that we ask when is a "man" never *also* raced, classed, sexed, gendered, and the like? Sara Hayden and D. Lynn O'Brien Hallstein in this volume attempt to sort out this kind of question. Moreover, it requires that we ask when is "a race" not *also* comprised of family histories and genealogies, political differences, varying social norms and expectations, individuals with personal quirks, as well as being gendered, sexed, classed, and the like? And, it requires that we ask when the amount of money available to a family over time or an individual at any point in time has not *also* influenced the amount of access, comfort, and resources available to that person or family, and also been raced, sexed, gendered, and the like. And, finally, as Kate Zittlow Rogness's development of intersectional style through the rhetoric of free lovers so aptly demonstrates in her chapter, taking up an intersectional approach requires that we ask why would, and when have, any of these factors not *also* affected, constrained, opened up, or even forced an individual's or group's styles, strategies, or choices of communication?

An intersectional approach to scholarship insists that we expand our research protocols, revisit our impressive storehouse of methodologies, refresh our understandings of how communication operates, and explain more comprehensively how communication and rhetoric work, and are at work, in the world.

DOING INTERSECTIONAL SCHOLARSHIP: THE DIFFICULT TASK OF RIGOROUS WORK

Intersectional work can feel difficult because at its center it requires that scholars interact with their own privilege (or lack of it) and theoretical blind spots. These are not always comfortable moments, but they are usually informative ones, to be sure. Intersectional work often challenges many of our basic assumptions about communication: those assumptions include the scope of communication—what it can or should do for people; the practice of communication—how communication is used effectively and how effective it actually is;

and the theorizing of communication—at what moments do we call a theory a "good" one, or even a "theory" at all. It also challenges who has the power to name, whose discourses can be heard, whose ways of knowing are valid, and whose approach to communication scholarship is rewarded.

We suggest that our discipline's push for conceptual neatness, its veneration of individual communicators, and the communication of homogenous groups do not serve us well. We can no longer pretend that we exist outside the web of complexity that makes us all raced, classed, gendered, sexed, and differently abled individuals who belong or don't belong to particular nation-states. We can no longer speak of "women" and "men" as if those categories, often assumed to be attached to cisgendered bodies, make any sense outside of complex relationships of identity, power, and privilege. We can only speak of individuals and groups as they exist in and in relationship to these ever-present aspects of self and society. If Althusser is correct, we always are hailed, and hail others, as curdled, and not fragmented, intersectional human beings.

OVERVIEW OF CHAPTERS IN
STANDING IN THE INTERSECTION

As Houston notes in the preface to this volume, our audience today is perhaps more progressive and willing to listen than the audience she faced after completing her Ph.D. three decades ago. Certainly, as the identities of the authors in this collection evidence, many white women are eager to engage and extend intersectional theories in their work. It is also necessary to note that the makeup of this collection lacks significant representation of women of color. All of our authors are also cisgendered and from the United States.[71] We think it is important to call attention to these factors because of ongoing absences of marginalized scholars in the pages of our books and journals. At the 2009 National Communication Association preconference seminar we organized in order to gather authors for this collection, the racial makeup of the group was quite diverse. Through the process of calling for complete essays, revisions, and the normal back and forth that goes into creating a book such as this, our makeup has drastically changed. As editors, we have reflected on why we have ended up with few authors of color: could it reveal the uneven demands for the time and energies of people of color, which lead them to have to be very selective in what they end up being able to complete? Could the dearth reflect some manner of editing in which we have engaged that worked against our contributors of color? Could it be, even now and with this volume, too risky for scholars of color to speak out about topics that challenge the foundations of our discipline? We are concerned by the dearth and what it might mean for us as feminist communication scholars. At the same time, we are excited that white women and one white man have so willingly and fruitfully entered this conversation with us, and with the scholars/activists who have come before us to make such a collection possible. Moreover, though the initial call for contributors at the preconference was general, all of the chapters reflect rhetorical approaches and methodologies. As such, we offer this volume as a rhetorical entry into intersectional ideas and practices in communication studies.

Although the ideas supplied by our authors in their chapters could have been organized in a number of ways, we settled on arranging this volume in two parts. In the first part, "Entering the Intersection," the chapters provide different theoretical points of entry as they address and explore the relationships between communication, rhetoric, and intersectionality. The insights the authors in this first half of the book offer assist us in complicating scholarly notions of style, mobility, and location and ask us to be aware of, and explicit, with regard to our theorizing of intersecting and contradictory identities. They model the doing of intersectional work, simultaneously exploring how agency is constrained and enacted as well as asking feminist scholars to be clear about their methodological choices and decisions. In the second part, "Audiences and Audiencing," each author takes up questions of audience in relation to intersectionality. Combined, the four authors here provide a more complex and nuanced understanding of the dimensions and roles of audiences, the difficulties of addressing audiences, the process of audiencing, as well as the ways subjects negotiate, achieve, and are denied audience recognition.

The first two authors in part one mark their entry point through an important concept in feminist rhetorical studies, that of style and more specifically "feminine style." We open our conversation and theorizing with Shanara Reid-Brinkley, who provides an explicit critique of the limitations of feminine style when considered in light of theories of intersectionality and through the lens of signifyin(g). Using the rhetorical practices of Senator Carol Moseley Braun, Reid-Brinkley uncovers significant weaknesses in any concept that assumes femininity can be separated from race and class. We follow this with Kate Zittlow Rogness's essay, which develops a theory of intersectional style—characterized by impropriety, possibility, and play—as a way to understand the rhetoric of the free love movement.

Through providing a close look at three free lovers' arguments for their political beliefs, Zittlow Rogness develops a framework with which to understand unconventional discourse and to challenge oppressive norms.

The collection then moves to Carly Woods, who suggests that mobility metaphors and shifting points of entry (as opposed to singular articulations) are an important way to engage rhetorical history and intersectionality. Woods argues that both theories of intersectionality and rhetorical history operate through spatial metaphors that could be enhanced by shifting to mobility metaphors. Through an analysis of three moments in the life of Barbara Jordan, Woods demonstrates how the metaphor of mobility illustrates the ways Jordan moved around and through the boundaries that may have otherwise prevented her from achieving success because of her race, gender, sexuality, and ability. The section closes with Sara Hayden and D. Lynn O'Brien Hallstein who maintain that gender and sex remain important entry points for theorizing intersectionality. Hayden and O'Brien Hallstein offer an intervention into much third wave theorizing on intersectionality that reduces the significance of gender in feminist thought and activism. Recognizing the necessity of addressing interlocking oppression and privilege, O'Brien Hallstein and Hayden provide a passionate "both/and" account of why, for them, it is necessary to do intersectional work *and* keep gender at the forefront of their work.

Our second section opens with Lester C. Olson, who continues his ongoing work on Black, lesbian feminist Audre Lorde, and here, demonstrates how audiences comprised of mostly white, middle-class, heterosexual women consumed Lorde's work in a way that precluded her radical emphasis on interlocking oppressions. Although Olson finds intersectionality a useful tool to examine the reception of Lorde's work, he further shows that thinking in terms of "interlocking oppressions" has more radical rhetorical potential for social change. Leslie A. Hahner adds to our conversation regarding audiences with a goal of extending intersectional theories by arguing that intersectionality shapes the way audiences receive addresses. In developing constitutive intersectionality, Hahner shows how discourses interact with a subject's existing affective investments, and that understanding this intersection helps us to see how specific identities become more salient in certain contexts.

The final two essays of our collection also center on questions of audience, but they point readers toward transnational contexts and attentiveness in intersectional work. Jennifer Keohane examines the ways in which feminist communist Betty Millard deployed a rhetoric that intersected transnationalism, space, gender, and social class in order to convince the male members of the American Communist Party that gender should impact communist analysis. Because many in the party at the time associated feminism with bourgeois sensibility, Keohane shows the careful intersectional maneuvering Millard employed in order to radically shift the party's perspective at the same time that she ignored the relevance of race, leading Black communist feminists to critique and extend her analysis. Sara L. McKinnon closes this collection with her development of an intersectional methodology to understand how audiences rely on essentialist discourses to recognize speaking subjects. Through her close analysis of a gender-based political asylum case in the U.S. immigration system, McKinnon argues that this particular audience—the immigration judge—relied on essentialized notions of race, class, gender, nation, and sexual relations between men and women in order to make his decision. As with Keohane, McKinnon reminds us of the importance of thinking outside of national contexts, or at the very least, thinking about the impact of nationalist logics in understanding the interplay between audience and intersectionality.

As with any collection, we hope these chapters coalesce to both enter and extend a scholarly conversation. As Carrillo Rowe writes, "I stand on the bridge built by those who have come before me and as a bridge to those who will follow, in relations of constant flux and movement, in which we are all constantly being remade."[72] In this feminist spirit, we offer *Standing in the Intersection*.

NOTES

1. Patricia Hill Collins, "Foreword: Emerging Intersections—Building Knowledge and Transforming Institutions," in *Emerging Intersections: Race, Class, and Gender in Theory, Policy, and Practice*, ed. Bonnie Thornton Dill and Ruth Enid Zambrana (New Brunswick, NJ: Rutgers University Press, 2009), vii–xiii.

2. Carol Blair, Julie R. Brown, and Leslie A. Baxter, "Disciplining the Feminine," *Quarterly Journal of Speech* 80 (1994): 383–409; Sonja K. Foss and Cindy L. Griffin, "Beyond Persuasion: A Proposal for an Invitational Rhetoric," *Communication Monographs* 62 (1995): 2–18; Sally Miller Gearhart, "The Womanization of Rhetoric," *Women's Studies International Quarterly* 2 (1979): 195–201.

3. Aimee Carrillo Rowe, "Subject to Power—Feminism without Victims," *Women's Studies in Communication* 32 (2009): 12–35; Olga Idriss Davis, "A Black Woman as Rhetorical Critic: Validating Self and Violating the Space of Otherness," *Women's Studies in Communication* 21 (1998): 77-89; Davis, "In the Kitchen: Transforming the Academy through Safe Spaces of Resistance," *Western Journal of Communication* 63 (1999): 364–381; Lisa A. Flores, "Creating Discursive Space through a Rhetoric of

Difference: Chicana Feminists Craft a Homeland," *Quarterly Journal of Speech* 82 (1996): 142–156; Marsha Houston, "The Politics of Difference: Race, Class, and Women's Communication," in *Women Making Meaning: New Feminist Directions in Communication*, ed. Lana F. Rakow (New York: Routledge, 1992), 45–59; Marsha Houston Stanback (now Houston), "What Makes Scholarship About Black Women and Communication Feminist Communication Scholarship?," *Women's Studies in Communication* 11 (1988): 28-31; Marsha Houston Stanback (now Houston), "Feminist Theory and Black Women's Talk," *Howard Journal of Communications* 1, no. 4 (1989): 187–194; Marsha Houston and Olga Idriss Davis, eds., *Centering Ourselves: African American Feminist and Womanist Studies of Discourse* (Cresskill, NJ: Hampton Press, 2002); Lester C. Olson, "Liabilities of Language: Audre Lorde Reclaiming Difference," *Quarterly Journal of Speech* 84 (1998): 448–470.

4. Flores, "Creating Discursive Space," 142.

5. Houston, "Politics of Difference," 46.

6. Marsha Houston and Olga Idriss Davis, "Introduction: A Black Women's Angle of Vision on Communication Studies," in *Centering Ourselves*, 7.

7. Chela Sandoval, *Methodology of the Oppressed* (Minneapolis: University of Minnesota, 2000).

8. Frances Beale, "Double Jeopardy: To Be Black and Female," in *The Black Woman: An Anthology*, ed. Toni Cade Bambara (New York: Washington Square Press, 1970/2005), 109–122.

9. Gloria Anzaldúa, *Borderlands/La Frontera: The New Mestiza* (San Francisco: Spinsters/Aunt Lute, 1987); Combahee River Collective, "A Black Feminist Statement," in *This Bridge Called My Back: Writings by Radical Women of Color*, ed. Cherríe Moraga and Gloria Anzaldúa (New York: Kitchen Table: Women of Color Press, 1983), 210–218; Patricia Hill Collins, *Black Feminist Thought: Knowledge, Consciousness, and the Politics of Empowerment*, 2nd ed. (New York: Routledge, 2000); Gloria T. Hull, Patricia Bell Scott, and Barbara Smith, eds., *All the Women Are White, All the Blacks Are Men, but Some of Us Are Brave: Black Women's Studies* (New York: Feminist Press, 1982); Hortense J. Spillers, "Mama's Baby, Papa's Maybe: An American Grammar Book," *Diacritics* 17, no. 2 (1987): 65–80; Barbara Smith and Lorraine Bethel, eds., "The Black Women's Issue," *Conditions* 5 (Nov. 1979). Audre Lorde, *Sister Outsider: Essays and Speeches* (Berkeley, CA: Crossing Press, 1984). As with all lists, this one is necessarily incomplete. It is also important to note that in most feminist intersectional scholarship, the category of "woman" refers to women born as female, as even discussions of gender transgression via lesbian identities still imagined gender as cisgendered.

10. Throughout the introduction, we will capitalize Black, while we continue to keep white in lowercase. A number of scholars have recommended capitalizing Black, even though it is normally thought of as a racial label, because it has a heritage and social meaning congruent with that of many ethnic groups. White, on the other hand, is more easily defined as only

a racial signifier. See Barrie Thorne, Cheris Kramarae, and Nancy Henley, eds., *Language, Gender, and Society* (Rowley, MA: Newbury House, 1983), vi; Kimberlé Crenshaw, "Race, Reform, and Retrenchment: Transformation and Legitimation in Antidiscrimination Law," *Harvard Law Review* 101 (1988): 1331, 1332 n. 2. Even as we have made this decision, we think it is important to mention that since all naming carries power, it may be productive to consider whether all identity categories should be capitalized given the significance of identity in people's lives. Some authors in this collection have opted to put black only in lowercase for their own political beliefs and reasons.

11. Kimberlé Crenshaw, "Mapping the Margins: Intersectionality, Identity Politics and Violence against Women of Color," *Stanford Law Review* 43 (1991): 1241–1299; "Demarginalizing the Intersection of Race and Sex: A Black Feminist Critique of Antidiscrimination Doctrine, Feminist Theory and Antiracist Politics," *University of Chicago Legal Forum* (1989): 139–167. See also Hull, Scott, and Smith, eds., *Some Are Brave.*

12. Olson, "Liabilities of Language."

13. Collective, "A Black Feminist Statement."

14. Moraga and Anzaldúa, eds., *This Bridge.*

15. Elizabeth Spelman, *Inessential Woman: Problems of Exclusion in Feminist Thought* (Boston: Beacon Press, 1988).

16. Iris Marion Young, *Intersecting Voices: Dilemmas of Gender, Political Philosophy and Policy* (Princeton, NJ: Princeton University Press, 1997).

17. María Lugones, *Pilgrimages/Peregrinajes: Theorizing Coalition against Multiple Oppressions* (Lanham, MD: Rowman & Littlefield, 2003).

18. Collins, *Black Feminist.*

19. Aimee Carrillo Rowe, *Power Lines: On the Subject of Feminist Alliances* (Durham, NC: Duke University Press, 2008).

20. Collective, "A Black Feminist Statement," 210.

21. Moraga, "La Güera," in *This Bridge,* 28–29.

22. Moraga, "La Güera," 29.

23. Moraga, "La Güera," 29. Italics in original.

24. These allies include Becky Thompson, Ann Russo, Ruth Frankenberg, Adrienne Rich, Mab Segrest, and Elizabeth Spelman.

25. Spelman, *Inessential Woman,* 133.

26. Spelman, *Inessential Woman,* 139.

27. Lugones, *Pilgrimages/Peregrinajes,* 122. The concept of "mestiza consciousness," also an intersectional approach, has been made most famous by Gloria Anzaldúa.

28. Lugones, *Pilgrimages/Peregrinajes,* 123. Italics in original.

29. Lugones, *Pilgrimages/Peregrinajes,* 127.

30. Lugones, *Pilgrimages/Peregrinajes,* 151.

31. Lugones, *Pilgrimages/Peregrinajes,* 140.

32. Cited in Lugones, *Pilgrimages/Peregrinajes,* 151.

33. Cited in Lugones, *Pilgrimages/Peregrinajes,* 151.

34. Cited in Lugones, *Pilgrimages/Peregrinajes,* 140.

35. Lugones, *Pilgrimages/Peregrinajes*, 173.

36. Sandoval, *Methodology of the Oppressed*, 56.

37. Carrillo Rowe, *Power Lines*.

38. Importantly, this overview is necessarily brief and incomplete as a comprehensive review of early scholarship on race, sexuality, gender, class, and ability would be well beyond the scope of this introduction. Our interest here is showing the ways in which most attempts to introduce a new dimension of identity into communication scholarship have occurred in ways that mark that identity as more or less singular. Moreover, we surely enact our own erasures here. We are not commenting, for example, on questions of nation, or on the fact that all of this scholarship emerges from within the United States about the United States. Intersectional scholarship does not charge us to do "everything," as if that would ever be possible; it calls on scholars to attend to multiple dimensions of power simultaneously. In spite of absences and our own blind spots, we hope to have accomplished that goal.

39. Houston, "Politics of Difference," 45; Edith Folb, "Who's Got Room at the Top? Issues of Dominance and Non-Dominance in Intercultural Communication," in *Intercultural Communication: A Reader*, 4th ed., ed. Larry A. Samovar and Richard E. Porter (Belmont, CA: Wadsworth, 1985), 119–127.

40. A few sporadic articles do exist as early as the 1930s that focus on individual identities, such as woman, and the rhetoric of various marginalized rhetors, such as African American men. For some of these earlier essays, see Karlyn Kohrs Campbell and Zornitsa D. Keremidchieva, "Race, Sex and Class in Rhetorical Criticism," in *The Sage Handbook of Rhetorical Studies*, ed. Andrea A. Lunsford, Kirt H. Wilson, and Rosa A. Eberly (Thousand Oaks, CA: Sage, 2009), 461–476. Although these earlier essays are important, we begin our conversation in this introduction with those essays that we see as beginning to address the politics of an identity. We also focused our attention on the field's academic journals as opposed to examining communication scholarship published in other interdisciplinary outlets or in books. The decision to limit our focus in this way was, in part, pragmatic as this made the texts we had to examine manageable. The decision also emerged from a belief that in communication, journals represent the foundation of much of the field, especially early on. We argue, additionally, that what was published "outside" the discipline, rather than "inside," tells us a great deal about the nonintersectional nature of academic publishing, historically as well as currently.

41. Franklyn S. Haiman, "The Rhetoric of the Streets: Some Legal and Ethical Considerations," *Quarterly Journal of Speech* 53 (1967): 99–114; Herbert W. Simons, "Patterns of Persuasion in the Civil Rights Struggle," *Today's Speech* 15, no. 1 (1967): 25–27; Parke G. Burgess, "The Rhetoric of Black Power: A Moral Demand?" *Quarterly Journal of Speech* 54 (1968): 122–133; and Mary G. McEdwards, "Agitative Rhetoric: Its Nature and Effect," *Western Speech* 32 (1968): 36–43.

42. Philip C. Wander, "The Savage Child: The Image of the Negro in the ProSlavery Movement," *Southern Speech Communication Journal*

37 (1971): 335–360. Importantly, at least one book of the time, by a Black scholar, also named racism: Arthur L. Smith (now Molefi Kete Asante), *Rhetoric of Black Revolution* (Boston: Allyn and Bacon, 1969).

43. Francis S. Dubner, "Nonverbal Aspects of Black English," *Southern Speech Communication Journal* 57 (1971): 361–374; Jack L. Whitehead and Leslie Miller, "Correspondence between Evaluations of Children's Speech and Speech Anticipated upon the Basis of Stereotype," *Southern Speech Communication Journal* 57 (1971): 375–386.

44. Jack L. Daniel, "Black Folk and Speech Education." *Speech Teacher* 19, no. 2 (1970): 123–129.

45. W. A. D. Riach, "'Telling It Like It Is': An Examination of Black Theatre as Rhetoric," *Quarterly Journal of Speech* 56 (1970): 179–186.

46. Arthur L. Smith (now Molefi Kete Asante), "Some Characteristics of the Black Religious Audience," *Speech Monographs* 37 (1970): 207–210.

47. Lloyd D. Powers, "Chicano Rhetoric: Some Basic Concepts," *Southern Speech Communication Journal* 38 (1973): 340–346.

48. Michael Victor Sedano, "Chicanismo: A Rhetorical Analysis of Themes and Images of Selected Poetry from the Chicano Movement," *Western Journal of Speech* 44 (1980): 177–190.

49. Alberto Gonzalez, "Mexican 'Otherness' in the Rhetoric of Mexican Americans," *Southern Journal of Communication* 55 (1990): 276–292.

50. Other early essays that take up questions of race and power include Marsha Houston Stanback (now Houston) and W. Barnett Pearce, "Talking to 'The Man': Some Communication Strategies Used by Members of 'Subordinate' Social Groups," *Quarterly Journal of Speech* 67 (1981): 21–30; Thurmon Garner, "Playing the Dozens: Folklore as Strategies for Living," *Quarterly Journal of Speech* 69 (1983): 47–57; John C. Hammerback and Richard J. Jensen, "The Rhetorical Worlds of Cesar Chavez and Reies Tijerina," *Western Journal of Speech* 44 (1980): 166–176.

51. James W. Chesebro, ed., *Gayspeak: Gay Male and Lesbian Communication* (New York: Pilgrim Press, 1981).

52. Barry Brummett, "A Pentadic Analysis of Ideologies in Two Gay Rights Controversies," *Central States Speech Journal* 30 (1979): 250–261; James W. Chesebro, John F. Cragan, and Patricia McCullough, "The Small Group Technique of the Radical Revolutionary: A Synthetic Study of Consciousness Raising," *Speech Monographs* 40 (1973): 136–146; Joseph J. Hayes, "Gayspeak," *Quarterly Journal of Speech* 62 (1976): 256–266; Julia P. Stanley, "Homosexual Slang," *American Speech* 45 (1970): 45–59.

53. Examples of other recent writing on LGBTQ themes include: Dan Brouwer, "The Precarious Visibility Politics of Self-Stigmatization: The Case of HIV/AIDS Tattoos," *Text and Performance Quarterly* 18 (1998): 114–136; Charles I. Nero, "Black Queer Identity, Imaginative Rationality, and the Language of Home," in *Our Voices: Essays in Culture, Ethnicity, and Communication*, ed. Alberto Gonzalez, Marsha Houston, and Victoria Chen (Los Angeles: Roxbury Publishing Company, 1997), 61–69; Frederick C. Corey and Thomas K. Nakayama, "Sextext," *Text and Performance Quarterly* 17 (1997): 58–68; James Darsey, "From 'Gay Is Good' to the Scourge of AIDS: The Evolution of Gay Liberation Rhetoric," *Communication Studies*

42 (1991): 43–66; Lisa Henderson, "Queer Communication Studies," *Communication Yearbook* 24 (2001): 465–484; E. Patrick Johnson, "Quare Studies, or (Almost) Everything I Know About Queer Studies I Learned from My Grandmother," *Text and Performance Quarterly* 21 (2001): 1–25; Charles E. Morris III, "'The Responsibilities of the Critic' F.O. Matthiessen's Homosexual Palimpsest," *Quarterly Journal of Speech* 84 (1998): 261–282; Olson, "Liabilities of Language."; Olson, "On the Margins of Rhetoric: Audre Lorde Transforming Silence into Language and Action," *Quarterly Journal of Speech* 83 (1997): 49–70; Jeffrey R. Ringer, ed., *Queer Words, Queer Images: Communication and the Construction of Homosexuality* (New York: New York University Press, 1994); R. Anthony Slagle, "In Defense of Queer Nation: From Identity Politics to a Politics of Difference," *Western Journal of Communication* 59 (1995): 85–103. For the most part, these essays approach sexuality as disconnected from other modes of identity. One main exception to this is Johnson's essay, "Quare Studies," where he examines the failures of queer scholarship to address the experiences of queers of color. Nero similarly offers a more intersectional approach to thinking of sexuality. Olson's work examines the speeches of Audre Lorde, who can be credited with some of the most important writing on difference, multiple oppressions, and change. After 2004, significant work in LGBTQ studies from a social-scientific and a queer perspective emerges in the field. The queer scholarship is notably led by white scholars including Charles E. Morris, III, John Sloop, Erin J. Rand, Daniel C. Brouwer, Jeffrey A. Bennett, Helene Shugart, and Michael D. E. Meyer. Queer scholars of color such as Thomas K. Nakayama, E. Patrick Johnson, Charles Nero, and Gust Yep also remain important voices, though their scholarship is not regularly featured on the pages of communication journals. Importantly, much of this scholarship imagines gender as cisgendered, since with the exception of work by scholars including Isaac West and Julia Johnson, trans theory and transgender identity is often not central to these analyses.

54. Scholarship on disability, like scholarship on LGBTQ experiences, is largely published outside the communication discipline. However, the special issue of *Text and Performance Quarterly* "Disability Studies/Performance Studies" (January–April 2008), and Petra Kuppers, "Performing Determinism: Disability Culture Poetry," *Text and Performance Quarterly* 27 (2007): 89–106, among a handful of other essays, are hopefully, changing that pattern.

55. Frederick Williams and Rita C. Naremore, "On the Functional Analysis of Social Class Difference in Modes of Speech," *Speech Monographs* 36 (1969): 77–105.

56. Jack Daniel, "The Poor: Aliens in an Affluent Society: Cross-Cultural Communication," *Today's Speech* 18, no. 1 (1970): 15–21.

57. Gerry Philipsen, "Speaking 'Like a Man' in Teamsterville: Cultural Patterns of Role Enactment in an Urban Neighborhood," *Quarterly Journal of Speech* 61 (1975): 13–22; Philipsen, "Places for Speaking in Teamsterville," *Quarterly Journal of Speech* 62 (1976): 15–26.

58. A number of communication scholars engage in Marxist critiques of rhetoric and communication, though these rarely focus on class as a

component of identity that impacts communicative practice. Exceptions include Dana L. Cloud, "Fighting Words: Labor and the Limits of Communication at Staley, 1993 to 1996," *Management Communication Quarterly* 18 (2005): 509–542.

59. Brenda Robinson Hancock, "Affirmation by Negation in the Women's Liberation Movement," *Quarterly Journal of Speech* 58 (1972): 264–271; Karlyn Kohrs Campbell, "The Rhetoric of Women's Liberation: An Oxymoron," *Quarterly Journal of Speech* 59 (1973): 74–86; Cheris Kramer (now Kramarae), "Women's Speech: Separate but Unequal?" *Quarterly Journal of Speech* 69 (1974): 14–24. As mentioned above, some much earlier scholarship attempted to bring women into the conversation, and it most certainly adopted a pop-bead approach. See Alice Donaldson, "Women Emerge as Political Speakers," *Speech Monographs* 18 (1951): 54–61; Wil A. Linkugel, "The Woman Suffrage Argument of Anna Howard Shaw," *Quarterly Journal of Speech* 49 (1963): 165–174; Elaine B. McDavitt, "Susan B. Anthony: Reformer and Speaker," *Quarterly Journal of Speech* 30 (1944): 173–180; Doris G. Yoakam Twitchell, "Pioneer Women Orators of America," *Quarterly Journal of Speech* 23 (1937): 251–259.

60. Houston, "Politics of Difference"; Houston Stanback (now Houston), "What Makes?"; Houston Stanback (now Houston), "Feminist Theory and Black Women's Talk."

61. This incomplete list includes Brenda J. Allen, "Black Womanhood and Feminist Standpoints," *Management Communication Quarterly* 11 (1998): 575–586; Karen Lee Ashcraft and Brenda J. Allen, "The Racial Foundation of Organizational Communication," *Communication Theory* 13 (2003): 5–38; Carrillo Rowe, "Subject to Power"; Carrillo Rowe, *Power Lines*; Karma R. Chávez, "Border (in)Securities: Normative and Differential Belonging in LGBTQ and Immigrant Rights Discourse," *Communication and Critical/Cultural Studies* 7 (2010): 136–155, Chávez, "Spatializing Gender Performativity: Ecstasy and Possibilities for Livable Life in the Tragic Case of Victoria Arellano," *Women's Studies in Communication* 33 (2010): 1–15; Carrie Crenshaw, "Women in the Gulf War: Toward an Intersectional Feminist Rhetorical Criticism," *Howard Journal of Communications* 8, no. 3 (1997): 219–235: Davis, "A Black Woman"; Flores, "Creating Discursive Space"; Houston, "The Politics of Difference"; Houston and Davis, *Centering Ourselves*; Sara L. McKinnon, "(in)Hospitable Publics: Theorizing the Conditions of Access to U.S. Publics," in *Public Modalities: Rhetoric, Culture, Media, and the Shape of Public Life*, ed. Daniel C. Brouwer and Robert Asen (Tuscaloosa: University of Alabama Press, 2010): 131–153; McKinnon, "Citizenship and the Performance of Credibility: Audiencing Gender-Based Asylum Seekers in U.S. Immigration Courts," *Text and Performance Quarterly* 29 (2009): 205–221; Shane T. Moreman and Bernadette Marie Calafell, "Buscando Para Nuestra Latinidad: Utilizing La Llorona for Cultural Critique," *Journal of International and Intercultural Communication* 1 (2008): 309–326; Shane T. Moreman and Dawn Marie McIntosh, "Brown Scriptings and Rescriptings: A Critical Performance Ethnography of Latina Drag Queens," *Communication and Critical/Cultural Studies* 7 (2010): 115–135; Aysel Morin, "Victimization of Muslim Women in *Submission*," *Women's*

Studies in Communication 32 (2009): 380–408; Patricia S. Parker, "Control, Resistance, and Empowerment in Raced, Gendered, and Classed Work Contexts: The Case of African American Women," *Communication Yearbook* 27 (2003): 257–291; Karla D. Scott, "Crossing Cultural Borders: 'Girl' and 'Look' as Markers of Identity in Black Women's Language Use," *Discourse and Society* 11 (2000): 237–248.

62. As a side note, in a recent essay, "Race, Sex and Class in Rhetorical Criticism," Campbell and Keremidchieva mention the "intersectionality debates" as calling attention to the "difficulty in isolating the complex discursive contexts framing speakers' experiences both with regard to their audiences and their self-understanding" (470). However, they minimize intersectionality's grounding in feminist theory and place it within a broader conversation about constitutive rhetoric and the critical-cultural approach to rhetoric. In addition to completely failing to mention scholarship on sexuality, their essay continues within the pop-bead approach by isolating, race, "sex," and class from each other. Thanks to Lester Olson for drawing our attention to this essay.

63. Stanley A. Deetz, *Democracy in an Age of Corporate Colonization: Developments in Communication and the Politics of Everyday Life* (Albany: State University of New York Press, 1992).

64. Bonnie J. Dow and Mari Boor Tonn, "'Feminine Style' and Political Judgment in the Rhetoric of Ann Richards," *Quarterly Journal of Speech* 79 (1993): 286–302; Karlyn Kohrs Campbell, "Style and Content in the Rhetoric of Early Afro-American Feminists," *Quarterly Journal of Speech* 72 (1986): 434–445.

65. Charles J. Stewart, "The Evolution of a Revolution: Stokely Carmichael and the Rhetoric of Black Power," *Quarterly Journal of Speech* 83 (1997): 429–446; Burgess, "The Rhetoric of Black Power"; Karlyn Kohrs Campbell, "The Rhetoric of Radical Black Nationalism: A Case Study in Self-Conscious Criticism," *Central States Speech Journal* 22 (1971): 151–160.

66. Darsey, "Gay Is Good."; Darsey, "From 'Commies' and 'Queers' to 'Gay Is Good'," in *Gayspeak*, 224–247; Slagle, "In Defense."

67. Fernando Pedro Delgado, "Chicano Movement Rhetoric: An Ideographic Interpretation," *Communication Quarterly* 43 (1995): 446–455; John C. Hammerback and Richard J. Jensen, *The Rhetorical Career of César Chávez* (College Station: Texas A&M University Press, 1998); John C. Hammerback, Richard J. Jensen, and José Angel Gutiérrez, *A War of Words: Chicano Protest in the 1960s and 1970s* (Westport, CT: Greenwood Press, 1985).

68. L. Takeo Doi, "Japanese Patterns of Communication and the Concept of *Amae*," *Quarterly Journal of Speech* 59 (1973): 180–186; Roichi Okabe, "Yukichi Fukuzawa: A Promulgator of Western Rhetoric in Japan," *Quarterly Journal of Speech* 59 (1973): 186–195.

69. Randall A. Lake, "Enacting Red Power: The Consummatory Function in Native American Protest Rhetoric," *Quarterly Journal of Speech* 69 (1983): 127-42; Lake, "Between Myth and History: Enacting Time in

Native American Protest Rhetoric," *Quarterly Journal of Speech* 77 (1991): 123–151.

70. This title of course references Gloria T. Hull, Patricia Bell Scott, and Barbara Smith's famous collection, *All the Women Are White, All the Blacks Are Men, but Some of Us Are Brave: Black Women's Studies*. Recently, the journal *Signs* (35, no. 4) hosted a special symposium on "Black Women's Studies and the Transformation of the Academy" where several of the essays refer to this important and groundbreaking collection. As Cheryl Clarke maintains, this collection changed how women's studies is taught, and like many other similar collections of the time, reflected the best of intersectional thought inside and outside the academy. See Cheryl Clarke, "*But Some of Us Are Brave* and the Transformation of the Academy: Transformation?," *Signs* 35 (2010): 779–788.

71. We do not know whether our contributors identify as able-bodied. These factors reflect who is absent/present in the wider discipline.

72. Carrillo Rowe, "Subject to Power," 12.

Part I

Entering the Intersection

Chapter 1

Mammies and Matriarchs: Feminine Style and Signifyin(g) in Carol Moseley Braun's 2003–2004 Campaign for the Presidency

Shanara Rose Reid-Brinkley

> The blacks won't vote for you because you're not part of the machine; the whites won't vote for you because you're black, and nobody's going to vote for you because you're a woman.
> —Senator Carol Moseley Braun[1]

The 2003–2004 race for the Democratic presidential nomination began with a barrage of candidates, which did not bode well for the democrats' chances at beating George W. Bush in the 2004 presidential election. Considering the increased rhetorical saliency of diversity and representation, the nominees included a Jewish American man (Joe Lieberman), an African American man (Reverend Al Sharpton), and an African American woman (Carol Moseley Braun). Senator Moseley Braun, the second African American to enter the race and the only woman, ran for the bid depicting President Bush as a violent, political leader that held America "hostage," contrasting herself as the calm, cooperative, and strong feminine alternative. Moseley Braun's rhetoric failed to produce a significant support base for the campaign and she conceded the race before the primaries. In an interview six years after the election, Moseley Braun said, "This is where being black and female comes in. Because black women have to work on being docile. . . . Because I missed some of the cultural cues, particularly with regard to both gender and race, I was not as sensitive as I should have been. And I paid the price for it."[2] Her inability to fit within appropriate frames of black femininity created a perceptual problem that made gaining support for campaign elections difficult. This chapter analyzes news media representation as well as Moseley Braun's presidential campaign discourse to identify the frames that not only constrained her effectiveness as a black female candidate, but also the frames to which she had access to resist dominant images of black femininity. Moseley Braun used feminine style as a rhetorical strategy to create an appropriate performance of femininity that was intelligible to a broad and diverse support base. However, given that black political candidates may be deemed single-issue candidates if they explicitly engage race, Moseley Braun used feminine style as a rhetorical cover for the African American practice of signifyin'. Intersecting the analysis of gender with race, class, and sexuality highlights the limitations of feminine style research, which largely ignores the various interactions of identity-based ideology. In the following sections, I review the contextual considerations associated with an analysis of Moseley Braun's rhetoric. Then I engage contemporary rhetorical theory on feminine style, illustrating the limited nature of this theory, when conceptualized from a non-intersectional framework. In the analysis section, I identify three frames—the Good White Mother, the Modern Mammy, and the Black Matriarch—as performance frames that Senator Moseley Braun negotiated during her campaign.

CAROL MOSELEY BRAUN'S RISE
TO THE NATIONAL STAGE

Before she ran for national office in 1992, Carol Moseley Braun served as an assistant U.S. attorney, a state legislator, and a county executive. Running during the "Year of the Woman," and arguing that she would be the first black woman senator in history, Moseley Braun beat her white male opponent, Richard Williamson, in her first bid for a congressional seat. Despite her victory politically and historically, Moseley Braun suffered a number of political scandals, including accusations of campaign money mismanagement and claims of a "mediocre" Senate record that led to her defeat after only one term in office.[3] Even though there had never before been an African American female member of the Senate, and she actually achieved a laudable Senate record during her years of service,[4] she lost her Senate seat in 1998 to Peter Fitzgerald, the republican who outspent Moseley Braun and ran a vicious campaign, with the assistance of republican strategist Karl Rove. Following the loss, President Bill Clinton appointed Moseley Braun ambassador to New Zealand.

On September 22, 2003, Moseley Braun formally announced her intention to seek the Democratic nomination for the presidency. Receiving support from notable women's organizations, including the National Organization for Women (NOW) and the National Women's Political Caucus (NWPC), Moseley Braun formulated her campaign discourse to be persuasive to women voters specifically and to the American public in general. Given the early support from women's organizations and Moseley Braun's use of gender as a rhetorical strategy, it is important to analyze the significance of feminine style in her campaign discourse. To do so, I have gathered the speeches, debates, interviews, and Internet chats that feature Moseley Braun, many of which were transcribed on her campaign site. Other artifacts were drawn from transcripts of news television and radio available online. As the number of actual artifacts for this analysis is quite large, I will not describe the context for each speech; instead, I am interested in the discourses constructed nationally through Moseley Braun's rhetoric and the fact that campaign speeches are never limited just to the immediate audiences to which they are delivered.

FOOTNOTING RACE AND CLASS TO BUILD A THEORY OF "FEMININE STYLE"

Karlyn Kohrs Campbell argues that women rhetors engage in the use of feminine style as a rhetorical strategy designed to create a space for women's participation in public deliberation.[5] Bonnie J. Dow and Mari Boor Tonn note that "the feminist agenda in rhetorical studies itself has been primarily liberal-feminist in orientation, a clear goal has been to revise the traditional 'great speaker' paradigm to include women rhetors."[6] Contemporary rhetorical study of feminine style has been used to study women's rhetoric across various rhetorical situations, including the study of women candidates and elected public officials. Feminine style "produce(s) discourse that displays a personal tone, uses personal experience, anecdotes and examples as evidence, exhibits inductive structure, emphasizes audience participation, and encourages identification between speaker and audience."[7]

Analysis of feminine style as a rhetorical strategy has largely been limited to studying the public discourse of white, middle-class women. This is partly a function of the focus of such scholarship on speeches representative of "feminist social reform."[8] As such, feminine style is a particularly raced and classed theory of criticism. As the women's suffrage and women's liberation movements have proven of great historical import, it is the famous voices of these movements, and the white women engaged in national politics, that have received the most attention in feminist rhetorical scholarship on feminine style. Various studies of feminine style note the need for further study into the diversity of "feminine styles."[9] Jane Blankenship and Deborah Robson suggest that such "study will be needed to fully address the salience of race, class, age, and ethnicity, etc., especially as it relates to women in politics."[10] Although their article "focuses only on the commonalities . . . found prominently placed in the discourse of women in settings of campaigns and governance,"[11] the authors argue that they do not "suggest that all women, monolithically, speak alike; rather, the intersections of gender with race, class, etc., mean that a multiplicity of voices help constitute variations within the feminine style."[12]

More recently, Victoria Pruin DeFrancisco and Catherine Helen Palczewski in *Communicating Gender Diversity* argue that "it is important to make room for diverse feminist theories" in the study of communication.[13] The authors note that there are multiple "feminine styles," with white, middle-class, straight femininity being but one version. However, the authors do not indicate that this particular style is a citation of a privileged performance of a culturally normative femininity. As a reiteration of a privileged performance of white femininity, it is no wonder that the study of feminine style in communication studies has been largely limited to the study of white, straight, middle-class women.[14]

Campbell's germinal essay analyzing feminine style in the rhetoric of Sojourner Truth, Ida B. Wells-Barnett, and Mary Church Terrell is one of the few rhetorical analyses of feminine style in black women's political rhetoric.[15] Campbell seeks to demonstrate that the theory of feminine style is explicative in studying diverse women's rhetoric. However, a reading of Campbell's analysis demonstrates the limited utility of the theory when race is not galvanized as an intersectional tool of analysis. Given that most women of the time period who spoke publicly in support of women's suffrage were white and middle class, Truth's race and class difference from such women is a critical space of evaluating her use of feminine style as a rhetorical strategy. The purpose of Truth's speech is not just to demonstrate that women deserve legal and political representation, but also to define womanhood, so that black women who have been traditionally defined outside of the feminine standard can be included. For Truth, the use of her *female* body cannot be disconnected from her use of her body as also *black* to make a political argument. To focus on her rhetoric as an example of feminine style functions to elide the difference that her race and class make.

In order to complicate this notion of feminine style, I argue that Moseley Braun spoke to African American discourse communities through the rhetorical strategy of "signifyin(g)," or "the African/African-American practice of Signification."[16] Henry Louis Gates Jr. notes that "Signifyin(g) is black double-voicedness; because it always entails formal revision and intertextual relation."[17] In interactions with white America, African Americans have often had to speak out of "two mouths." They developed rhetorical practices designed to communicate with white people according to accepted norms of social interaction. "Double voice" as a rhetorical practice can refer to the rhetorical use of indirection in which the racial other depends on the shared knowledge of blackness being "brought to bear upon the manifest content of the speech act."[18] Such a rhetorical strategy is dependent upon a simultaneity: training in black discourse communities, its values, beliefs, and sociolinguistic rituals, but also a mastery of the discursive practices of whiteness. Given the history of the enslavement and subjugation of black people in the U.S. context, it has been a critical strategy of resistance to develop language and communication strategies that would allow African Americans to convey information and messages while under the surveillance of whites. Although white audience members may often read the rhetoric of black people literally, black discourse can function to produce underlying messages designed to be heard by members of the discourse community, but also misdirect non-members from interpreting or attaching significance to the message. Given the recognizability of feminine style as a rhetorical strategy for women candidates, the "double voice" of feminine style can function as a strategy of misdirection to create a cover for African American signification. As Gates argues, "Repetition, with a signal difference, is fundamental to the nature of Signifyin(g)."[19]

BLACK FEMININITY AND THE RHETORICAL CONSTRAINTS OF POLITICAL CAMPAIGNING

Because she was one of the highest-ranking black officials in the country during her tenure in the Senate and the first black woman elected to that position, Moseley Braun is an important sociopolitical figure on the American political landscape. Her race and gender increased her public visibility. Thus, any hint of scandal surrounding her campaign captured media attention. Before her election, Moseley Braun, and her siblings, were accused of taking a $28,000 Medicaid disbursement intended for their mother. Moseley Braun was required to pay the state back $15,000.[20] Following her election to the Senate in 1992, an article in *Time* notes that after winning her seat, Moseley Braun rented an expensive penthouse apartment, bought a new SUV and a new wardrobe, and left for a month-long vacation with her fiancé (Kgosie Matthews) and son.[21] During her unsuccessful run for reelection to the Senate in 1998, the *St. Petersburg Times* referenced "Allegations that Matthews and Moseley Braun improperly spent several hundred thousand dollars of campaign donations on luxury vacations, jewelry, and clothing."[22] A writer for *The Economist* wrote that it was "rumored" that Moseley Braun's fiancé used campaign money "to cover Braun's personal credit card bills."[23] During Moseley Braun's campaign for the presidency, the *Christian Science Monitor* noted: "From the start of the race, Moseley Braun was plagued by charges that her office was mismanaged; that she misused campaign funds, spending donated dollars on dresses and jewelry; and missed important Senate functions, like orientation."[24] The financial issue concerning Moseley Braun's misuse of her mother's Medicaid disbursement was leaked to the press during her 1992 Senate campaign. If this problem had been her only financial hiccup, the senator may not have faced the political difficulties that developed in the 1998 Illinois Senate race and the 2004 presidential race. However, Moseley Braun was not just accused of mishandling campaign funds, she was accused of purposefully misusing those funds for her own personal gain. Her personal gain was constructed as feminine as she violated the public trust by allegedly using campaign contributions to purchase clothes and jewelry. However, her missteps were also constructed within ideologies of race, as Moseley Braun violated acceptable norms of performance for black women in her position.

The Black Lady Overachiever

The ideologies of race, gender, class, and sexuality are productive of "dynamic" images of black womanhood.[25] Such images are changeable over time and space and are intertextual in their references to one another. Thus, historical stereotypes of black femininity recirculate and influence available subject positions for contemporary black femininity. For professional, middle-class, black women, how one negotiates historical and contemporary discourses that shape the images of black womanhood is important to successful integration into majority white working environments.[26] In addition, the scrutiny that black women political candidates and public officials face further complicates their performance of black femininity. While professional black women face forms of surveillance at work, black female public officials often have few safe spaces outside of the public purview. Black feminist theorist Patricia Hill Collins, citing Wahneema Lubiano's concept, notes that the "Black Lady Overachiever" is "a new controlling image applied to middle-class professional Black women."[27] The Black Lady Overachiever is first and foremost a "black lady."[28] The black lady is middle-class, straight, and either bound by heterosexual marriage or is single and asexual. The building of a social performance of black femininity within the black middle class that could provide a course for the resistance of dominant narratives constraining black women produced a strategy that required a close reiteration of white, middle-class, heterosexual, American femininity. Collins writes: "According to the cult of true womanhood that accompanied the traditional family ideal, 'true' women possessed four cardinal virtues: piety, purity, submissiveness, and domesticity."[29] As black women exited the bonds of slavery, historical characterizations of their sexuality, along with black men, operated to constrain their freedom. Narratives constructing black women as sexually deviant, black men as sexually violent, and white women as the object of black male sexual desire, were reproduced postslavery to deny black women the protection associated with acceptable femininity. Black women's response was the development of a politics of respectability that mimicked white, middle-class, heterosexual femininity as a means to resist the ideological narratives objectifying black femininity.[30]

The black lady as a strategic representation of black, middle-class respectability must have the "manners and morals of good black women."[31] The modern day black lady professional, or the Black Lady Overachiever, must perform a "comforting" representation of black femininity that marks dissociation from negative images of black womanhood.[32] This black woman speaks standard English and is well educated, "free of dreadlocks, braids, and other indicators of nappy hair," gracious and accommodating, loyal to the institution that employs her, asexual, and unraced in any manner that might disrupt the establishment.[33] Black women who violate these tenets in majority white settings face various forms of censure.

Moseley Braun often fit this model: she is well educated with both a college and law degree. Throughout her time in public office, she spoke standard English, demonstrating a strong mastery of language and vocabulary. She was usually pictured with straight (non-kinky) hair, pulled back into a tight bun or conservatively styled. Her suits were also usually conservative in style and color. Her performance of black femininity during campaign races responded to the dominant negative ideologies that construct available subject positions for black women. As a Senate candidate, Moseley Braun needed to demonstrate her loyalty to her constituents, her willingness to work on their behalf while subjugating her own needs, her trustworthiness, and her ability to lead. I will engage Moseley Braun's sexuality later in the chapter, but for now I focus on why questions of loyalty, commitment, and hard work may have derailed public support for the Senator's campaign rather than helped her.

All black women's performances of appropriate femininity are always already suspect within white supremacist discourse. In other words, black women must engage in a persistent, performative replication of propriety. At times, however, Moseley Braun violated the appropriate frames of the black lady and the Black Lady Overachiever. The black lady is a caretaker for both home and community. She is often portrayed as frugal, while maintaining the appearance of middle-class successfulness. The accusations that Senator Moseley Braun, both purposefully and possibly unknowingly, misused campaign funds for her own personal gain is evidence that she violated the trust of her constituents. In that her gain represents the accoutrements of material wealth, she became a political gold digger or hustler who "tricked" the U.S. public into paying for her clothes, jewelry, cars, and homes.

In the news media, Senator Moseley Braun's fiancé, Kgosie Matthews, is referenced as a participant in the misuse of the senator's campaign funds. Matthews was Moseley Braun's campaign manager for the 1992 Senate campaign, having had no prior experience. A lawyer and Nigerian lobbyist, Matthews faced other allegations during his tenure as the senator's campaign manager: he was accused of sexually harassing female members of then candidate Moseley Braun's office staff. After a brief investigation, Moseley Braun found the "charges" to be "baseless."[34] It has also been insinuated that Moseley Braun's decision to visit Nigeria, without approval from the State Department, early in her Senate career was because of Matthews's influence, as a Nigerian lobbyist, over her political decision making. While Moseley Braun explained the trip as attending the funeral of a friend, human rights groups accused her of consorting with officials of a violent dictatorship that the U.S. government had shunned.

Moseley Braun's romantic attachment to a black man outside the sanctity of marriage also made her an untrustworthy political figure. In order to maintain the favor or affection of her fiancé, media assumed that she was willing to make his wants and needs her priority, over the interests of her constituents, the nation, and evidently her female office workers:

The big irony for Moseley-Braun, 51, is that the woman who became a feminist icon on a platform of "I believe Anita Hill" seems to have shipwrecked her career over a man. "It's a tragedy that she ever met him," moaned Kay Clement, a former close friend of Moseley-Braun from Hyde Park. "Him" is Kgosie Matthews, 41, the senator's former fiancé and 1992 campaign manager. Although Moseley-Braun and Matthews broke off their engagement in January 1994, the abrasive South Africa native continues to haunt her career.[35]

The final aspect of the Black Lady Overachiever that confounded Moseley Braun's campaign is sexuality. Although the Black Lady Overachiever can be a sexual being, that sexuality must be contained within the confines of traditional heterosexual marriage. Collins notes, "all systems of oppression rely on harnessing the power of the erotic."[36] A black woman's heteronormative marriage operates as a control mechanism to offset the normative, historical description of black women's hypersexuality. The single Black Lady Overachiever must be asexual or risk the casting of her identity within dominant discourse as the hypersexual jezebel reinforcing the social belief in the abnormality of black female sexuality. Her lack of a husband feeds into the social belief that successful black women are masculine and aggressive, making them unattractive to men. Without marriage to contain her hypersexuality, Moseley Braun's choice to date a black man and to give him power over her campaign and the Senate office without the benefit of marriage positioned her as a figure of ridicule: Moseley Braun became an out-of-control jezebel willing to pass on control of the levers of power to an untrustworthy man.

Questions of Race Loyalty

The previously mentioned difficulties were not the only problems Moseley Braun faced in the 2004 presidential race. She was not the only African American seeking the Democratic nomination as she entered the presidential race months after the Rev. Al Sharpton began campaigning, and the news media represented Moseley Braun as a political counter to him.[37] The *Michigan Citizen* noted that Senator Moseley Braun's "candidacy has . . . been characterized as a 'stop Sharpton' bid."[38] A staff writer for *Human Events* wrote: "On January 27, Moseley-Braun had held a hush-hush meeting with Democratic National Committee Chairman Terry McAuliffe, it is believed, [he] encouraged her to run. Why? Fear that Al Sharpton, who was already running, would win a sizeable share of the black vote in the primaries and become a major power broker in the national Democratic Party."[39] Sharpton's acerbic style and his confrontational ethic in discussing racial issues may have made the party establishment nervous. The *New York Beacon* notes that Sharpton consistently garnered the majority of black support in national polls, while Moseley Braun often trailed behind General Wesley Clark, Joe Lieberman, and Howard Dean.[40] Despite mounting opposition to the wars in Iraq and Afghanistan, President Bush remained popular with the U.S. public. The party establishment likely was concerned that Sharpton's campaign would destabilize support of the African American voting bloc, which the democrats depend upon in presidential elections. Positing the seemingly calmer Senator Moseley Braun as a counter served as a means of discrediting Rev. Sharpton's campaign.

This meant, however, that Moseley Braun could be characterized as a sellout to the black community and a willing political pawn of the white establishment. In addition, Moseley Braun targeted her campaign rhetoric to women voters. Her upper middle-class status, the fact that she was married to a white man (prior to her engagement to Kgosie Matthews), and her use of feminine style may have made her unpersuasive to a national black audience. Black feminist Evelyn Simien argues:

> A long-standing debate exists within the black community about the relationship between black feminist consciousness and race loyalty. Black civil rights organizations and their predominantly male leadership have argued that feminism detracts from race loyalty and divides its membership into separate camps. From this perspective, a focus on sex discrimination inhibits, or even precludes, the development of racial awareness and black empowerment.[41]

Black women who challenge the traditional spaces of black male authority are considered traitors to the black community and face its censure, and the Anita Hill/Clarence Thomas sexual harassment scandal stands as a contemporary example.

With these constraints in mind, in the following section, I explore the rhetorical strategies Moseley Braun used during her campaign: shoring up support from women voters, particularly white women; negotiating between the Good White Mother, Modern Mammy, and Black Matriarch frames; and rehabilitating her image. Indeed, Moseley Braun walked a rhetorical tightrope as she negotiated between various constituencies across differences of race, class, and gender within the presidential space that has been historically hostile to any invasion by black femininity as Shirley Chisholm's experience demonstrates.

FEMINIST SENSIBILITY AND THE GOOD WHITE MOTHER

From the beginning of the campaign, the media dubbed her candidacy a long shot: Moseley Braun trailed far behind in almost every national poll, and received few nationally significant endorsements from organizations or individuals. However, she did receive national endorsements from both NOW and the NWPC, news media sources noting: "women's groups are cheering her on."[42] Moseley Braun had already established feminist credentials, and Kim Grady, the president of NOW in 2003, stated: "Feminists are delighted that Carol Moseley-Braun is exploring a presidential run in 2004. A woman's place is definitely in the White House. Moseley-Braun is a long-time women's rights supporter with a record to back up her rhetoric."[43]

Moseley Braun's focus on gender difference functioned to shore up what she hoped would be her base of female support. Numerous scholars note that the office of the U.S. Presidency is a particularly gendered space, a masculine space.[44] Parry-Giles and Parry-Giles note that presidential space is "hegemonically masculine."[45] Thus, as female presidential candidates attempt to compete in this masculine space, they are often constrained by images and practices that define them as "other" in that space. And yet, black women are Othered in multiple ways in this space. Moseley Braun is only the second black woman to run for president, Shirley Chisholm being the first. Although femininity may be out of place on the presidential landscape, white middle-class women have race and class privilege that can help to offset their gender difference. Also, as white middle-class, heterosexual femininity represents the normative standard for U.S. women, acceptable performances of that femininity by white, middle-class, straight women may provide greater access to political authority.

Consistent with the neo-liberal white feminist frame expressed by Kim Grady, Moseley Braun referenced the lack of gender diversity at the highest levels of national government. She referred to the glass ceilings she broke as "the first woman on the Senate finance committee."[46] In response to a question about whether she was a long shot in the presidential race, Senator Moseley Braun quipped, "obviously I'm the only woman in the race . . . we've not had a woman president."[47] It is important to note that Moseley Braun identified gender and not race as "obviously" holding her back, even though no black person or woman of any race had occupied the position of U.S. president, given that her candidacy preceded President Barack Obama's successful run in 2008.

Yet, for Moseley Braun gender difference was quite relevant to her candidacy. Moseley Braun explained: "Being a woman I think gives me a slightly different take on a lot of the issues and on a lot of the solutions to the problems we face. Women have to be very results-oriented, very practical-minded, and approach things in terms of collaboration instead of competition."[48] Moseley Braun positioned herself as a feminine alternative with femininity as an important aspect of leadership. Additionally, "practicality" and "consensus-building" are characteristics associated with feminine style in women's public rhetoric. These characteristics, according to Moseley Braun, are "feminine assets . . . we learn as girls."[49] Her emphasis on "feminine assets" and her lack of reference to race functioned to assure her audience that all little girls have the same or similar learning experience.

Beyond constructing a rhetoric of sameness across women's experiences, Moseley Braun referenced motherhood and homemaking in constructing her identity for the campaign. Specifically, she made use of the Good White Mother frame in her campaign discourse. Various scholars have discussed motherhood as a powerful rhetorical symbol in political discourse.[50] In the U.S. context, however, motherhood has various symbolic associations, particularly when intersected by race, class, sexuality, nationality, and religion. Not all women have equal access to the rhetorical saliency of the motherhood frame. Women political candidates may use anecdotes and analogies that reference their identities as homemakers and wives to indicate that they engage in acceptable performances of white, straight, middle-class femininity (i.e., the Good White Mother). The Good White Mother in the U.S. social imagination stands as an idealized standard for femininity that constrains all women across various intersections, although in markedly different ways. Emerging from the tradition of the Cult of True Womanhood, the Good White Mother is committed to family (which includes husband and children), caretaking, and homemaking. The Good White Mother is a member of a religious community, even if not devout. She is an active community member, developing good relations with her neighbors. The Good White Mother also supports efforts to protect the rights of women and children. The 1990s "soccer mom," a popular symbol of women's political participation, characterized as white, middle class, and suburban with a sizable discretionary income, is a contemporary example of the Good White Mother.[51]

Moseley Braun negotiated this frame in important ways, defining herself through a particular version of femininity: "Following my time in the assistant U.S. Attorney's office, I married and started a family, and I was home, being a homemaker, when my neighbors got me engaged in a local environmental effort to save the bobbilinks in Jackson Park. We were protesting the removal of the bobbilinks' habitat (Laughter)."[52] Her characterization of herself as a mother, wife, and homemaker before entering the space of politics demonstrates an adherence to this heteronormative frame. Moseley Braun met her heterosexual obligation as a straight woman, proved she was a "real" woman and thus unlikely to disrupt heteronormativity by her presence in the masculine space of politics. Specifically, the mother/homemaker/wife is the representation of the normative social position of the middle-class U.S. woman. That Moseley Braun and her husband could afford for her to refrain from working and yet maintain a middle-class lifestyle is a significant marker of class privilege. In addition, her reference to bird conservation as her first entry into local politics is important. The face of environmental activism in the imagination of the U.S. public is most likely white and middle class. And, failing to save the bird habitat in her local neighborhood park did not pose any direct threat to her family or community.[53] Thus, her environmental activism is packaged as quite different from the grassroots movements started by poor and working-class women across race as they combat hazardous waste and emissions.

Narratives of the Bad Black Mother in the discourse of both public and popular media culture denigrate the mothering traditions of black women.[54] The image of the welfare queen, and the Bad Black Mother, institutionalized through the "Moynihan Report," are shaped by an intertextual relationship with the discourses of European colonialism and U.S. slavery that characterize black women as sexually licentious, aggressive, and domineering. In these narratives black women are cast as the downfall of poor, working-class black communities. Middle-class, professional, black women face similar accusations: that their time spent working outside the home is said to contribute to the poor academic achievement of black children and the pursuant problems with black criminality.[55]

Although utilizing the symbol of the Good White Mother is a strategy that might help to recuperate black femininity, black women still face ideologies at the intersection of race, gender, class, and sexuality that cause them to disrupt that frame. A black woman's performance of normative white femininity is always already read against her black female body. Thus, her performance is always spectacularly suspect and must then be continuously reperformed to sustain readability, and even then may remain unintelligible. If the Good White Mother was an uncomfortable fit for Moseley Braun, her rhetorical use of motherhood also could be read as a repetition of the image of the Modern Mammy.

MODERN MAMMY AND BUILDING COALITIONS IN A NATIONAL CAMPAIGN

In order to reap the rewards of professional success, the Black Lady Overachiever is often required to play the role of a "Modern Mammy."[56] As a historical representation of black femininity constructed during American slavery, mammy is "the faithful, obedient, domestic servant."[57] Mammy, as a trusted figure by the white family she cares for, relinquishes her responsibility to her own family, in favor of loyalty to the white family. She is wholly committed to the physical, spiritual, and emotional health of the white family, and her love for the family is unconditional, signifying a safe space for the family under her protection. Even outside the context of slavery, "the mammy symbolizes the dominant group's perceptions of the ideal Black female relationship to elite White male power."[58] Even though black women have entered other vocations, including professional positions, "now they are mammies to the workplace and are expected to intervene in every crisis."[59]

Indeed, Moseley Braun's campaign rhetoric can be read productively through the Modern Mammy frame. As a senator, Moseley Braun made the following statement at the DNC fall meeting: "it is going to take a woman to transform it [the presidency] into a recipe of success for America; I can create jobs and get this economy working for everybody and take a new broom to the mess Bush has left, and put our economic house in order."[60] Complicating her use of the mother/wife/homemaker frame, Moseley Braun is not just a "woman" repairing the damage done to the United States during the Bush administration. A gender-only reading of Moseley Braun's rhetoric would ignore the manner in which race intersects and alters signification. It is not that it takes just a "woman" to resolve the "mess," it takes a practical and hardworking black woman with a "new broom."

If the Modern Mammy is loyal and trustworthy, she also can be depended upon to take whatever actions are necessary to protect her white family. Here, the United States becomes the white family in the metaphor, requiring Moseley Braun's nurturance and support. The word "mess" indicates uncleanliness and disorder created by carelessness or ineptitude. The president and his emissaries are then characterized as spoiled, white children; their privilege having made them selfish and uncontrollable. Moseley Braun, as the Modern Mammy figure, would take control of the situation and bring order back to chaos.

In addition, the tool for solving the crisis is a "new broom," a familiar item that Mammy uses to clean the white household. Moseley Braun articulates that it must be a "new" broom because it is firm and stiff, rather than bendable and supple. Just as mammy knows which broom is most effective for the job, Modern Mammy knows what tools are needed to "put" the political and "economic house in order." If mammy is responsible for maintaining the orderliness of the house, then Moseley Braun's reference to the "economic house" is significant. As Mammy is trusted with access to the white family's resources, she must act responsibly and prove that the family's trust is well placed. To this end, the Modern Mammy frame may have helped Senator Moseley Braun respond to the accusation that she previously misused campaign funds. If the Modern Mammy is loyal and trustworthy, then Moseley Braun's rhetoric may have tapped into this symbolic framing to alleviate any lingering distrust among voters. Moreover, Moseley Braun explained that she had "an inclusive approach to politics."[61] She is everybody's mammy, all of America becomes the white family.

Not only are Mammies trustworthy caretakers, they also nourish bodies and souls. Responding to the endorsement of NOW and the NWPC, Moseley Braun explained:

> And I have a recipe for Democrats to win the White House in 2004. . . . First, you start with the people who elected Gore in 2000. . . . Then you add the people who voted for Bush who are out of work, out of money and out of hope. . . . And so you add a pinch of those voters who are distressed about the deficits, dismayed about the costs of Iraq. . . . And you stir all this up with tax cuts for the rich, Enron, Worldcom and Haliburton and you have a powerful stew.[62]

The recipe metaphor indicates that Moseley Braun knows the right ingredients, in the correct proportions, to produce the necessary balance. And, according to Olga Davis, "Although it was work, the creation of food was a rhetorical act of nurturance and care, creative genius, and survival. African dishes placed on the master's table proved that in the kitchen it was the African cook, not the mistress who was the teacher."[63] In this political context, Moseley

Braun becomes the "creative genius" who has developed a "recipe" or strategy for democrats to win the presidency.

In identifying the particular constituencies that are a part of her "recipe" for winning the presidency, Moseley Braun simultaneously demonstrates why the Modern Mammy frame may seem to be a useful strategy in producing a coalition to elect a black female president. With her "stew" she brings together variously situated groups of U.S. citizens and their positions on the political landscape. She calls out to the Gore democrats from the 2000 election. She also attempts to appeal to the middle to working-class republican family who has seen jobs shipped overseas and the cost of everyday expenses rising. Finally, she adds independent voters who are issue driven rather than candidate focused and are angry over the Bush tax cuts and the incentives given to big businesses at the expense of the taxpayer.

To ensure the right "recipe" and proportion of ingredients come to bear on the presidential race, Moseley Braun's metaphor implies that a culinary master is needed in the political kitchen. She is not referring to an Iron Chef or a Top Chef Master. Instead, she likens her political strategy to the preparation of a "powerful stew" and, in so doing, classes the frame. A "stew" resonates with an ethic of "making do" with whatever ingredients are available. It signifies a poor or working-class experience with financial struggle and feeding a family with limited food resources. It represents the sacrifices mothers make to provide what is necessary for their families. Moseley Braun's "stew"—designed to nourish the national body with a healthy meal of inclusive politics—is a gendered, raced, and classed solution to caring for, and leading, the nation.

However, the Modern Mammy frame may also have been unpersuasive to black voters given the questions concerning Moseley Braun's racial credibility. Although her political and legislative career indicate a commitment to sponsoring, passing, and implementing various policies that benefit communities of color, news media focus remained on the potential conflict between the senator and Rev. Al Sharpton. The Mammy is often portrayed as disconnected from the interests of black communities because she is permanently entrenched in the white family. Similarly, the Modern Mammy is supposed to prioritize the white male power structure within which she participates. When asked by interviewers from both *National Public Radio* and the *TriState Defender* about her loyalties, Moseley Braun explained: "I did not get in this to take on one candidate . . . that has been a rumor."[64] She argued that the presidential race was a "competition" and she was "campaigning to take votes from all the candidates."[65] Moseley Braun identified the "rumor" as representing a malicious narrative designed to harm and discredit her candidacy and defined the nature of political campaigning as competitive, indicating that she was simply playing the game as it was intended to be played. Moseley Braun never referred to Sharpton directly nor did she explicitly respond to the race claim. Instead, she sidestepped the accusation and broadened the issue to all party hopefuls signifying that Sharpton was no more significant than any of the other candidates.

In sum, the Modern Mammy, as a frame for black female political candidates seeking a broad and diverse base of support, may operate as a double bind, constraining the possibility of success in a national election. If black female candidates need the support of black and white voters, the Modern Mammy frame limits their ability to speak explicitly to race issues or to directly reference racial difference in campaign rhetoric. The Modern Mammy, in the political context, is supposed to remain politically unraced in order to engender a level of comfort within the white male power structure. She can be raced as long as race is limited to cultural expressions in spaces outside the political sphere. Although race is allowed limited visibility on occasions like African American history month, cultural celebrations, or office potlucks to which black women are expected to bring soul food, the Modern Mammy's race should never influence her decision making or be an excuse for demonstrating disloyalty to the white male power structure. Moseley Braun's reticence to negotiate directly the relevance of race and gender ideology in U.S. politics may have offered her protection from becoming the "race candidate," but it also may have alienated potential white voters. Yet, such a stance may also have indicated to black voters that she was unwilling to represent black America or have their best interests at heart. Given the specific problems she faced as a result of the rumors surrounding Sharpton, the Modern Mammy frame may have done more to strengthen Moseley Braun's appearance as a race traitor.

SIGNIFYIN(G) ON THE GOOD WHITE MOTHER AND THE MODERN MAMMY

Both the Modern Mammy and the Good White Mother are frames associated with significations of black female identity. Each depends on a limiting of blackness as a rhetorically or politically relevant identity category for black candidates. As I argue in the previous section, black female political candidates are situated in political discourse across various ideological differences, making it difficult to achieve identification with the diverse constituents needed to win a national election. However, the Modern Mammy and the Good White Mother may offer a rhetorical cover for black female candidates who engage in the African American practice of signifyin(g), to reach out to black communities without having to implicitly speak to or from those home places. Moseley Braun's campaign rhetoric is not only an example of a feminine style intersected by race, class, and sexuality, but it is peppered with signifyin(g) rhetoric that distinguishes her from the Modern Mammy and the Good White Mother. For Moseley Braun, the Black Matriarch became a signifyin(g) frame from which she could speak to African Americans, all the while under the narrative guise of feminine style, simultaneously signifying on elite white America.

Davis argues that both slave women and black female domestic workers, who were assigned to kitchen duties and the daily care of the master's or employer's home, developed a "cultural space . . . to recover" black women's "dignity and power of tradition."[66] During and following slavery, black women created the kitchen as the safe space from which to buttress the material realities of raced and gendered subjugation. As many black women "emerged from the kitchen of black dominated space into the dining room of white dominated space," they brought narrative strategies from "the kitchen" into spaces from which they were previously excluded.[67] Like others before her, Moseley Braun used the traditional authority of black women in the kitchen as a space safe from white domination to construct a double-voiced narrative. This strategy illustrates the intersectional tensions inherent in the rhetorical frames at Moseley Braun's disposal.

Contrary to the myth of the Black Matriarch described above, within African American communities, black women who have held the sole responsibility for the survival of their families are often characterized as the Strong Black Woman. Rather than denigrating black women for having children outside of marriage, black communal discourse signifies the Black Matriarch as a positive image of the black superwoman. This version of the Black Matriarch signifies black women's commitment to family and community, hard work, and a willingness to make sacrifices for the betterment of those she cares about. The Black Matriarch may perform Modern Mammy under the white gaze, while maintaining a critical orientation that provides a means of resisting the effects of white privilege.

In her announcement speech at Howard University, one of the most prestigious historically black colleges and universities in the country, Moseley Braun stated: "I can fix the mess they have created, because I am practical."[68] Although her reference to the "mess" from above placed the blame on President Bush, her use of "they" in this example may indicate a broadening of the blame for the current crisis. Moseley Braun is, of course, referring to the entire administration and the Congress, which includes members of the Democratic Party and sections of the U.S. public. Her reference, however, also could refer to economically privileged whites whose influence and control over government created the "mess." In this one pronoun switch, Moseley Braun communicated that the "mess" had grown to such proportions that it required an industrious and strong black woman to clean up after financially well-off white people. Thus, we cannot assume that it is the subservient and obedient Mammy who is the savior. Instead, if we read Moseley Braun as signifyin(g) on the Mammy, her stance is really one that sees through the illusion of the loving white family to the reality that the white family cannot really be loved because of its subjugation of black people.

In addition, the practicality that Moseley Braun often referenced as a feminine characteristic can also represent the wisdom of older black women within the discourses of black communities. For example, when referencing the Bush tax cuts and the wars in Iraq and Afghanistan, Moseley Braun repeated the phrase: "it didn't make a whole lot of sense."[69] This rhetorical stance could signify the tough love both children and adults receive from older black female family and community members. In the context of the black community, older black women are respected and revered for their knowledge and particularly their commonsense. In addition, age provides older black women with the wisdom and leeway to "tell it like it is." The older black woman has seen enough to avoid being easily fooled. Thus, her perspective allows her to see beyond the illusions created to pacify her and her people. This sage figure in the African American tradition depends on her experiential knowledge and has a healthy skepticism toward establishment rhetoric.

If the Good White Mother and the Modern Mammy operate as a cover for the Black Matriarch, and it appears they do so in Moseley Braun's campaign rhetoric, then they may also allow her a means to signify on her white female and feminist supporters. Despite the fact that both black and white women face gender oppression, white women's racial privilege has often discouraged unity over issues of gender subjugation. As the kitchen, according to Davis, was "preeminently the domain of black women," it became a safe space for black women away from the racism of white women.[70] In other words, when Moseley Braun argued that "they" have created a "mess," she indicated that white women's participation in the elite white male power structure made them responsible for the crisis as well. Senator Moseley Braun repositioned black women as being privy to a practical wisdom not shared with white women because of their racial privilege.

CONCLUSION

What does it mean for black female political candidates to find themselves negotiating the Modern Mammy and Black Matriarch frames? Both representations afford black women limited maneuverability around identity performance. The Modern Mammy frame requires a direct participation in systems of institutional power that reproduce racism, sexism, classism, and heterosexism. The Modern Mammy reconstitutes a deferential relationship to whiteness and may tie the hands of black female candidates. The Black Matriarch frame violates the Modern Mammy frame as this black woman is anything but docile and obedient. The Black Matriarch is more confrontational regarding whiteness and economic privilege. If the performance of this frame was more explicit during the campaign, Moseley Braun may have had no chance of developing a diverse support base. Instead, the conflict between the Modern Mammy and the Black Matriarch demonstrates why signifyin(g) may be a necessary rhetorical strategy for black female candidates. Even as the Modern Mammy may make non-blacks more comfortable, if the black female political candidate can achieve a double-voiced communication strategy, she may be able to maintain identification with black communities without sacrificing the support of non-blacks.

Although Moseley Braun engaged in the performance of feminine style to generate a persuasive message, her identity as a black woman limited her ability to perform that style. For black women to perform feminine style, they must perform the white feminine ideal that, by its very definition, poses black femininity as its antithesis. Despite a mimicking of the ideals of white femininity, black women are trapped in a performance that is in opposition to the blackness of their bodies. In as much as the standard of feminine style as a rhetorical position is built within a discourse of white, middle-class femininity by definition, black women whose discourse is reflective of that style may receive both recognition and be penalized for their performance.[71]

Gender is always already raced and classed. As this analysis of Moseley Braun demonstrates, a gender-only reading of women's discourse ignores the manner in which feminine style is predicated on the reiteration of normative performances of white femininity. To date, studies of feminine style have focused exclusively on the discourse of white women, as if white women remain unraced. Race is not only a significant consideration in feminist rhetorical analysis when the rhetor is a person of color. Our silence with regard to race, class, and sexuality is a methodological cover story that reinforces white feminist performances as the norm and disciplines the speech of nonwhite feminists, further shrinking the rhetorical space of resistance. Thus, as feminist communication scholars write feminist accounts of white female rhetoricians, particularly those using feminine style, we should always and explicitly consider how race, class, and heteronormative sexuality intersect with gender to help or hamper their rhetorical position.

NOTES

1. Dayo Omolade, "The Root Interview: Carol Moseley-Braun," *The Root*, March 9, 2010, accessed March 10, 2011, http:www.theroot.com/views/root-interview-carol-moseley-braun.

2. Cited in Omolade, "The Root."

3. Alexandra Marks, "The Quest of Carol Moseley Braun," *Christian Science Monitor*, November 20, 2003, 1; Mary Jacoby, "'98 Is Not Sen. Moseley-Braun's Year," *St. Petersburg Times*, October 31, 1998, 1A; Ann Gerhart, "What Makes Carol Run? Moseley Braun Is Short on Campaign Cash and Staff but Long on Determination," *Washington Post*, November 12, 2003, C01; Monica Davey, "To Some, Ex-Senators Campaign Is Effort to Set Record Straight; Road to the White House/Braun's Long-Shot Bid," *International Herald Tribune*, December 19, 2003, 2.

4. Senator Moseley Braun was the first woman to serve on the Finance Committee and passed legislation for women's pension equity, environmental remediation, school modernization, and interest rate deduction for college loans. She also delivered a speech on the Senate floor in 1993 opposing the extension of a patent to the United Daughters of the Confederacy insignia, which included the confederate flag. The reaction from Senator Jesse Helms, who sponsored the legislation, demonstrated the difficulties that Moseley Braun faced in the Senate as one of two African Americans and the only black woman. Following the defeat of the legislation, Senator Helms cornered Moseley Braun in a Senate elevator and whistled the tune to "Dixie," threatening to continue to do so until he had forced Moseley Braun to cry. She did not cry.

5. Karlyn Kohrs Campbell, *Man Cannot Speak for Her*, 2 vols. (New York: Greenwood Press, 1989).

6. Bonnie J. Dow and Mari Boor Tonn, "'Feminine Style' and Political Judgment in the Rhetoric of Ann Richards," *Quarterly Journal of Speech* 79 (1993): 286.

7. Dow and Tonn, "Feminine Style," 287.

8. Dow and Tonn, "Feminine Style."

9. Bonnie J. Dow, "Feminism, Difference(s), and Rhetorical Studies," *Communication Studies* 46 (1995): 106–118; Jane Blankenship and Deborah C. Robson, "A 'Feminine Style' In Women's Political Discourse: An Exploratory Essay," *Communication Quarterly* 43 (1995): 353–366; Victoria Pruin DeFrancisco and Catherine Helen Palczewski, *Communicating Gender Diversity: A Critical Approach* (Thousand Oaks, CA: Sage, 2007); Sara Hayden, "Re-Claiming Bodies of Knowledge: An Exploration of the Relationship between Feminist Theorizing and Feminine Style in the Rhetoric of the Boston Women's Health Book Collective," *Western Journal of Speech Communication* 61 (1997): 127–163; Jennifer A. Peeples and Kevin M. DeLuca, "The Truth of the Matter: Motherhood, Community and Environmental Justice," *Women's Studies in Communication* 29 (2006): 59–87.

10. Blankenship and Robson, "Feminine Style," 354.

11. Blankenship and Robson, "Feminine Style. "

12. Blankenship and Robson, "Feminine Style," 363.

13. DeFrancisco and Palczewski, *Communicating Gender*, xii.

14. DeFrancisco and Palczewski, *Communicating Gender*, 42.

15. Karlyn Kohrs Campbell, "Style and Content in the Rhetoric of Early Afro-American Feminists," *Quarterly Journal of Speech*, 72 (1986): 434–444.

16. Henry Louis Gates, Jr., *The Signifying Monkey: A Theory of Afro-American Literary Criticism* (New York: Oxford University Press, 1988), 97.

17. Gates, *Signifying Monkey*, 51.

18. Gates, *Signifying Monkey*, 86.

19. Gates, *Signifying Monkey*, 97.

20. Steve Chapman, "Chicago Hopeless," *New Republic*, 219, no. 16 (1998): 19–21.

21. Nancy Traver, "This Is a Honeymoon?" *Time*, January 18, 1993, 10–11.

22. Jacoby, "'98 Is Not."

23. "Calamity Carol," *The Economist*, August 30, 1997, 18.

24. Marks, "The Quest of Carol Moseley Braun," 1.

25. Patricia Hill Collins, *Black Feminist Thought: Knowledge, Consciousness, and the Politics of Empowerment*, 2nd ed. (New York: Routledge, 2000), 69–70.

26. Patricia Hill Collins, *Black Sexual Politics: African Americans, Gender, and the New Racism* (New York: Routledge, 2004), 140–141.

27. Patricia Hill Collins, *Fighting Words: Black Women and the Search for Justice* (Minneapolis: University of Minnesota Press, 1998), 39.

28. Collins, *Fighting Words*.

29. Collins, *Black Feminist*, 72.

30. E. Frances White, *Dark Continent of Our Bodies: Black Feminism and the Politics of Respectability* (Philadelphia: Temple University Press, 2001), 14. While black women may have found a useful strategy in

mimicking white femininity, they do not attempt to replicate it exactly. It is a repetition that allows black women to build a version of black femininity that adheres to norms of white femininity while producing a strategy solidly situated in black women's experience and cultural knowledge.

31. White, *Dark Continent*, 36.

32. Collins, *Fighting Words*, 39.

33. Collins, *Fighting Words*.

34. Jacoby, "'98 Is Not."

35. Jacoby, "'98 Is Not."

36. Collins, *Black Feminist*, 128.

37. "Welcome to the Club, Carol," *Chicago Defender*, February 25, 2003, 8; Hazel Trice Edney, "Moseley-Braun Campaigns against Sharpton—and Everyone Else," *Tri-State Defender*, June 25, 2003, 3A; Gerhart, "What Makes Carol Run?"

38. Ron Walters, "Vantage Point; a Possible Strategy for Two Black Presidential Candidates," *Michigan Citizen*, March 8, 2003, A7.

39. "Crowd of One Greets Moseley-Braun," *Human Events*, February 24, 2003, 6.

40. "Poll Shows: Rev. Al Sharpton Leads among Black Voters," *New York Beacon*, November 5, 2003, 4.

41. Evelyn M. Simien, *Black Feminist Voices in Politics* (Albany: State University of New York Press, 2006), 48.

42. Allison Stevens, "Moseley Braun Runs for President and More," *Womens eNews* March 4, 2003, accessed March 13, 2011 http://www.womens enews.org/story/campaign_trail.

43. Stevens, "Moseley Braun."

44. Shawn J. Parry-Giles and Trevor Parry-Giles, "Gendered Politics and Presidential Image Construction: A Reassessment of the 'Feminine Style,'"*Communication Monographs* 63 (1996): 337–353; Murray J. Edelman, *Constructing the Political Spectacle* (Chicago: University of Chicago Press, 1988); Michael S. Kimmel, *Manhood in America: A Cultural History* (New York: Free Press, 1996).

45. Parry-Giles and Parry-Giles, "Gendered Politics," 337–338.

46. Bob Edwards, "Former Sen. Carol Moseley Braun," *National Public Radio: Morning Edition* May 6, 2003, accessed March 13, 2011 http://www .npr.org/programs/specials/democrats2004/transcripts/braun_trans.html.

47. Edwards, "Former Sen."

48. Edwards, "Former Sen."

49. Carol Moseley Braun, "Politics," *Washington Post*, May 12, 2003, accessed March 13, 2011 www.washingtonpost.com/wp-srv/liveonline/03/ special/politics/sp_politics_braun051203.htm.

50. Karrin Vasby Anderson, "From Spouses to Candidates: Hillary Rodham Clinton, Elizabeth Dole, and the Gendered Office of the U.S. President," *Rhetoric and Public Affairs* 5 (2002): 105–132; Dow and Tonn, "Feminine Style"; Peeples and DeLuca, "The Truth."

51. Anderson, "From Spouses."

52. Carol Moseley Braun, "Remarks before the Iowa Health Care Forum," August 14, 2003, accessed November 10, 2004 http://www.carolfor president.com. This website is no longer active.

53. Peeples and DeLuca, "The Truth."

54. Collins, *Black Feminist*.

55. Collins, *Fighting Words*.

56. Collins, *Black Feminist*, 74

57. Collins, *Black Feminist*, 72.

58. Collins, *Black Feminist*.

59. Collins, *Black Feminist*, 74.

60. Carol Moseley Braun, "Remarks before the Democratic National Committee Fall," October 23, 2003, accessed November 10, 2004 http://www.carolforpresident.com.

61. Edwards, "Former Sen."

62. Carol Moseley Braun, "Statement of Ambassador Moseley-Braun at the Endorsement by National Organization for Women and the National Women's Political Caucus," August 26, 2003, accessed November 12, 2004 http://www.carolforpresident.com.

63. Olga Idriss Davis, "In the Kitchen: Transforming the Academy through Safe Spaces of Resistance," *Western Journal of Communication* 63 (1999): 368.

64. Edney, "Moseley Braun"; Edwards, "Former Sen."

65. Edwards, "Former Sen."

66. Davis, "In the Kitchen," 365.

67. Davis, "In the Kitchen."

68. Carol Moseley Braun, "Announcement Speech at Howard University," September 22, 2004, accessed November 12, 2004 http://www.carol forpresident.com.

69. Cited in Edwards, "Former Sen."

70. Davis, "In the Kitchen," 368.

71. All U.S. female political candidates are constrained by the idealized version of femininity, but across different avenues of power. It is that difference that makes visible the race, gender, class, and sexual ideologies that operate in tandem to subjectify and subjugate.

Chapter 2

The Intersectional Style
of Free Love Rhetoric

Kate Zittlow Rogness

A s an oxymoron, feminist rhetorical theory and criticism offers unique opportunities to study how sociocultural constructions of "woman" influence discourse, opinion, policy, and subjectivity.[1] Patriarchy reinforces a condition of lack by socializing women to strive toward an image of ideal womanhood that is unattainable.[2] By limiting ourselves (physically, sexually, emotionally, intellectually), we are led to believe that we will realize professional, personal, and intimate fulfillment. Women are thus faced with the riddle: How can I become a "whole" woman through subtraction?

This riddle reinforces what Elizabeth Spelman refers to as "pop-bead metaphysics."[3] Women's identities are compartmentalized into categories of race, sexuality, nationality, or otherwise, as if there is some core essence of "woman" with which all women could (or should) relate. For Spelman, this way of thinking implies that "being a woman means the same whether [she is] white or Black, rich or poor, French or Jamaican, or Jewish or Muslim."[4] Pop-bead feminism often translates into one-size-fits-all solutions to the discrimination women experience. These solutions address the needs of some women, while creating or reinforcing prejudicial practices that put at risk the well-being of other women. As Kimberlé Crenshaw warns, for example, policies and laws established to protect women from domestic abuse and rape can increase the discrimination experienced by married immigrant women, whose partners may threaten divorce and deportation should the abuse be reported.[5] Such rhetoric serves to separate "women from their potential as members of society as well as their existences within that order and offer[s] women a limited framework from which to operate."[6]

Feminist rhetorical scholars work toward changing the face of culture, politics, and the academy by incorporating feminism into the rhetorical canon and by using women's voices to challenge those patriarchal norms that exclude women by translating or silencing their experiences. To include women into the rhetorical canon, some scholars have focused on "inventing woman."[7] Women have been able to transform their public and civic subjectivity through discourse, from creating a feminine public persona to facilitating the passage of the Nineteenth Amendment. For instance, Karlyn Kohrs Campbell describes how women were able to invent a public space from which they could legitimately speak when they did not have a history of participating in public conversations or debate.[8] Scholars have also invented the rhetorical woman (who is markedly different from the supposedly ungendered rhetorical actor) by describing how women have developed ways to exercise their influence while simultaneously reinforcing and challenging cultural norms of femininity—even when they have been historically prohibited from education, public forums, or civic subjectivity.[9] Finally, scholars describe how "woman" has been invented through cultural norms and public discourse by tracing the development of "woman" and "man" as sociocultural phenomena that shape, enable, and restrict individuals and their experiences.[10]

An overarching goal of feminist rhetorical criticism, as suggested by Carole Spitzack and Kathryn Carter, is to complicate the ways we communicate gender and communicate about gender, because "unless investigations of women serve to challenge and complicate depictions of human communication, the insights gained by gender and feminist scholars are easily placed back into the pre-established frameworks that have been found to distort women's communication."[11] Thus, the purpose of feminist rhetorical analysis has not only been to record women's discourse and include them into the annals of public address, but also to use those texts to challenge patriarchal assumptions that have dominated the field of rhetoric and shaped our cultural landscapes. Feminist rhetorical analysis, then, is a form of rhetorical criticism committed to social justice through dissolving patriarchal forces that have silenced women's voices, while also providing insights for rethinking the social construction of gender from a rhetorical perspective.

An underlying principle in feminist rhetorical criticism has been the public and private sphere dichotomy. The private sphere, the space of the home and family, was "woman's space" where she could develop her "natural" talents for nurturance and domesticity by being pious and submissive.[12] Counter to the private, the public sphere was considered a masculine space where men might use their "innate" reason to participate in political debate. The dichotomy of public/private has informed much of what we know about feminist activism, from the nineteenth-century development of a "feminine style" of speech, to more contemporary performances of feminist activism, such as the second-wave mantra: "the personal is political."

The inequality derived from separating the personal from the political has been most intimately felt by white, middle-class, heterosexual women. The experiences of women who have been cast as Other have "never fit the logic of work in the public sphere juxtaposed to family obligations in the private sphere."[13] Historically, immigrants, women of color, and poor white women found it necessary to take work outside their own home in order to supplement their families' income. This work was often domestic, fulfilling the domestic duties of their white, upper-class counterparts as maids, cooks, or child care providers. As a result, white, upper-class, married women were able to appear more "feminine" because of hired and forced help in the home. This environment created the opportunity for white, middle-class women to protest their oppressed condition, fulfilling Patricia Hill Collins's assertion that: "In such frameworks, all individuals and groups possess varying amounts of penalty and privilege in one historically created system . . . depending on the context, individuals and groups may be alternately oppressors in some settings, oppressed in others, or simultaneously oppressing and oppressed."[14] Thus, while aptly informing the experience and discourse of one group (white, upper-class, heterosexual, U.S. women), the dichotomy of the public/private sphere has also served to reinforce racial, class-based, and sexual hierarchies that oppress immigrants, women of color, LGBTQ individuals, and poor people.

The discrimination created and reinforced by the private/public dichotomy sheds light on the challenge that the differences among women and between genders poses for feminist scholarship. Unifying theories of feminism with coordinating "solutions" requires women to subtract from who they are, or transform themselves altogether, in order to best fit an "emancipating" ideal of womanhood. Reflecting on this experience, Audre Lorde states, "I find that I am constantly being encouraged to pluck out some one aspect of myself and present this as the meaningful whole, eclipsing or denying the other parts of the self."[15] Scholars warn that the "whole" Lorde refers to is often the image and experience of heterosexual, white, U.S. women.[16] The consequential tension between difference and unity "has left many feminists uneasy or misunderstood, others silenced, and no small measure of us uncertain about whether we can have productive conversations about our differences."[17] In many cases, particularly for white scholars, this tension has been interpreted as a *problem* to feminist theorizing.[18]

Rather than a weakness or problem of feminism, difference is "that raw and powerful connection from which our personal power is forged."[19] By acknowledging our differences in a spirit of equality, we might "devise ways to use each other's difference to enrich our visions and our joint struggles."[20] Intersectionality provides a way to account for the complex, nuanced, lived experiences of women that lie beyond the boundaries of traditional theory. Intersectionality does not replace the white, middle-to-upper class, heterosexual, U.S. female experience that is represented through established theories, such as feminine style. Instead, it *displaces* the centrality that experience has held in our academic circles and social activism by recognizing that women's and men's experiences are shaped by their gender *and* race, class, sexuality, and nationality.

Theories of intersectionality reject unifying conceptualizations of woman, womanhood, and their related solutions. Instead, we are called to "explore plural differences among women, both celebrating women's differences and criticizing reductionist representations of an everywoman."[21] Thus, intersectionality presents us with the challenge to generalize from personal experience in a way that resists concretizing "woman" into a static subject position.

Intersectionality is often evoked as a perspective or lens through which feminist scholars identify how cultural subjectivities, such as gender, race, sexuality, or nationality, interact to shape the structural, political, and representational aspects of experience.[22] Intersectionality holds that our subject positions are imbued with the oppressive power to discriminate against one group in order to (further) empower ourselves. To counter this trend, intersectionality aims to develop "politically empowering alliances [that] resist subordination."[23] Intersectionality thus may "be used by rhetoricians to analyze critically how differences among women are discursively constructed to hierarchically privilege the experience of heterosexual, white, U.S. women."[24] Intersectionality may also guide scholars to consider how one's subject position informs and lends rhetorical power to her discourse.[25] Such analyses focus on one's experience of being "woman," for instance, as a raced, gendered, sexed, classed, and nationalized cultural construction, and womanhood as a temporary, ever-evolving, and fluid experience.

Though intersectionality provides perspective and guidance to feminist scholars, it has largely been an abstract ideal toward which we orient our theorizing and criticism. This abstraction resists totalizing women's experience, yet we may be left wondering: How does one *do* intersectional criticism? To answer this question, I turn toward the public discourse of free love at the turn of the century. To show how free lovers embodied an *intersectional style*, I first describe their discourse through the perspective of intersectionality, paying specific attention to the ways that intersecting forces shaped their critique of marriage and influenced their visions of free love. I then use this description as the basis for my argument: The discourse of free lovers embodied an intersectional style that is characterized by impropriety, play, and possibility. I conclude by explaining how the characteristics of an intersectional style of discourse may be used as a critical rhetorical instrument to examine the agentic possibility of those discourses that do not fit into the parameters of traditional feminist rhetoric, and to challenge those theoretical norms that oppress individuals on the basis of sex, sexuality, gender, race, and class.

THE INTERSECTIONAL STYLE OF FREE LOVE

The discursive ideal for public discourse has largely been aligned with masculine norms of rationality and disembodiment. Echoing Aristotle and Cicero, Jürgen Habermas highlighted this ideal in his description of a healthy public sphere, which is characterized by critical publicity.[26] Critical publicity rests on members of the public's ability to access information and their capacity to shape public arguments. In order for arguments to be "public," they must be "depersonalized so that, in theory, any person would have the ability to offer an opinion about them and submit that opinion to the impersonal test of public debate without personal hazard."[27] As this suggests, the particularized body and personal experience is abstracted from rational thought, and the speaking subject occupies a space of "utopian universality."[28] In order to participate in the public sphere, then, "one must abstract from the positivities of race, gender, sexuality, and class along with other corporeal specificities in order to enact one's agency as citizen-subject through proper protocols of speech and bodily deportment."[29]

Utopian universality is conveyed through a specific rhetorical style. Style refers to the "initial encounter through which auditors apprehend meaning," or the way a rhetor shapes his or her "presentation of self to the roles established for speaker, subject, and audience."[30] Style is often reflected through word choice, the form of argument, the evidence one uses to justify claims, and delivery.

As it reflects audience expectations, situational constraints, and the purpose of the speech, style is typically characterized by norms of decorum. Cicero referred to this as the "golden mean"; the speaker's capacity to adhere to some norms of decorum while transgressing others in order to persuade an audience. Thus, style is often the deliberate response to rhetorical constraints, but also, is a constraint in itself, as it shapes how an audience might interpret and respond to a message.

As the public sphere has typically been gendered masculine, the rhetorical style of the universal subject position is stereotypically masculine—"the male, the white, the middle class, the normal."[31] On the other hand, women—the physical aberration to the universal subject—have been encoded in emotionality, irrationality, and embodied civic subjectivity. This means that men do not need to account for the positivity of their bodies in public debate because they are assumed to be inherently rational compared to their emotional female counterpart. As a result, "self abstraction from male bodies confirms masculinity" while "self abstraction from female bodies denies femininity."[32] Generally accepted norms of decorum thus express a fear of the body, or somatophobia.[33]

As described above, women have accounted for their bodies by adopting a feminine style of discourse. Reflecting the means by which women learned the crafts of housewifery and motherhood, women's speech in the nineteenth century embodied a feminine style by presenting arguments inductively and by offering personal experience as the justification for claims.[34] By affirming the qualities of femininity, particularly piety, women were able to account for the positivity of their bodies in public spaces by becoming the moral arbiters of public reason. Yet this morality, as it was embodied through feminine style, celebrated the unmarked woman, the prototypical bead in Spelman's metaphysical pop-bead jewelry. The specific feminine qualities embodied in feminine style (purity, piety, domesticity and submissiveness) translated into a particular vision of a "true woman": dainty, weak, and *pale*.[35] In this regard, some women were able to abstract from their particular selves in order to fulfill an abstract feminine subjectivity, while other women were excluded altogether. Fear of the body thus translates into fear of the female body.

Responding to this public pubic psychosis, an ever present theme within feminist discourse and activism has been the desire for a fullness of expression and experience—or a return to the body. Gloria Anzaldúa describes this desire as the path of El Mundo Zurdo, Lorde describes it as the erotic, and, at the turn of the twentieth century, Victoria Woodhull, Voltairine de Cleyre, and Emma Goldman described this desire as free love.[36] Each conceptualization is unique and transformative, focusing on the "lifeforce of women; of that creative energy empowered, the knowledge and use of which we are now reclaiming in our language, our history, our dancing, our loving, our work, our lives."[37] While advocates of free love did not agree on a unifying definition of free love, the nature of their public discourse suggests that agreement was secondary, even insignificant, for women's and men's movement toward liberation. Woodhull, de Cleyre, and Goldman privileged the personal rather than the political, demonstrating how one's personal experience shapes her or his vision of freedom. Their attention to the personal, specific experiences of women and men conveys an openness to the multiple ways equality might be envisioned and embodied through free love within intimate, social, and political relationships. These accounts may be read as a precursor to later critiques of power that inform intersectionality.

Reading free love discourse from an intersectional perspective lends insight into how women respond to the constraint that their bodies are always gendered, sexualized, raced, classed, and nationalized. Not quite straight, not quite American, and not quite white, Woodhull, de Cleyre, and Goldman transgressed cultural norms of femininity that were defined through heterosexuality, a patriarchal republican civic ideal, and whiteness. While their trajectories toward wholeness differed, Woodhull, Goldman, and de Cleyre communicated a common emancipatory spirit that might be fulfilled through free love. As I argue below, Woodhull, de Cleyre, and Goldman not only articulated a vision of free love that resisted a concrete or static sense of womanhood, but the way they articulated that vision also suggests an intersectional style of discourse that is characterized by impropriety, play, and possibility.

Free love began as a lifestyle, a central organizing ideal among utopian communities that were scattered across the United States. As a lifestyle, free lovers believed that the legal institution of marriage was unnatural because it inhibited individuals from developing and ending relationships on the basis of desire and emotion. Free love transformed from a lifestyle into a feminist issue in the 1870s with Victoria Woodhull's 1871 speech, "The Principles of Social Freedom." As a feminist issue, free love viewed the institution of marriage as unnatural: marriage disrupted the social order and created conditions of dependency, servitude, despotism, prostitution, and a sexual double standard. As an alternative to marriage, free love would liberate women and men from the roles of husband

and wife and the cultural assumptions of gender that were politically and socially policed through those roles. Free love would restore social order, creating the conditions for true freedom. Over its
tenure as a movement, free love began as a supplement to suffrage
alongside the debates on divorce, and evolved into a core argument
of anarchist feminism. Unlike suffrage, which primarily addressed
women's civic rights, free love considered the force of both politics
and culture in women's condition and liberation. Three important
proponents of free love are Victoria Woodhull, Voltairine de Cleyre,
and Emma Goldman.

VICTORIA WOODHULL: THE IMPROPRIETY
OF FREE LOVE

Victoria Woodhull, the first woman to speak to a congressional hearing (1870), worked as a stock and gold broker on Wall Street (1871)
and ran for president of the United States (1871). Woodhull's actions,
largely inspired by her own experiences, were motivated by her desire to transform women's oppressed position in society and politics.
Like many other women who came from poor and working-class
backgrounds, Woodhull believed that her quality of life would im-
prove through marriage. Lured into marriage at fourteen, Woodhull
assumed the burden of caring for her family both financially and
emotionally, as her husband was absent and an alcoholic. By supporting her family as a clairvoyant, Woodhull encountered more women
whose marriages left them incapacitated and unhappy. These experiences led her to conclude that the institution of marriage was
severely flawed, and Woodhull came to believe that marriage would
need to be fixed or ameliorated for women to realize true indepen-
dence.[38] From this conclusion, Woodhull began associating herself
with, and working toward, "free love." Woodhull integrated this
perspective into her work and her political commitments, introducing and arguing for free love at meetings for the National Women's
Suffrage Association, the American Association for Spiritualists,
and the International Workers Association.[39]

In November 1871, Woodhull described the "Principles of Social
Freedom" to a sold out Steinway Hall in New York City. There, she
argued that love was "a right higher than Constitutions or laws . . .
a right which Constitutions and laws can neither give nor take."[40]
Woodhull believed that the abolition of marriage would free women
from the despotic relationship of husband and wife and help them
realize their social freedom. This social freedom included increased
access to higher education, unlimited career opportunities, lifestyle

choices, and, ultimately, the freedom to express desire and experience sexual pleasure without consequence from state or society. Through free love, women would be able to express their sexual desires in a way that would not result in public scorn because, "women as much as men are personalities, responsible to themselves for the use which they permit to be made of themselves."[41]

The pinnacle of Woodhull's speech occurred when she came out as a free lover. Cued by an audience member's question of whether she practiced free love, Woodhull affirmed: "I am a Free Lover. I have an inalienable, constitutional and natural right to love whom I may, to love as long or as short a period as I can; to change that love every day if I please, and with that right neither you nor any law you can frame have any right to interfere."[42] Because purity was a feminine virtue that women were expected to demonstrate through the appearance of asexuality, Woodhull's announcement that she practiced free love was a serious transgression against social mores. By professing her own sexuality on stage, she transformed the public nature of her speech into an intimate moment. Rather than being a pure, asexual cipher for man's love and sexual desire, Woodhull embodied a feminine sexuality—one where she, a white woman, expressed desire and initiated sexual acts. In doing so, she disrupted the ideal of heteronormative intimacy that celebrated the double sexual standard that applauded men's (hetero)sexuality while penalizing women for any expression of sexual desire. In this space she twisted "normal notions of gender and sexuality,"[43] asserting that white women not only experienced sexual desire, but might also pursue that desire in order to restore order and cure social ills like prostitution.[44] Drawing attention to the ways that prescribed sexuality inflects women's experience as gendered subjects, Woodhull's feminist deviance constituted what we now might call a queer space, one that "contained, played with, and used deviance to create new possibilities."[45]

Melissa Deem argues that "intimacy structures publics in ways that often go unexamined, unacknowledged, and untheorized," and "this structuration has such normative force as to condemn those who do not conform to normative intimacy as unfit for citizenship and public participation except through abjection and shame."[46] From this perspective, we might read Woodhull's improper testimony of free love, sexuality, and desire as a tactical strategy, an "incarnate, sensorially open, ability to have depth of insight into the complexities of the social."[47] Woodhull was likely conscious that her affirmation of free love contradicted the ideal of white femininity; although a financially successful stockbroker, she stood there as a deviant working-class prostitute, a dichotomy that called into being her own working-class upbringing, further justifying her vision of free love.

Impropriety, in the context of decorum, has often been explored for the ways that it leads toward social change by shifting discursive and cultural norms. These discussions focus on the "fix," rather than the flux. Woodhull's impropriety, grounded in an argument of embodied rationality, was in flux as her testimony resisted reincorporating women's sexuality into a collective experience. As it contradicted overriding norms of gender in relationship to race, class, and sexuality, Woodhull's impropriety satisfied an ideal of intersectionality. From this we might conclude that impropriety is a stylistic form through which intersectionality may thrive; impropriety relies on the body in a way that makes the public stutter, and through its logic of flux, resists totalizing woman's experience.

VOLTAIRINE DE CLEYRE: AN ENACTMENT OF PLAY

Born in 1866, in the midst of the suffrage movement, Voltairine de Cleyre became an ardent anarchist after the Haymarket Affair in 1886, when five anarchists were wrongly arrested and convicted for throwing a bomb during a labor rights protest that killed eight people. An independent thinker, de Cleyre passionately studied and advocated "anarchism without adjectives." Believing that any government intervention violated natural law and disrupted social order, de Cleyre vehemently espoused free love as a means to realizing true freedom. De Cleyre's anarchist civic subjectivity strongly inflects her description of marriage and her abstract vision of free love.

From the standpoint of feminist anarchism, de Cleyre conceptualized marriage as any permanent dependent relationship between a man and a woman. As a permanent dependent relationship, marriage "ruined the soul" because it inhibited desire, restricted sexual development and reduced one's potential to parentage.[48] De Cleyre argued that marriage created the conditions for "sex slavery" because it enacted a gendered hierarchy developed by the church and reinforced by the state through a prevalent notion of republican civic virtue. Civic virtue confined women's political agency to the restrictive role of mother, or Republican Motherhood. Marriage required that women submit their bodies to their husbands' desires and to their children's needs. Thus, instead of protecting the weak and pure woman from the immoral and violent man, physical and emotional abuse of women was "done quietly, beneath the shelter-shadow of home, and sanctified by the angelic benediction of a piece of paper, within the silence-shade of a marriage certificate."[49]

De Cleyre's free love was informed by her austere philosophy of anarchism, which argued against a citizenship enforced through the unnatural virtuous ideals of republicanism advocated by the church and state. In contrast to these ideals, we might read her anarchism as a cultural form of citizenship, one that relies on (local) community agreement rather than an allegiance to a nation-state. True to her anarchist philosophy, de Cleyre did not prescribe a specific vision of free love, but strategically abstracted free love, leaving her audience to interpret what "free love" could be through what it was *not* (marriage). As a result, de Cleyre did not impose a monolithic characterization of "woman" onto the possible movement toward freedom. By articulating it as an individual decision about how one relates on an intimate level (with implications for one's public relationships), de Cleyre intensely personalized free love, fulfilling the goal in intersectionality that we avoid generalizing experiences of womanhood.

In her description of free love, de Cleyre describes a dichotomy between the reality of women's experience (shaped by sexuality, nationality, race, and class and policed through the institution of marriage) and the possibility of free love. What the Sophists referred to as play, Anzaldúa describes as "the pull between what is and what should be."[50] As marriage shaped the reality of woman's experience, de Cleyre describes free love as the radical possibility that woman could be liberated in a way that realized her individual needs and desires. As a critical tool, de Cleyre's undefined free love functioned as the *question* of women's liberation rather than the answer; a question that was without available criteria or knowledge to render judgment.

Without available criteria, the question requires our imagination. In the context of feminism, "imagination, when it is considered in its freedom . . . is not bound to the law of causality, but is productive and spontaneous, not merely reproductive of what is already known, but generative of new forms and figures."[51] In this regard, the question, or play, of free love becomes the catalyst for dialogue that reinforces an intersectional feminist ethic where we might describe, if temporarily, the gap between women's lived experience and the politics or theory that defines the experience.[52] This rhetorical styling of play creates the conditions for considering the possible, which is evidenced more clearly in Goldman's free love discourse.

EMMA GOLDMAN: POSSIBILITY GENERATED
THROUGH INTERSECTIONALITY

At the age of sixteen, Emma Goldman emigrated to the United States from Eastern Europe in search of her American Dream: to become a doctor. However, as a Jewish, Eastern European immigrant, Goldman experienced the racist policies of immigration that were supported by the thriving eugenics movement. Examined for tuberculosis, or "Jewish disease," Goldman's body was subjected to close scrutiny to determine whether she would infect or threaten the "genetically strong" citizens of the United States. On securing entry into the United States, Goldman found work in a textile factory, where she was subjected to unhealthy and often dangerous working conditions. Like de Cleyre, the Haymarket Affair inspired Goldman to get involved in the anarchist movement; becoming known as "Red Emma," Goldman believed that anarchism would only succeed with the liberation of the most oppressed populations.

Goldman criticized marriage for making "a parasite of woman," because "it incapacitates her for life's struggle, annihilates her social consciousness, paralyzes her imagination, and then imposes its gracious protection, which is in reality a snare, a travesty on human character."[53] Goldman specifically highlighted how intersections of race, class, and gender shaped women's experiences by repeating a theme of motherhood. Whereas white women were considered "pure" and asexual (as indicated in Woodhull and de Cleyre's criticism), their immigrant and Black sisters were characterized as "feeble minded" and "hypersexual."[54] In the context of the eugenics and birth control movements, "nativists" feared that white women's abstinence or use of contraception would result in a race suicide. In response, white upper-class women were (further) encouraged to fulfill their femininity through motherhood, while their working-class, immigrant and Black sisters were encouraged (sometimes forcefully through involuntary sterilization) to abstain from motherhood altogether. Thus, Goldman recognized that the way women could portray their virtue was contingent upon their race. Motherhood represented the fulfillment of the feminine ideal for white upper-class women, and the rejection of virtue (or the embodiment of immorality) for immigrant and Black women who gave in to their "natural" deviant sexuality.

Contrary to marriage, Goldman described free love as passion, enacted through action and emotion: a *process* of *producing*.[55] Goldman described free love as something that could not be bought, subdued, conquered, or commanded.[56] Instead, free love was personified; it was "the harbinger of hope, of joy, of ecstasy," because it defied laws and conventions and was "the freest, the most powerful moulder of human destiny."[57] Through free love, women's value to society would not be determined by their capacity to perform "true womanhood" through marriage, motherhood or abstinence, or gendered roles determined for them by sex and race. Women's value would instead be determined by how they invented themselves and prospered through their expression of passion, occupying a positive space of production. Goldman thus described motherhood as a "free choice, of love, of ecstasy, of defiant passion."[58]

Goldman's critique of marriage and vision of free love recognized how women's experiences were shaped by race, class, gender, sexuality, and nationality. She drew distinctions between the working-class experiences of the factory girl and the expectations of the upper or middle-class married socialite. Her final vision of free love encourages all women to experience their bodies in a way that is positive and passionate—a fullness of experience.

In her article, "Marriage and Love," Goldman concludes with a visual description about the possibility of a world informed by free love: "Some day men and women will rise, they will reach the mountain peak, they will meet big and strong and free, ready to receive, to partake, and to bask in the golden rays of love. What fancy, what imagination, what poetic genius can foresee even approximately the potentialities of such a force in the life of men and women."[59] As mentioned above, the possibility of free love aligns with Lorde's notion of the erotic, or the "measure between the beginnings of our sense of self and the chaos of our strongest feelings," and Anzaldúa's idea of El Mundo Zurdo, where "I with my own affinities and my people with theirs can live together and transform the planet."[60]

As a style of intersectionality, possibility may be read as the form of the argument, rather than the content. While Goldman, Lorde, and Anzaldúa articulate similar visions, they do so by destroying the dichotomy between the masculine rational mind and the embodied feminine psychosis. Instead of this dichotomy, they embrace an embodied rationality, where the sensations of women's lived experience, as gendered, sexualized, raced, and nationalized, are not silenced, erased, or inoculated, but realized through a positive affirmation of difference. This possibility is evidenced through Lorde's assertion of the erotic: "once we begin to feel deeply all the aspects of our lives, we begin to demand from ourselves and from our life-pursuits that they feel in accordance with that joy which we know ourselves to be capable of. Our erotic knowledge empowers us, becomes a lens through which we scrutinize all aspects of our existence, forcing us to evaluate those aspects honestly in terms of their relative meaning within our lives."[61]

Goldman acknowledged the experiences of womanhood as they were shaped by class and race while rejecting prescribed gender roles. Her conception of freedom through free love focused on the way individuals could realize their potential as individuals, to grow, experience, love, and produce. Possibility may thus be read as the culmination of impropriety and play. It is that fullness of body, mind, and politic that guides our imagination to conceptualize what could be.

Free love, in both its more conservative form (as articulated through Woodhull) and its more radical forms (articulated by anarchist-feminists like de Cleyre and Goldman), encountered deep-seated resistance from the majority of the United States because it advocated the rejection of cultural norms of femininity and the hidden norms of heterosexuality, whiteness, and citizenship that inform that femininity. Yet, free lovers pushed against marriage and posed arguments for free love that spoke to their experiences as women. Their intersectional style perpetuated the debate, which required their audiences to continue making decisions about who "woman" was and what she should, or could, be. This continuous play created the condition for what might be considered as possible. Free lovers evoked radical notions of the possible by challenging their audiences to consider "woman" as a transitional construct that is gendered, raced, and sexualized.

CONCLUSION

As I have described above, the discourse of free love embodies an intersectional style characterized by impropriety, play, and possibility. The intersectional style of free love challenged the gendered construction of "woman" by focusing on the actuality of women's experience, as well as the possibility of becoming woman. This intersectional style multiplied the identification of woman by locating personal subjectivities at the intersections of sexuality, race, class, and citizenship. Woodhull, Goldman, and de Cleyre recognized that gender has never been a "pure" construction of identity, but has always been complicated by the multiple subjectivities embodied by individual women.

With their focus on the dynamic association between personal, intimate relationships and public, collective notions of gender, sexuality, race, class, and citizenship, Woodhull, de Cleyre, and Goldman embodied an intersectional style to disrupt dominant assumptions of "femininity" that limited women (and men) from realizing their freedom. Further, rather than debilitating the rhetorics of free love, the contradictions that exist among the varying definitions of free love in relationship to feminism (such as the support or rejection of suffrage, eugenics, and long-term relationships) demonstrate how Woodhull, de Cleyre, and Goldman each responded to their experience with patriarchy from their unique positions at the intersections of sexuality, citizenship, class, and race. In so doing, their intersectional style of feminist rhetoric relates their "ways of knowing" or their experiences of being oppressed as women. However, their intense focus on individually generated visions of free love risks shifting attention away from interlocking systems of oppression.

Examining rhetorics for an intersectional style participates in the goals of feminist criticism by using specific texts to describe conceptions of woman that challenge the patriarchal invention of "woman." This takes up the aim of the Combahee River Collective by developing an "integrated analysis and practice based upon the fact that the major systems of oppression are interlocking."[62] Incorporating intersectionality as an approach and a style of criticism may repair the white solipsism that has informed feminist rhetoric and criticism within the field of communication studies. In doing so, we might truly "rethink fundamental assumptions in our theory, criticism, and pedagogy."[63]

Finally, as scholars and activists, we might recognize how the intersectional style of free love realizes the emancipatory possibility imbued in the celebration of difference. Woodhull, de Cleyre, and Goldman focused on an imperfect and incomplete vision of freedom that relied more on the *feeling* of freedom than policies to create the conditions for that feeling. Their embodied rationality demonstrates how we might imagine a rhetoric that enjoins the body with the mind in order to harness the "raw and powerful connection from which our personal power is forged."[64] Although consciousness raising facilitates a collective recognition that individuals' lived experiences are shaped by cultural notions of race, gender, sex, sexuality, nationality, class, or otherwise, generating visions of freedom is impaired by generalized experiences of womanhood. Instead, as we learn from the intersectional style of free love, freedom may require a commitment to impropriety and play in order to imagine possibility.

NOTES

My thanks to everyone who offered support in the writing of this chapter. I especially thank Karma Chávez and Cindy Griffin for their insightful feedback.

1. Karlyn Kohrs Campbell, "The Rhetoric of Women's Liberation: An Oxymoron," *Quarterly Journal of Speech* 59 (1973): 74-86.

2. Christina R. Foust and Kate Zittlow Rogness, "Beyond Rights and Virtues as Foundations for Women's Agency: Emma Goldman's Rhetoric of Free Love," *Western Journal of Communication* 75 (2011): 148–167.

3. Elizabeth Spelman, *Inessential Woman: Problems of Exclusion in Feminist Thought* (Boston: Beacon Press, 1988).

4. Spelman, *Inessential Woman*, 136.

5. Kimberlé Crenshaw, "Mapping the Margins: Intersectionality, Identity Politics, and Violence Against Women of Color," *Stanford Law Review* 43 (1991): 1241–1299.

6. Cindy L. Griffin, "Rhetoricizing Alienation: Mary Wollstonecraft and the Rhetorical Construction of Women's Oppression," *Quarterly Journal of Speech* 80 (1994): 302.

7. Karlyn Kohrs Campbell, "Inventing Women: From Amaterasu to Virginia Woolf," *Women's Studies in Communication* 21 (1998): 111–121.

8. Campbell, "Inventing Women."

9. Karlyn Kohrs Campbell, "The Rhetoric of Women's Liberation"; Campbell, "The Sound of Women's Voices," *Quarterly Journal of Speech* 75 (1989): 212–258; Bonnie J. Dow and Mari Boor Tonn, "'Feminine Style' and Political Judgment in the Rhetoric of Ann Richards," *Quarterly Journal of Speech* 79 (1993): 286–302; Shawn Parry-Giles and Diane Blair, "The Rise of The Rhetorical First Lady: Politics, Gender Ideology and Women's Voice, 1798–2002," *Rhetoric and Public Affairs* 5 (2002): 565–600; Mari Boor Tonn, "Militant Motherhood: Labor's Mary Harris 'Mother' Jones," *Quarterly Journal of Speech* 82 (1996): 1–21.

10. Barbara Biesecker, "Towards a Transactional View of Rhetorical and Feminist Theory: Rereading Helene Cixious's *The Laugh of the Medusa*," *Southern Communication Journal* 57 (1992): 86–96; Jane Sutton, "The Taming of the *Polos/Polis*: Rhetoric as an Achievement without Woman," *Southern Communication Journal* 57 (1992): 97–119.

11. Carole Spitzack and Kathryn Carter, "Women in Communication Studies: A Typology for Revision," *Quarterly Journal of Speech* 73 (1987): 401.

12. Barbara Welter, "The Cult of True Womanhood: 1820–1860," *American Quarterly* 18 (1966): 151–174.

13. Patricia Hill Collins, *Black Feminist Thought: Knowledge, Consciousness, and the Politics of Empowerment*, 2nd ed. (New York: Routledge, 2000), 128.

14. Collins, *Black Feminist*, 246.

15. Audre Lorde, "Uses of the Erotic: Erotic as Power," in *Sister Outsider: Essays and Speeches*, ed. Audre Lorde (Berkeley, CA: Crossing Press, 1984), 120.

16. Collins, *Black Feminist*; Carrie Crenshaw, "Women in the Gulf War: Toward an Intersectional Feminist Rhetorical Criticism," *Howard Journal of Communications* 8 (1997): 219–235, esp. 220; Marsha Houston, "The Politics of Difference: Race, Class and Women's Communication," in *Women Making Meaning: New Feminist Directions in Communication*, ed. Linda Rakow (New York: Routledge, 1992), 45–59.

17. Karma R. Chávez and Cindy L. Griffin, "Power, Feminisms, and Coalitional Agency: Inviting and Enacting Difficult Dialogues," *Women's Studies in Communication* 32 (2009): 2.

18. María Lugones, *Pilgrimages/Peregrinajes: Theorizing Coalition against Multiple Oppressions* (Lanham, MD: Rowman & Littlefield, 2003), 77.

19. Audre Lorde, "The Master's Tools Will Never Dismantle the Master's House," in *Sister Outsider*, 112.

20. Lorde, "Age, Race, Class and Sex: Women Redefining Difference," in *Sister Outsider*, 122.

21. C. Crenshaw, "Women in the Gulf War," 221.

22. K. Crenshaw, "Mapping."

23. C. Crenshaw, "Women in the Gulf War," 223.

24. C. Crenshaw, "Women in the Gulf War," 220.

25. Foust and Rogness, "Beyond Rights"; Linda Horwitz, Diane Kowal, and Catherine Palczewski, "Anarchist Women and the Feminine Ideal: Sex, Class, and Style in the Rhetoric of Voltairine de Cleyre, Emma Goldman and Lucy Parsons," in *The Rhetoric of Nineteenth-Century Reform: A Rhetorical History of the United States: Significant Moments in American Public Discourse* (Vol. 5) ed. Martha Watson and Thomas R. Burkholder (East Lansing: Michigan State University Press, 2008), 308–354.

26. Jürgen Habermas, *The Structural Transformation of the Public Sphere: An Inquiry into a Category of Bourgeois Society*, trans. T. Berger and F. Lawrence (Cambridge, MA: MIT Press, 1962/1991).

27. Michael Warner, "The Mass Public and the Mass Subject," in *Habermas and the Public Sphere*, ed. Craig Calhoun (Cambridge, MA: MIT Press, 1999), 382.

28. Warner, "The Mass Public," 382.

29. Melissa Deem, "Stranger Sociability, Public Hope, and the Limits of Political Transformation," *Quarterly Journal of Speech* 88 (2002): 450.

30. Neil Leroux, "Perceiving Rhetorical Style: Toward a Framework for Criticism," *Rhetoric Society Quarterly* 22 (1992): 29; Robert Hariman, "Decorum, Power, and the Courtly Style," *Quarterly Journal of Speech* 78 (1992): 33.

31. Warner, "The Mass Public," 383.

32. Warner, "The Mass Public," 383.

33. Elizabeth Spelman, "Gender & Race: The Ampersand Problem in Feminist Thought," in *The Feminist Philosophy Reader*, ed. Alison Bailey and Chris Cuomo (New York: McGraw Hill, 2007), 273.

34. Karlyn Kohrs Campbell, *Man Cannot Speak for Her: A Critical Study of Early Feminist Rhetoric*, Vol. 1 (New York: Praeger, 1989), 13.

35. Campbell, *Man Cannot Speak for Her.*

36. Gloria Anzaldúa, "La Prieta," in *This Bridge Called My Back*, 3rd ed. ed. Cherríe Moraga and Gloria Anzaldúa (Saline, MI: Third Woman Press, 2002), 220–233; Lorde, "Uses of the Erotic"; Victoria Woodhull, "The Principle of Social Freedom, Involving Free Love, Marriage, Divorce," *New York Times*, November 21, 1871; Voltairine de Cleyre, "They Who Marry do

Ill," in *The Voltairine de Cleyre Reader*, ed. A. J. Brigati (Oakland, CA: AK Press, 2004), 11–20; Emma Goldman, "Tragedy of Women's Emancipation," *Anarchism and Other Essays* (New York: Mother Earth Publishing Association, 1917); Goldman, "Marriage and Love," *Anarchism and Other Essays*; Goldman, "Marriage," in *Emma Goldman: A Documentary History of the American Years Made for America, 1890–1901* (Vol. 1), ed. Candace Falk (Urbana: University of Illinois Press, 2008), 269–273.

37. Lorde, "Uses of the Erotic," 55.

38. Mary Gabriel, *Notorious Victoria* (Chapel Hill, NC: Algonquin Books, 1998).

39. Amanda Frisken. *Victoria Woodhull's Sexual Revolution: Political Theater and Popular Press in Nineteenth-Century America* (Philadelphia: University of Pennsylvania Press, 2004).

40. Woodhull, "Principles of Social Freedom" 16.

41. Woodhull, "Principles," 37–38.

42. Woodhull, "Principles," 23.

43. John Nguyet Erni, "Queer Figurations in the Media: Critical Reflections on the Michael Jackson Sex Scandal," *Critical Studies in Mass Communication* 15 (1998): 160.

44. Woodhull argued that prostitution was a social ill created by women's limited career choices and inequality of pay; women had the choice between marriage (which Woodhull characterized as legalized prostitution since women were trading their bodies for financial security) or prostitution.

45. Karen Foss, "Harvey Milk and the Queer Rhetorical Situation," in *Queering Public Address: Sexualities in American Historical Discourse*, ed. Charles E. Morris, III (Columbia: University of South Carolina Press, 2007), 88.

46. Deem, "Stranger Sociability," 452.

47. Lugones, *Pilgrimages/Peregrinajes*, 218.

48. De Cleyre, "They Who Marry Do Ill," 18.

49. Voltairine de Cleyre, "Sex Slavery," in *The Voltairine de Cleyre Reader*, 94.

50. Anzaldúa, "La Prieta," 232.

51. Linda Zerilli, *Feminism and the Abyss of Freedom* (Chicago: University of Chicago Press, 2002), 163.

52. Drucilla Cornell, "What Is Ethical Feminism?" in *Feminist Contentions: A Philosophical Exchange*, ed. Seyla Benhabib, Judith Butler, Drucilla Cornell, and Nancy Fraser (New York: Routledge, 1995), 75–106.

53. Goldman, "Marriage and Love," 235.

54. Collins, *Black Feminist*.

55. Foust and Rogness, "Beyond Rights."

56. Goldman, "Marriage and Love."

57. Goldman, "Marriage and Love," 236.

58. Goldman, "Marriage and Love."

59. Goldman, "Marriage and Love," 240.

60. Lorde, "Uses of the Erotic," 54; Anzaldúa, "La Prieta," 233.

61. Lorde, "Uses of the Erotic," 57.

62. Combahee River Collective, "A Black Feminist Sentiment," in *This Bridge*, 210.

63. Campbell, "The Sound of Women's Voices," 214.

64. Lorde, "The Master's Tools," 112.

Chapter 3

(Im)mobile Metaphors: Toward an Intersectional Rhetorical History

Carly S. Woods

Metaphors not only "structure our experience"[1] but "by orga-nizing reality in particular ways, our selected metaphors also prescribe how we are to act."[2] As the opening chapter of this volume notes, feminist scholars have long grappled with the figurative lan-guage of intersectionality in order to find the conceptual framing that best accounts for varied relationships between power, oppres-sion, and privilege. Similarly, rhetorical historians have an obliga-tion to think critically about the metaphors we use. One cluster of metaphors, in particular, characterizes both intersectional and rhetorical-historical research: the spatial and geographic. Moreover, critiques of both research approaches essentially point to the same problem; that the language of intersections and maps suggests a fixed location that does not fully account for the fluidity and shift-ing of human relationships.[3]

In her overview of feminist perspectives on the history of rheto-ric, Kate Ronald notes that there has been an "explosion of research in women's rhetoric over the last decade and a half."[4] Much of the early research in this area concentrated on the primary analytical category of "woman" in documenting, recovering, and interpret-ing rhetorical texts.[5] Since then, major methodological debates have centered on the question of how best to ensure that feminist rhetorical historians do not focus too narrowly on a single axis of identity (woman) to the exclusion of others.[6] This chapter uses com-mon critiques of the metaphors of intersectionality and rhetorical history as a starting point to articulate a forward-looking vision for intersectional rhetorical history. To that end, I offer a way for communication scholars to animate our methodological and conceptual metaphors with an eye toward motion and mobility.

In line with contemporary feminist theorizing that favors a coalitional (relational) rather than individual (locational) politics, I argue that an intersectional approach to rhetorical history should be concerned with shifting webs of relationships rather than singular articulations of identity in historical contexts. The first section identifies overlapping spatial and geographic language in key texts on intersectionality and feminist rhetorical history. I then suggest how metaphors that capture motion and mobility better address the relational complexity of the historical practices and people we study. Finally, I offer examples of the themes of coalitional belonging, movement, and travel in the life of politician Barbara Jordan to demonstrate the possibilities of intersectional rhetorical history. In taking mobile metaphors seriously, intersectionality can inform rhetorical-historical research, while feminist rhetorical history can explore innovative spaces for the extension of intersectionality studies.

INTERSECTING SPACES AND PLACES

Theorists such as Kimberlé Crenshaw, Patricia Hill Collins, Gloria Anzaldúa, and Chandra Talpade Mohanty have persuasively argued for consideration of how the intersections of gender, race, class, sexuality, geography, religion, and ability create unique modes of being in the world. In their germinal works, these theorists have relied on the language of space and geography to attend to the multidimensional aspects of identity. In her pioneering work on critical legal theory, Crenshaw demonstrates the necessity of the "intersectional thesis" as an alternative to simplistic identity politics in the context of violence against women of color. Crenshaw maintains that when identity-based activism forces a choice between embodied allegiances to multiple identity groups, it becomes ineffectual and forgoes possibilities for coalitional politics. To force such choices is to "relegate the identity of women of color to a location that resists telling."[7] Crenshaw offers instead, "Mapping the Margins," a geographic metaphor that lays the groundwork for her intersectional thesis and allows for complexities of identities. Similarly, Hill Collins discusses the interlocking systems of race, gender, and class oppression as a "matrix of domination." She borrows from Nira Yuval-Davis's concept of transversal politics, in which individuals are rooted in their own experiences but shift to exhibit empathy for a range of perspectives in order to advance coalitional strategies for African American women's groups.[8] Taken literally, a transversal line on a graph or a map is visual representation of an intersection: a line that cuts through two parallel lines.

Spatial and geographic metaphors are also extended in the work of theorists considering nation and ethnic origin as fundamental axes of identity. Anzaldúa's *Borderlands/La Frontera* highlights the shifting and manifold identities of living on borders and in margins. As her poem "To Live in the Borderlands Means You" states, "to survive the Borderlands / you must live *sin fronteras* (without borders) / be a crossroads."[9] Mohanty works with the metaphors of home as well as borders in her reconceptualization of transnational feminist practice.[10] She draws on the imagery of borders, explaining that,

> Feminism without borders . . . acknowledges the fault lines, conflicts, differences, fears, and containment that borders represent. It acknowledges that there is no one sense of a border, that the lines between and through nations, races, classes, sexualities, religions, and disabilities, are real—and that a feminism without borders must envision change and social justice work across these lines of demarcation and division.[11]

These scholars advocate an intersectional approach that acknowledges difference and works to transcend borders that separate and divide. It enables, rather than restricts, research by feminist scholars wishing to attend to the particularities of communication in transnational contexts.

Similar language shapes critical approaches to rhetorical history. Many studies in rhetorical history could be charged with focusing on elite individuals; often famous, powerful, white, class-privileged, and heterosexual men. Historical studies of oratory and public address have attended narrowly to the rhetorical contributions of the "great white straight male,"[12] and, as such, reify the notion that there is a singular and fixed rhetorical tradition.[13] Pivotal debates in feminist rhetorical historiography center on the issue of whether such work should similarly create a canon of great women orators, employing a type of academic "affirmative action" to rectify an unjust tradition.[14] Since those early exchanges, feminist rhetoricians have argued for expanded thinking about what counts as legitimate evidence of rhetorical performance and the spaces where we can look for that evidence. Instead of solely attending to traditional rhetorical situations, we are now encouraged to pay attention to "gendered rhetorics of bodies, clothing, space, and time."[15]

Indeed, this growing body of literature indicates a fruitful interdisciplinary intersection. Roxanne Mountford suggests that feminist approaches to rhetorical history offer a promising "prospect of rapprochement" between like-minded scholars in English and communication because they have the shared experience of being "routinely marginalized," are committed to paying attention to differences across communities, and have a history of "reading one another's work."[16] Another striking aspect of this subfield is the pattern of metaphors used in order to articulate the goals of feminist rhetorical history.

Spatial and geographic metaphors are used both to describe the role of the contemporary researcher *and* to describe the historical people we study. Feminist rhetorical historians are positioned as cartographers, called on to map the silences or "rema[p] rhetorical territor[ies]."[17] Cheryl Glenn uses the language of replacing the "neatly folded history of rhetoric" with "new, often partially completed maps that reflect and coordinate our current institutional, intellectual, political, and personal values."[18] Lisa Ede, Cheryl Glenn, and Andrea Lunsford urge the refiguration of "canonical mappings," urging scholars to "stan[d] at the border" of rhetoric and feminism, and ultimately, to traverse those borderlands.[19] Lindal Buchanan and Kathleen Ryan's recent compilation of crucial feminist rhetorical texts is an endeavor to "walk and talk feminist rhetorics" where there are "no established paths to follow."[20]

At the same time that scholars inhabit the role of mapmakers, we describe the people we study as explorers of rhetorical space, border-crossers, and navigators of difference. Feminist rhetorical history creates a space to study the way that marginalized populations in history both literally and figuratively traversed boundaries meant to limit public discourse. Historian Mary P. Ryan uses the language of navigation in her work on the sometimes unorthodox ways that nineteenth-century women found avenues to enter public debates. She refers to these avenues as "circuitous routes"[21]; an influential metaphor that is taken up by rhetorical historian Susan Zaeske to describe women's antislavery activism through petitioning in the antebellum period.[22] Lisa A. Flores describes how the experience of living on literal borders has prompted Chicana feminists to "cross rhetorical borders through the construction of a discursive space or home."[23] Indeed, some rhetorical historians have been able to extend such analysis in a variety of overlooked people and spaces, including but not limited to nineteenth-century women's rhetorical performances in the domestic space of the parlor,[24] literacy practices among African American women,[25] teachers of African American,

Native American, and Chicano/a students,[26] post-Mao women writers,[27] and "queer figurations" in rhetorical history.[28]

Feminist rhetorical history, in borrowing and extending spatial and geographic metaphors, *intersects* with the aims of intersectionality studies. In drawing from the intersections of feminisms and rhetorics, it comes as no great surprise such texts would employ similar metaphors. As Thomas K. Nakayama and Robert L. Krizek note, such metaphors "consider the milieu present at the intersection of differing 'realities' while recognizing the variance within each of the 'realities.'"[29] The language of space and location—and especially, seeing oneself as a critical cartographer of underexplored territories—is evocative. It grounds our historical explorations and provides a motivating purpose for our research endeavors. The ability to see ourselves as active participants in such metaphors forges a connection with the historical people and discourses we study; we would like to see ourselves as fellow travelers.

My aim is not to reject such points of identification by abandoning spatial and geographic metaphors. Intersectionality functions as an important instrument of critique. However, like feminism itself, intersectionality is sometimes misinterpreted as a punishment or an unavoidable land mine ("Sure, you considered X identity, but you didn't consider Y identity") rather than an affirmative discussion of available possibilities going forward. What we now need are well-developed ways of "doing" intersectional rhetorical history.[30] To gain a wider appreciation for the synergistic relationship between rhetorical histories and intersectionality, we must consider how common metaphors of space and place can be shifted to better analyze the dynamics of historical experience in motion.

METAPHORS IN MOTION

Since the first "generation" of groundbreaking work, usually theorized through the metaphor of interlocking oppressions, metaphors of identity and intersectionality have been questioned in light of numerous critiques. Such critiques trouble representations of identity as a "closed, bordered, and fixed entity" seeking instead to recast it as "open, flexible, and changeable."[31] As Anna Carastathis argues, the conceptual model of intersectionality always places individuals at a crossroads, where "the claim that the identity of the Black woman produced by the intersection of gender and race is viable only if we can think 'Black' without thinking 'woman,' and if we can think 'woman' without thinking 'Black.'"[32] Indeed, the idea of an "intersection" is a spatial/locational metaphor. Though cars can move through, there is the danger (as with traditional approaches to identity) that an intersection will have stoplights, where individuals are forced to decide if they want to turn "right" into their gender, "left" into their ethnicity, or "straight" into their sexuality (pun intended). In later articulations of her theory, Kimberlé Crenshaw reminds readers that we are not dealing with one four-way stop. Instead, we should envision "*multiple intersections* that often cross each other, creating complex crossroads where two, three, or more of these routes may meet in overlapping dimensions."[33] Intersectional affiliations are thoroughfares that individuals and groups move through; traffic is the "activity of discrimination"—those decisions and policies that slow movement and cause collisions.[34] The metaphor of the intersection works only insofar as we see it not as a static space where paths diverge or get jammed, but as a fluid and multidimensional space of travel that facilitates the mobility of disparate individuals and groups.

Conversations about the best way to integrate feminist perspectives into rhetorical history also question the value of spatial and geographic metaphors. Barbara E. L'Eplattenier suggests that there are two problems with the now-dominant metaphor of mapping and remapping the history of rhetoric to include women. First, the mapping metaphor may fail to adequately account for the messy process of doing rhetorical history—it "implies that we have a complete map—a complete picture to discuss, present, and interpret."[35] We may be cartographers, but we need to acknowledge the gaps and silences that accompany any historical narrative. Furthermore, L'Eplattenier argues for metaphors that "give us a way to include and consider the external pressures which occur both systematically and intermittently and push/pull on the people we study."[36] In other words, historical actors deploy rhetorical strategies based on a wide range of intersectional tensions and concerns—and our metaphors for conducting research ought to take these into account. Instead of just locating women on a map of the history of rhetoric, we must theorize how they moved through the intersections of class, race, sexuality, ability, and other axes of belonging.

It is possible and desirable to attend to these critiques and do intersectional rhetorical history without abandoning spatial and geographic metaphors. Mapping and remapping can be useful in conceptualizing feminist rhetorical work, but the missing link is motion—the ability to capture the ways in which the historical people we study were complex, multifaceted beings. No matter what historical period is being studied, an intersectional rhetorical history must acknowledge that the people we study may have navigated "routes" into public culture, but they were also always negotiating their "roots." Roots imply being tied to a particular space. If people are rooted, they have identity-based affiliations; they may feel the pull of their roots toward a home. Routes, of course, indicate motion and travel, the ability to move between spaces, affiliations, and homes.[37]

Aimee Carrillo Rowe offers a compelling case for replacing a politics of location with a politics of relation. A politics of location, as demonstrated by Adrienne Rich's essay, articulates an individual sense of self with "a notion of identity that begins with 'I'—as does the inscription 'I-dentity,' which announces itself through its fixity: 'I am . . . '." By contrast, a politics of relation acknowledges the ways in which "the subject arrives again and again to her own becoming through a series of transitions—across time and space, communities and contexts—throughout the course of her life . . . constituted not first through the atomized self, but through its own longings to be with."[38] The body in motion is the representative metaphor for a politics of relation. To imagine the body—like the subject—in motion underscores the ways in which the self is constituted through "a shifting set of relations that we move in and out of."[39]

What does this focus on movement—on roots and routes, bodies in motion—mean for intersectional rhetorical history? It answers Crenshaw's call by asking scholars to consider the multidimensional movement of people and discourses rather than discovering or locating them on a map. First, it encourages feminist rhetorical historians to resist seeing the people we study as similarly frozen in time. Instead, we should recognize the ways in which historical research affords us the ability to study relational movements and shifts over time. How did an individual's early life experiences as part of a particular community shape her later rhetorical performances? When and how did they establish affiliational ties, and were those ties strategic or fleeting? How are their longings to be with particular people and communities articulated "behind the scenes" and what does this tell us about the rhetorical choices made in public fora? Instead of making claims about fixed identity, we can focus on those moments where a sense of affiliation, love, or belonging influenced communicative practice within a particular historical moment.

Second, it bears on the very way that rhetorical historians select relevant materials to study. Carrillo Rowe argues that a politics of relation can function to "reverse, or better, to multiply the sites of power that hail us, urging us to consider the ways in which power becomes intelligible through a politics of love."[40] As rhetorical historians, what power do we wield? Are we hailing the dead based on a particular articulation of identity—Black, woman, lesbian, able-bodied, working class? If so, we fail to "interrogat[e] the *conditions* that enable[d], or would potentially disrupt, those communal sites which hail [their] affective investments."[41] Without the fluidity that an intersectional approach allows, rhetorical historians too easily use stable identity categories as terministic screens that direct our attention toward certain types of archival materials and away from others. In our quest to study the history of women's rhetoric, for example, we may focus exclusively on correspondence between women, overlooking the ways they shifted in and out of in a complex web of other relationships, coalitions, and alliances that help us to understand their lives and rhetorical choices.

By focusing on historical bodies in motion, this approach has much to bring even to the most-studied figures in rhetorical history. Instead of asking how Barbara Jordan became the first and only African American woman to accomplish so many political feats," the next section demonstrates the possibility of mobile metaphors by asking how Barbara Jordan's multiple and shifting relational belongings and longings shaped her rhetorical choices and performances.

BARBARA JORDAN: POLITICS IN MOTION

The first African American woman to serve in the Texas state legislature and the first African American woman from the South to be elected to the U.S. Congress, Barbara Jordan is famous for her political savvy, oratorical fireworks, and legislation to help the underprivileged. As Molly Ivins states, "the words, the first and only, came before Barbara Jordan so often that they almost seemed like a permanent title."[42] Indeed, media commentary so often focused on the two primary ways that Jordan was an anomaly in politics—her sex, her skin color—that she had to craft a savvy rhetorical strategy for discussing those aspects of her identity in public interviews and speeches.

Past rhetorical scholarship has focused on Jordan's 1976 keynote address to the Democratic National Convention (DNC). Most noted is this part of the speech's opening:

> But there is something different about tonight. There is something special about tonight. What is different? What is special? I, Barbara Jordan, am a keynote speaker. When—A lot of years passed since 1832, and during that time it would have been most unusual for any national political party to ask a Barbara Jordan to deliver a keynote address. But tonight,

here I am. And I feel—I feel that notwithstanding the past
that my presence here is one additional bit of evidence that
the American Dream need not forever be deferred.[43]

In this brief articulation, Jordan accomplished the necessary task of
commenting on her "first and only" status at the DNC. However,
instead of providing a verbal taxonomy of the ways that she was different and special, the invocation of her name and the visual cues
of her very presence on the stage were enough to fill in the argument. This has been theorized as a prototypical moment of *rhetorical enactment*, in which a person is an incarnation of her argument:
"the very fact that she, a black woman, had achieved the stature to
be asked to give the address was proof that blacks and women can
reach the highest levels of achievement in America here and now."[44]

Some conventional rhetorical analyses of the speech attempt, in
limited ways, to comment on Jordan's identity. However, because
such commentary is limited to the immediate rhetorical situation of
the address, it falls short in providing a more complex understanding
of intersectionality. Wayne Thompson, for example, argues that the
speech was successful because Jordan balanced the dual purposes
of affirming her "Blackness" and "womanliness" without speaking
too much about them or invoking unfavorable stereotypes. Indeed,
he even goes so far as to comment on her status as an unmarried
woman: "Never having married, Barbara Jordan lacked some of Ella
Grasso's opportunities to capitalize on womanliness. The next best
course was to keep the quality from being a liability."[45] This interpretation unquestioningly links the assumption of compulsory heterosexuality to Jordan's communication of a static gender identity.
It suffers from a narrow view of what constitutes relevant evidence
for rhetorical criticism. Published in 1979, Thompson's analysis is
historically time-bound in itself.

By contrast, an intersectional rhetorical history approach to
studying Barbara Jordan benefits from a broader, longitudinal view.
This approach provides greater insight into how Jordan's lived experiences may have precipitated her communicative choices and complicates public commentary that focuses too narrowly on singular or
dual articulations of her identity. Scholars need to broaden our ratio
of text-to-context, looking to those behind-the-scenes machinations
that made rhetorical performances possible.[46] Jordan acknowledged
this necessity herself, stating, "People always want you to be born
where you are. They want you to have leaped from the womb a public figure. It just doesn't go that way. I am the composite of my experience and all the people who had something to do with it."[47] In

what follows, I offer evidence of the complexity of Jordan's experience and relationships during two periods in her life, highlighting
travel, motion, and (im)mobility as literal and conceptual themes.

The first way that intersectional rhetorical history can aid in
understanding Jordan's case is through an exploration of her participation on the debate team at Texas Southern University (TSU) in
the 1950s and how it helped to cultivate her rhetorical sensibilities.
Beyond just honing her speaking, writing, and reasoning skills, Jordan's desire to travel to debate tournaments is an apt case study for
the negotiation of difference in a historical setting. First, she had
to gain access to TSU's traveling debate team, which did not allow
women to attend intercollegiate debate competitions out of a sense
of gendered decorum: they did not want to risk ruining the reputa-
tions of the women students who would have to "ride in cars with
boys" in order to attend.[48] Jordan had been a stand-out competitor
on the speech and debate team at Phillis Wheatley High School,
and she viewed the traveling college team as a important activity to
challenge her where her college classes did not. In order to convince
TSU's debate coach that her presence on the team would not risk
impropriety, she

> gave up the scoop-neck dresses and costume jewelry of high
> school, cropped her waved hair short above her ears, affected
> bulky, boxy jackets and flat shoes. Gaining twenty pounds,
> her buxom figure took on the squared lines of androgyny.
> She became a no-nonsense presence, someone it was all
> right to take across the country in a car full of males and not
> worry about chaperonage.[49]

In doing so, Jordan altered her body so that she could ensure its mobility through travel to debate tournaments. If we consider her desire to be on the intercollegiate debate team as an articulation of a
desire to belong, we see that Jordan was able to play with, queer,
and transgress modes of gendered expression in order to enable affiliation with a particular community. The decision to forgo more
conventional signs of heterosexual femininity was one that she
maintained throughout her career in state and national politics, and
her boxy paint suits were often commented on in descriptions of her
physical appearance.

Jordan gained access to the intercollegiate debate competition,
and her experience within "the debate community" was largely
shaped by her race, class, and geographic ties. Once she overcame
this instance of sex-based discrimination by convincing her debate

coach to allow her to travel, Jordan was able to literally travel outside of her neighborhood in Houston, seeing firsthand the realities
of the racially segregated world. As one of few historically Black colleges participating in interracial debates at the time, TSU debaters
experienced both the exhilaration of travel and the sting of racist discrimination as they traveled through the South to other parts of the
country. Speech and debate were literal and figurative vehicles that
allowed them to travel across communities. The ability to travel to
competitions created a space of encounter where those axes of difference were constantly negotiated. In 1956, TSU made history by
participating in the first integrated speech and debate tournament
in the South at Baylor College. Glenn Capp, the director of debate
at Baylor, was a proponent of the race and sex-based integration of
debate, but many in the Waco, Texas, community disagreed with
the decision to admit TSU to the tournament.[50] The team had to
stay outside of town because there was no place that would lodge
them. This discrimination, however, seemingly did not carry over
to the competition at Baylor: Jordan won the junior division's first
place prize in oratory and third place in extemporaneous speaking.
Pitted against white students in speaking and debate competitions
and emerging victorious time and again, Jordan began to see herself
as a star in both worlds. She thought, "why, you white girls are no
competition at all. If this is the best you have to offer, I haven't
missed anything."[51] Because of her participation on the debate team,
she was able to cultivate longings for a future beyond the world she
knew in Houston, a desire that led her to pursue law school at Boston University after she graduated from TSU.

The second representative anecdote comes from Jordan's later
political career. As one of few African American women in national
politics, her policy positions and affiliations were closely monitored,
especially with regard to civil rights, women's rights, and legislation
benefiting her Texas constituency. She rooted her advocacy for social change in her affiliations: as a person born and raised in Texas,
as a legal scholar who believed in equality through legal change for
racial minorities, and as a woman who believed in women's ability
to make choices for themselves.[52] Intersectional rhetorical analysis and access to Jordan's own accounts in her autobiography, *Barbara Jordan: A Self Portrait*, provide crucial insights on how another
aspect of her experience came to bear on her shifting and mobile
affiliations.[53] Jordan developed multiple sclerosis in 1973, but, realizing that she was already marked with the visual cues of a large,
dark-skinned, female body, she kept her medical condition under
wraps until later in her life when she required a wheelchair. One

cannot fully understand Jordan's role as a political figure without acknowledging the way that Jordan's disability shaped her rhetorical choices—and the ensuing public commentary.

In Washington, Jordan chose a seat in the center aisle of the House floor rather than with the liberals or the congressional Black Caucus, stating that she wanted to be in the line of vision of the presiding officer.[54] She rarely left her seat to talk to others, instead waiting for her colleagues to approach her. As journalist Walter Shapiro put it in his cover story for *Texas Monthly*,

> Much of her day is spent just sitting on the floor of the House, listening and waiting for people to come to her. (She rarely leaves her seat to talk to someone else.) Originally this may have been a mechanism for quick digestion of the rules of the House, but now it is a more convenient way for her to hold court. There may also be physical reasons for her staying close to the floor during a legislative day: she simply isn't nimble enough to be sure of getting from her office to the chamber in the fifteen minutes allotted for a roll call vote. Her administrative assistant confirms that she has "a damaged cartilage behind the knee which causes her to limp when she doesn't have time to get to therapy." Her sheer bulk also limits her mobility, although she has lost at least 50 pounds since the beginning of the year on a strict diet.[55]

Although this account acknowledges her physical limitations, it links them to Jordan's large bodily size. Like other commentators, Shapiro largely interprets her immobility as a queenly power move of political royalty, a way to "hold court," a point framed and underlined by the *Texas Monthly*'s cover image that month: a drawing of Jordan with a crown on her head, buttressed with the words, "Is Barbara Jordan for Real?" Jordan's biography reveals that the actual reason for her stationary position in the House was linked to her struggle with multiple sclerosis: "she had begun to feel an occasional numbness in her feet and a weakness in her legs that she thought might be the beginning of arthritis. . . . Jordan always wanted to be physically comfortable."[56] The intersectional dynamics of this choice are rich: Jordan's choice not to physically share space with possible coalitional allies among liberals and in the Black Caucus was mediated by an axis of her personal experience that was not immediately and visually legible. Power and privilege are manifested in multiple ways in this example. Jordan wished not to lose power by speaking publicly about her physical ailment, and so she played

with the ambiguity that came along with her immobile body; public
commentators read her stationary position on the House floor as
one imbued with power.[57] This account resists an easy telling, in
which Jordan was deliberately attempting to shirk her coalitional
bonds. It demonstrates how consideration for multiple axes of identity can manifest in public spaces. Ironically, then, Jordan's physical immobility provides one other example of her movement across
communities. Jordan never existed as, and never could be, simply an
African American, a woman, a liberal.

There are, of course, many other examples emanating from
Jordan's personal experience that are relevant to her rhetorical
contributions and deserve further complication beyond static articulations of identity. So far, an intersectional analysis prompts us
to study the ways that Jordan transgressed gender, race, and abil-
ity/disability systems. Like many political figures, Jordan spoke
publicly about certain aspects of her life and valued her privacy on
others. In a public communication strategy that paralleled her treatment of her multiple sclerosis diagnosis, Jordan rarely discussed
her romantic relationships in political contexts. Though her long-
term relationship with educational psychologist Nancy Earl is narrated in the language of love, companionship, and home building in
her autobiography,[58] mainstream media outlets only began to raise
questions about Jordan's sexuality when covering an incident that
demonstrates the inextricable link between her personal experience
and everyday (be)longings. It was not until 1988, after Jordan retired
from national politics, that Earl was mentioned in the media. Jordan
nearly drowned as she was doing physical therapy exercises in a pool
and Earl jumped in to save her. Media accounts described Jordan and
Earl as "housemates" at that time.[59] After her death in 1996, the
Advocate published a cover story titled, "Barbara Jordan: The Other
Life—Lesbianism Was a Secret the Former Congresswoman Chose
to Take to Her Grave." This public outing explained that "Jordan's
attitude about discussion of her sexual orientation paralleled her attitude about talking about her health. . . . [Jordan's friend said] 'She
was not defined by her physical conditions, her sexual orientation,
or the color of her skin. If you were to define her by any of those
areas, Barbara Jordan would roar.'"[60] The *Advocate*'s next issue
published letters to the editor showcasing readers' conflicted views
on the article: some were outraged about the violation of Jordan's
civil liberties and personal privacy, while others lamented that she
did not use her public position to more vociferously advocate for
LGBTQ rights. Most illuminating for our purposes is a letter from
Josh LaPorte, one of Jordan's former students at the University of

Texas, who wrote about doing a presentation on the ethics of outing in Jordan's political ethics course:

> Professor Jordan agreed with my premise that outing is a clash of values between freedom of speech and the right to privacy. She also agreed with my conclusion: that the right to privacy supersedes freedom of speech except when it is in the public interest to know. Gay and closeted public officials who actively pursue an antigay agenda need to be outed because they are misrepresenting themselves to voters and to the public. Jordan never pursued that kind of agenda, so her outing is only fodder for the public appetite. . . . What your publication did was un-ethical.[61]

This brief exploration of Barbara Jordan's public life has shown that she is far from a one- or two-dimensional figure: her experience can be read as a queer engagement with public life. Her journeys—into pant suits, into politics, and into the public sphere—harnessed the power of the supposedly incongruous to form the rhetorical power that she yielded. Jordan played with expectations at every turn, gaining access to and power within exclusionary institutions. Without an intersectional approach to rhetorical history, these insights have been obscured, the richness of her behind-the-scenes personal experience left to gather historical dust. Rather than locating Jordan's "true identity," we ought to view Jordan as an intersectional rhetorical figure who, as she notes, was the composite of multiple experiences, affiliations, and relationships. As such, we gain fuller understandings of the complicated choices (and the influences on those choices) that make up rhetorical history.

MOVING FORWARD: TOWARD AN INTERSECTIONAL RHETORICAL HISTORY

How do multiple, overlapping oppressions affect rhetorical performances? This chapter has argued for the synergistic relationship between rhetorical history and intersectional research, first highlighting common spatial and geographic metaphors and then suggesting that we shift our focus to account for the unique dynamics of mobility and immobility that historical figures navigate. Rhetorical historians are not simply cartographers who locate women frozen in time on an already-printed map of rhetoric. We are travel companions who study the movement of people and discourses across rhetorical space and time. We search for those roads untaken, seeking

to better understand the queer aspects of rhetorical-historical figures and of ourselves as researchers intimately tied to the people
and subjects we study. This conceptualization is full of possibilities:
by refusing to narrow the focus of research to a single axis of identity, we can open ourselves up to more serendipitous findings[62]; by
focusing on movement across and between communities, we can
better account for the complexity of intersectional experience and
integrate critical insight about the value of relational politics; by
understanding aspects of mobility and immobility, we can better
explain the choices individuals make or are forced to make.

Communication scholarship in general, and rhetorical history in
particular, provides new spaces and materials from which to extend
and study intersectionality. As my analysis of Barbara Jordan demonstrates, rhetorical-historical research brings with it the benefit
of longitudinal analysis and the ability to gain broader perspective
through acknowledgment of articulations of belonging to particular communities. This means that in addition to telling the stories
of those everyday people whose voices were lost in the history of
rhetoric, we can also revisit the rhetoric of prominent public figures
with an intersectional lens. Rhetorical history and feminist intersectional work have much to contribute to each other: a blending of
perspectives and goals that travel together to better understand the
people and discourses we study.

NOTES

I thank Karma Chávez, Cindy Griffin, and Damien Pfister for their helpful
feedback at various stages of this project. Portions of this chapter are drawn
from my dissertation (University of Pittsburgh, 2010, directed by Gordon
Mitchell) and supported by a Student Research Fund Award from the University of Pittsburgh's Women's Studies Program.

1. George Lakoff and Mark Johnson, *Metaphors We Live By* (Chicago:
University of Chicago Press, 1980), 158.

2. Sonja K. Foss, *Rhetorical Criticism: Exploration and Practice* (Prospect Heights, IL: Waveland, 1989), 189.

3. For example, Anna Carastathis critiques intersectional models in
her "The Invisibility of Privilege: A Critique of Intersectional Models of
Identity," *Les Ateliers de L'Ethique* 3, no. 2 (2008): 23–38, while Barbara E.
L'Eplattenier draws attention to the problem of static geographic metaphors
in feminist rhetorical history in "Questioning Our Methodological Metaphors," in *Calling Cards: Theory and Practice in the Study of Race, Gender,
and Culture*, ed. Jacqueline Jones Royster and Ann Marie Mann Simpkins
(Albany: State University of New York Press, 2005), 133–146.

4. Kate Ronald, "Feminist Approaches to the History of Rhetoric," in *The Sage Handbook of Rhetorical Studies*, ed. Andrea A. Lunsford, Kirt H. Wilson, and Rosa A. Eberly (Thousand Oaks, CA: Sage, 2009), 140.

5. This is not to say that all rhetorical histories overlook intersectional dynamics. Indeed, as this chapter highlights, rhetorical historians have led the charge in studying the situated communicative practices of a variety of marginalized groups that might otherwise be obscured by the dominant narrative of a rhetorical tradition.

6. Barbara Biesecker and Karlyn Kohrs Campbell's exchange in *Philosophy and Rhetoric* about the value of studying the individual speaking subject as opposed to a radical contextualizing of collective rhetorical practices remains a significant methodological rift in feminist rhetorical history. See Biesecker, "Coming to Terms"; Karlyn Kohrs Campbell, "Biesecker Cannot Speak for Her Either," *Philosophy and Rhetoric* 26 (1993): 153–159; Barbara Biesecker, "Negotiating with Our Tradition: Reflecting Again (Without Apologies) on the Feminization of Rhetoric," *Philosophy and Rhetoric* 26 (1993): 236–241. Kate Ronald identifies the exchange as one of two major methodological issues in the development of feminist rhetorics, while Lindal Buchanan and Kathleen J. Ryan feature Biesecker's original article and Campbell's reply as a landmark controversy in their volume, *Walking and Talking Feminist Rhetorics* (West Lafayette, IN: Parlor Press, 2010). Hui Wu has extended this troubling of singular identity focus, urging methods that better address the experiences of Black and Third World rhetorical women in her "Historical Studies of Rhetorical Women Here and There: Methodological Challenges to Dominant Interpretative Frameworks," *Rhetoric Society Quarterly* 32 (2002): 81–97.

7. Kimberlé Crenshaw, "Mapping the Margins: Intersectionality, Identity Politics, and Violence Against Women of Color," in *Identities: Race, Class, Gender and Nationality*, ed. Linda Alcoff and Eduardo Mendieta (Malden, MA: Wiley-Blackwell, 2003), 175.

8. Patricia Hill Collins, *Black Feminist Thought: Knowledge, Consciousness, and the Politics of Empowerment*, 2nd ed. (New York: Routledge, 2000), 245. Nira Yuval-Davis develops the concept of transversal politics in *Gender and Nation* (London: Sage, 1997).

9. Gloria Anzaldúa, *Borderlands/La Frontera: The New Mestiza*, 3rd ed. (San Francisco: Aunt Lute Books, 2007), 217.

10. Chandra Talpade Mohanty, *Feminism Without Borders: Decolonizing Theory, Practicing Solidarity* (Durham, NC: Duke University Press, 2003), chap. 3, "What's Home Got to Do With It?"

11. Mohanty, *Feminism*, 2.

12. Charles E. Morris III, "Introduction: Portrait of a Queer Rhetorical/ Historical Critic," in *Queering Public Address: Sexualities in American Historical Discourse*, ed. Charles E. Morris III (Columbia: University of South Carolina Press, 2007), 3.

13. Kathleen J. Turner's edited volume *Doing Rhetorical History* articulated the need for a more critical approach, casting rhetorical history as a

process of social construction. See her "Rhetorical History as Social Construction: The Challenge and the Promise," in *Doing Rhetorical History: Concepts and Cases*, ed. Kathleen J. Turner (Tuscaloosa: University of Alabama Press, 1998), 1–18.

14. See the Biesecker-Campbell exchange discussed in note 6.

15. Jordynn Jack, "Acts of Institution: Embodying Feminist Rhetorical Methodologies in Space and Time," *Rhetoric Review* 28 (2009): 286.

16. Roxanne Mountford, "A Century After the Divorce: Challenges to a Rapprochement Between Speech Communication and English," in *The Sage Handbook of Rhetorical Studies*, 419.

17. A phrase borrowed from Cheryl Glenn's "Remapping Rhetorical Territory," *Rhetoric Review* 13 (1995): 287–303 and her book, *Rhetoric Retold: Regendering the Tradition from Antiquity Through the Renaissance* (Carbondale: Southern Illinois University, 1997), especially chap. 1.

18. Glenn, "Remapping Rhetorical Territory," 287.

19. Lisa Ede, Cheryl Glenn, and Andrea Lunsford, "Border Crossings: Intersections of Rhetoric and Feminism," *Rhetorica* 12 (1995): 401–402.

20. Buchanan and Ryan, *Walking and Talking Feminist Rhetorics*, xiv.

21. Mary P. Ryan, "Gender and Public Access: Women's Politics in Nineteenth-Century America," in *Feminism, the Public and Private*, ed. Joan B. Landes (Oxford: Oxford University Press, 1998), 218.

22. Susan Zaeske, *Signatures of Citizenship: Petitioning, Antislavery and Women's Political Identity* (Chapel Hill: University of North Carolina Press, 2003), 5.

23. Lisa A. Flores, "Creating Discursive Space Through a Rhetoric of Difference: Chicana Feminists Craft a Homeland," *Quarterly Journal of Speech* 82 (1996): 143.

24. Nan Johnson, *Gender and Rhetorical Space in American Life, 1866–1910* (Carbondale: Southern Illinois University Press, 2002).

25. Jacqueline Jones Royster, *Traces of a Stream: Literacy and Social Change Amongst African American Women* (Pittsburgh: University of Pittsburgh Press, 2000).

26. Jessica Enoch, *Refiguring Rhetorical Education: Women Teaching African American, Native American, and Chicano/a Students, 1865–1911* (Carbondale: Southern Illinois University Press, 2008).

27. Hui Wu, "The Alternative Feminist Discourse of Post-Mao Chinese Writers: A Perspective from the Rhetorical Situation," in *Alternative Rhetorics: Challenges to the Rhetorical Tradition*, ed. Laura Gray-Rosendale and Sibylle Gruber (Albany: State University of New York Press, 2001), 219–234.

28. Morris, *Queering Public Address*.

29. Thomas K. Nakayama and Robert L. Krizek, "Whiteness: A Strategic Rhetoric," *Quarterly Journal of Speech* 81 (1995): 291–309.

30. The title of this chapter plays on Carrie Crenshaw's work in laying out an intersectional approach to rhetorical criticism. See her "Women in the Gulf War: Toward an Intersectional Feminist Rhetorical Criticism," *Howard Journal of Communications* 8, no. 3 (1997): 219–235.

31. María Martínez Gonzáles, "Feminist Praxis Challenges the Identity Question: Toward New Collective Identity Metaphors," *Hypatia* 23, no. 3 (2008): 23.

32. Carastathis, "The Invisibility of Privilege," 27.

33. Kimberlé Crenshaw, "Traffic at the Crossroads: Multiple Oppressions," in *Sisterhood Is Forever: The Women's Anthology for a New Millennium*, ed. Robin Morgan (New York: Washington Square Press, 2003), 47, emphasis in original.

34. Crenshaw, "Traffic at the Crossroads," 47.

35. L'Eplattenier, "Questioning," 138.

36. L'Eplattenier, "Questioning," 141.

37. In her discussion of locational feminism as "narratives of encounter," Susan Stanford Friedman stresses the interplay between routes and roots. See her *Mappings: Feminism and the Cultural Geographies of Encounter* (Princeton, NJ: Princeton University Press, 1998), 151–178.

38. Aimee Carrillo Rowe, *Power Lines: On the Subject of Feminist Alliances* (Durham, NC: Duke University Press, 2008), 27. See Adrienne Rich's "Notes toward a Politics of Location," in *Blood, Bread, and Poetry: Selected Prose 1979–1985* (London: Little, Brown, 1984), 210–231.

39. Carrillo Rowe, *Power Lines*, 27, 25.

40. Carrillo Rowe, *Power Lines*, 26.

41. Carrillo Rowe, *Power Lines*, 28.

42. Molly Ivins, "The First and Only," interviewed by Charlayne Hunter-Gault, *Newshour* with Jim Lehrer transcript, PBS, January 17, 1996, accessed March 1, 2010 http://www.pbs.org/newshour/bb/remember/jordan_1-17.html.

43. Barbara C. Jordan, "1976 Democratic National Convention Keynote Address," *American Rhetoric*, 2010, accessed September 1, 2010 http://www.americanrhetoric.com/speeches/barbarajordan1976dnc.html.

44. Karlyn Kohrs Campbell, *The Rhetorical Act* (Belmont, CA: Wadsworth, 1982), 273.

45. Wayne N. Thompson, "Barbara Jordan's Keynote Address: Fulfilling Dual and Conflicting Purposes," *Central States Speech Journal* 30 (1979): 276.

46. E. Michele Ramsey elaborates on this argument in her article, "Addressing Issues of Context in Historical Women's Public Address," *Women's Studies in Communication* 27 (2004): 352–376.

47. Barbara Jordan and Shelby Hearon, *Barbara Jordan: A Self Portrait* (New York: Doubleday, 1979), 2.

48. Ann Crawford Fears, *Barbara Jordan: Breaking the Barriers* (Houston: Halycon Press, 2003), 20.

49. Jordan and Hearon, *Barbara Jordan*, 78.

50. Capp received irate letters and reports that there were editorials published against the integration of the tournament. See his *Excellence in Forensics: A Tradition at Baylor University* (Waco, TX: Baylor University, 1986), 49.

51. Mary Beth Rogers, *Barbara Jordan: American Hero* (New York: Bantam Books, 1998), 55.

52. Jordan explains in her autobiography that though she had not experienced the legal restrictions of "chattel status" that married women faced, and "not having borne infants, she did not interpolate how it might feel to have no control over whether or not your body reproduced" she "intellectually endorsed" women's rights. See Jordan and Hearon, *Barbara Jordan*, 213–214.

53. The case for studying the rhetorical dynamics of autobiographies has been made by Martha Watson in *Lives of Their Own: Rhetorical Dimensions in Autobiographies of Women Activists* (Columbia: University of South Carolina Press, 1999), especially chap. 1.

54. Jordan and Hearon, *Barbara Jordan*, 180–181.

55. Walter Shapiro, "What Does This Woman Want: Is Barbara Jordan Really Worth All the Fuss?" *Texas Monthly* (October 1976): 204.

56. Rogers, *Barbara Jordan*, 184.

57. Disability has been slowly integrated into feminist rhetorical and rhetorical-historical work. See Jay Dolmage and Cynthia Lewiecki-Wilson, "Refiguring Rhetoric: Linking Feminist Rhetoric and Disability Studies," in *Rhetorica in Motion: Feminist Rhetorical Methods and Methodologies*, ed. Eileen E. Schell and K. J. Rawson (Pittsburgh: University of Pittsburgh Press, 2010), 23–38; Davis W. Houck and Amos Kiewe explore the carefully orchestrated treatment of FDR's disability and its relationship to the body politic in their text, *FDR's Body Politics: The Rhetoric of Disability* (College Station: Texas A&M Press, 2003).

58. See Jordan and Hearon, *Barbara Jordan*, 237–240. As other scholars have noted, the goal of rhetorical-historical scholarship is not to prove a figure's "true sexuality" but rather to see how that aspect of their identity is negotiated and remembered in public culture. See especially Dana Cloud and Lisbeth Lispari's contributions to *Queering Public Address*.

59. J. Jennings Moss, "Barbara Jordan: The Other Life: Lesbianism Was a Secret the Former Congresswoman Chose to Take to Her Grave," *Advocate*, March 5, 1996, 44–45.

60. Moss, "Barbara Jordan," 42.

61. Josh LaPorte, "Je m'appelle Barbara." *Advocate*, April 16, 1996, 8.

62. For tales of serendipity and dead ends in historical research, see Gesa E. Kirsh and Liz Rohan's *Beyond the Archives: Research as Lived Process* (Carbondale: Southern Illinois University Press, 2008).

Chapter 4

Placing Sex/Gender at the Forefront: Feminisms, Intersectionality, and Communication Studies

Sara Hayden and D. Lynn O'Brien Hallstein[1]

> The problem with calling this work third-wave feminism is not that it isn't necessarily feminist; the problem is that how the work is feminist is not articulated in most cases. If the new feminism means that gender is not always the central category of analysis, then more work needs to be done to specify when and why it should or should not be.
> —Carissa Showden[2]

Over the past several decades, scholars in communication studies have incorporated intersectional thinking into our work. Stemming from feminist theorizing, intersectional thinking involves attending to the multiple and intersecting axes of power that form identities and upon which instances of oppression and resistance are enacted. As feminist rhetorical scholars, we are intrigued by and committed to participating in efforts to engage in intersectional work. At the same time, however, our commitment to feminism *specifically*—the exploration of sex/gender and the eradication of barriers to women's agency—means that our efforts to engage in intersectional work are coupled with a commitment to placing sex/gender at the forefront of our research, albeit always in the context of multiple axes of power.

We recognize that the previous statement may cause some readers to pause; indeed, to some it may even seem to be an oxymoron. After all, one of the goals of intersectional work is to offer a corrective to the racist, classist, and heterosexist assumptions that undergird some earlier feminist scholarship—scholarship that focuses on "women" but discusses only women who are white, straight, cis-gendered,[3] able bodied, and middle class. Yet we do not believe that the foregrounding of sex/gender *necessarily* reflects such assumptions, and we maintain that a sustained commitment to exploring sex/gender can be held in the context of intersectional work. In this chapter, then, one of our goals is to explain what a commitment to placing sex/gender at the forefront of our scholarship means to us, why we make this commitment, and what we believe is to be gained from this approach. Ultimately, we make the case that foregrounding sex/gender can be compatible with intersectional thinking.

Equally important, however, is a related goal: to explore intellectual and methodological concerns we have about how intersectionality functions in practice. In brief, our decision to maintain a focus on sex/gender (again, always in the context of other forms of power) also stems from our concern over the ways that some third-wave feminist scholars and activists have engaged in intersectional work. As we discuss in detail below, in an effort to address the multiple axes of power within which identities are formed and instances of oppression and resistance are enacted, some third-wave feminists turn their attention away from gender such that it is not clear what is feminist about their work. Indeed, some third-wave feminists short shrift issues related to sex/gender, ironically replicating a sexist system in which women's issues are considered of lesser importance than other issues.

The tendency of some third-wave feminists to minimize sex/gender points to a lacuna in discussions of intersectionality. That is, while there has been much work discussing what intersectionality means as a *theory*, less has been done to ferret out what it means to engage intersectional scholarship *in practice—as a method*. Intersectionality calls on scholars and activists to consider multiple and intersecting axes of power, yet because it is impossible to consider "everything," or to assume a "god's eye view," scholars must always make choices about where and how to focus on intersecting axes of power. Those choices are best made reflexively and transparently.[4] Our concern with third-wave intersectional thinking, then, is that it needs more justificatory grounds and explanation when put into practice. In other words, we suggest that we all would do well to provide justificatory grounds to explain our foci, including in intersectional scholarship.

In the case of the third-wave feminist scholarship discussed below, we suggest that it is a lack of reflexivity that leads to the short shrifting of sex/gender. In contrast, as we incorporate intersectional thinking into our work, we choose to reflexively and transparently foreground sex/gender, but we do so *not* because we believe it is the central or most important axis of power, nor does our choice assume white, middle-class, heterosexual, cisgender normativity. Instead, our decision begins with a recognition that scholarship always reflects a perspective and requires active and reflexive choice making about the standpoint[5] from which we think, write, and speak. And, as feminist scholars, our standpoint is *as feminists*: feminists who are interested in continuing to do work to eradicate sex/gender oppression with all of its complexities. Support for and explanation of these claims unfolds as follows: First, we offer an overview of the specific form of intersectionality to which we are responding, drawing attention to moments when sex/gender is downplayed or dismissed. Second, we discuss three examples of feminist scholarship in an effort to flesh out some of the different, specific reasons scholars might place sex/gender at the forefront of their analyses. Finally, we conclude by exploring the implications and the justification for the choice to foreground sex/gender in the three examples, while also revealing why we believe that doing so is well matched with, rather than contrary to, intersectional thinking.

THIRD-WAVE INTERSECTIONALITY

Third-wave intersectionality is a more recent strand of third-wave writing[6] that focuses on interlocking forms of oppression in the service of social justice.[7] As scholars Heywood and Drake argue, third-wave intersectional analyses emerged in direct response to the critiques of essentialism of white second-wave feminism.[8] Third-wave intersectional analyses also are grounded in the historical legacy of postmodern and poststructural theories and their focus on dispersed micropractices of power, emphasizing paradox, conflict, multiplicity, and "critiques of essentialism and exclusion within second-wave debates, especially developed by women of color and lesbian feminists (including contemporary queer theory)."[9] In doing so, third-wave intersectional thinking shifts the epistemological focus of feminist theorizing and activism.

In particular, as Showden argues, and is worth quoting at length:

> While intersectionality is not itself a "politics," it is an attempt to shift the epistemological standpoint of feminism, providing a new subject position from which feminist critique is articulated. The position from which knowledge is articulated can have dramatic implications for the kinds of

politics that are then seen as viable and valuable. So as intersectionality shapes feminist activism, new possibilities for coalitions become visible, and the specific goals or political projects of feminism are fruitfully reconceived as well.[10]

This means that, as intersectional thinking considers various components of identity as interdependent and codeterminative rather than additive and discrete, it also shifts the epistemological ground of politics to coalitional politics. In other words, unlike most white second-wave scholars whose epistemology was grounded in women's oppression and political action in the name of women as a group, intersectional analyses develop ways of thinking and political action that recognize the intersection of various multiple, shifting bases of oppression, primarily around race, class, gender, sexuality, and (dis)ability, and aim to create coalition politics based on interlocking, yet always shifting and changing, forms of oppression and axes of identity.

We agree with much of this third-wave theorizing; in particular, we accept that identities and instances of oppression/resistance are formed and enacted within multiple axes of power. We maintain, however, that once the multiplicity of identity, oppression, and resistance are acknowledged, the difficulty resides in developing ways to *analyze* and *discuss* these multiplicities. It is the exploration of this difficulty—the doing of intersectional work or the practice of intersectionality—that requires much more discussion and attention. Many third-wave feminists have responded to this difficulty by shifting their focus from "women's issues" to a broader concern for social justice. It is in this move that we begin to see both a tendency to minimize sex/gender and a lack of attention to methodological issues.

For example, Labaton and Martin, editors of *The Fire This Time*, argue that "intersectionality suggests those issues that have traditionally been associated with the feminist movement—reproductive rights, domestic violence, date rape, and equal pay for equal work—are not the only issues that should define it."[11] Although Labaton and Martin claim that they are not suggesting that these "traditional" second-wave issues no longer matter, they also argue, and are worth quoting at length, that:

> we should not become *so distracted by the core issues* that we neglect other social justice concerns. The borders of feminism need to be split open, both so that we are freed from ideological rigidity and so that other identity claims of

race, sexuality, class, nationality, and geography can move beyond being simply "tolerated" or "included."[12]

A similar sentiment is articulated by Lisa Jervis, cofounding editor of the third-wave feminist magazine *Bitch*: "gender isn't always the primary mode of analysis. . . . Anti-poverty work, international human-rights work, and labor are all issues that are feminist issues, but they aren't all about women."[13]

Thus for some third-wave feminists, gender no longer is always the primary category of analysis, and when gender is no longer in the forefront, the range of issues open to feminist inquiry, as well as the means through which feminist activism proceeds, expand exponentially. Again according to Labaton and Martin, "Unlike second wave feminism, which has operated from a monolithic center, multiplicity offers the power of existing insidiously and simultaneously everywhere. 'Woman' as a primary identity category has ceased to be the entry point for much young activist work. Instead, it has become one of the many investigatory means used to affect an indefinite number of issues and cultural analyses."[14] Thus, as much third-wave intersectional analyses shift focus away from gender as the primary analytic category, they fundamentally resituate the epistemological, methodological, and political foundations of feminism.

Although these epistemological shifts are exciting and intriguing, they raise key questions for feminist thinkers, most importantly around the issue of feminism itself. More pointedly, for us the question that arises is: When the issues addressed are so varied and the modes of analysis so broad, what makes the work feminist? We are not the first scholars to raise this question. In exploring the politics of third-wave intersectionality, Showden points out, "if third-wave feminism cannot articulate a gendered analysis of these cultural shifts and their responses to them, then one might ask in what sense it is still feminism."[15] Thus Showden calls on third-wave feminists to explain how and why their work should be considered feminist, while also drawing attention to the seeming dismissal of the significance of traditional feminist issues implied in some third-wave activists' work. She writes: "If reproductive rights and violence against women are a 'distraction' from (more?) important feminist issues, then third-wave activists need to supply some justificatory measure for deciding what makes an issue feminist, and why."[16]

Along with Showden, one of our central concerns with much intersectional work is its lack of clarity around which issues are placed in the forefront and why. In particular, we are troubled by the fact that many intersectional activists and scholars fail to make apparent when and why they claim that their work is feminist. This lack of clarity is compounded, and becomes even more startling and troubling, when intersectional scholars claim that intersectional work "has become one of many investigatory means," and that intersectional work is "insidiously and simultaneously everywhere."[17] Although we appreciate the move to open the borders of feminism to include various and interlocking forms of gendered oppression, to be "insidiously and simultaneously everywhere" seems to suggest that feminism is anything, anywhere, at any time. We simply do not understand how and why intersectional work should be considered *feminist* when sex/gender is one of many possible investigatory tools, sometimes employed, sometimes not. As a result, we believe much more work needs to be done to address these issues as feminist communication scholars continue to explore intersectional ideas. It is important to clarify that we do not make this call for more discussion and precision because we have an ideologically rigid understanding of feminism. Rather, we do so because as feminisms continue to develop and change—as the borders of feminisms are expanded—new and important questions about the implications of those changes must be addressed if we hope to maintain a feminist standpoint. Thus, again, we urge feminist communication scholars to be transparent, indicating clearly on which issues they choose to focus and how and why such foci should be considered feminist.

Like Showden, we also are troubled that some feminists frame issues rooted in sex/gender, including reproductive justice and patriarchal oppressions, as "distractions." We cannot help noticing that such claims echo a sexist system in which "good women" are charged to put their own issues and needs last. Moreover, a similar downplaying of the significance of sex/gender can be found in the work of some communication scholars who engage in intersectional work. An example can be found in John Sloop's recent review of four books, each of which, Sloop maintains, productively invokes an intersectional lens. Indeed, he asserts "while one might first open these texts with an interest in questions of gender/sexuality and contemporary culture, to varying degrees, each one raises intersecting questions about race, class, and occupation."[18] Sloop's discussion of each book is thoughtful and generous; however, he finds some fault with Judith Halberstam's *In a Queer Time and Place*, suggesting that "her focus on intersectionality all too often is undermined by the fullest focus remaining on sexuality/gender."[19] Yet we would argue that Halberstam's emphasis on sexuality/gender is no more pronounced than is E. Patrick Johnson's emphasis on race in *Appropriating Blackness*, a book for which Sloop has nothing but praise.

Indeed, Sloop writes: "If anyone has given us an example of how intersectional analyses may proceed . . . it is Patrick Johnson."[20]

To be clear, we agree with Sloop that Halberstam's analyses, while engaging in intersectional thinking, typically begin from and return to questions of sex/gender. However, Johnson's analyses similarly utilize an intersectional focus while typically beginning from and ending with questions of race. For example, Johnson devotes a chapter in the book to a discussion of his grandmother, with particular attention to her history as a live-in domestic worker. There are clearly sex/gender-based issues that Johnson could have mined in this chapter, and at times he does address such issues. However, the *focus* of his attention is on race. He notes, for instance, that in spite of the low wages she was paid by her employers, his grandmother, Mary, received nonmonetary compensation in the form of "gifts" and "nice" treatment. He writes:

> In addition to receiving material goods (i.e., hand-me-downs), Mary felt that because the Smiths were *"very* nice people" who treated her with respect, the job was worth keeping. . . . Based on the experiences that Mary recounts, I interpret the term "nice" to reflect a mutual understanding between her and the Smiths concerning her position within the home and her relationship to the family. In brief, she was an "outsider-within." On one level, she was treated as an adult member of the family and she claimed authority (and responsibility) accordingly. On another level, however, her "familial" position and authority was [sic] constantly qualified by the fact that she was a paid employee and she was *black*.[21]

In a study based on her experiences as a domestic worker and interviews with 40 other domestics, Judith Rollins offers a gendered analysis of similar interpersonal relations between employers and employees. She writes:

> All of the domestics I interviewed stressed the importance of the treatment they received from employers in their job satisfaction. The female employer understands the power of emotional rewarding and punishing in a way that the typical male employer does not, and she knows such rewarding will be more effective with a female employee than with a male. Her use of the emotions to control domestics is another aspect of the maternalist dynamic.[22]

Johnson draws extensively on Rollins's work in his chapter, yet he bypasses a gendered analysis of this particular issue, instead focusing on how the interpersonal relationship established between his grandmother and her employer reflects both women's construction of what they recognize as "authentic" blackness:

> Ultimately, the point I wish to communicate is two-fold: on the one hand "authentic" blackness is constructed by Mary's white mistress vis-à-vis her construal of what a "real good mammy should be." Mary performs and obliges that construction in various ways. On the other hand, within her narrative performance, she also performs her own version of "authentic" blackness by drawing on black cultural performance traditions that reposition and ground her authority as a "black" subject.[23]

Once again, we want to be unambiguous. We point out Johnson's focus on race over gender not to suggest that Johnson is in *error*; rather, we are simply suggesting that as a scholar engaging in intersectional work, Johnson had to choose his focus and his method of analysis, and while his book admirably addresses the intersections of race, class, sexuality, and gender, in this instance and elsewhere, he tends to *foreground* race. Indeed, he is both explicit and reflexive about such choices, writing in an earlier chapter that "although theories of performativity focus primarily on the performativity of gender, I engage a discussion about the performativity of race."[24]

When engaging in intersectional work, such choices are not only *inevitable*, they are also *necessary* in order to put intersectional thinking into practice, to develop a method of analysis. Indeed, as we learned from feminist standpoint theorists[25] and the postmodern turn, all writing necessarily reflects a perspective; it is not possible to take a "god's eye view" of the world either in our thinking or in our actual methods of analysis. Our disagreement with Sloop, then, is with his characterization of Johnson's work as more consistently intersectional than Halberstam's. *Both* Johnson and Halberstam provide examples of intersectional work that begin with two different foregrounded nubs: for Johnson, questions of race; for Halberstam, questions of sex/gender. Both Johnson's and Halberstam's works are powerful and important intersectional analyses. The difference is what is at the forefront of those analyses. Because we believe that all work, even intersectional analysis, is always, already and inevitably focused in some way, the key difference between the two is one of focus and methodological practice rather than which is more authentically intersectional.

Both Showden's critique as well as our discussion of Sloop's work thus return us to a key methodological question about intersectional work—a question to which all rigorous work must attend—which provisions are attended to, when, and why. The third-wave feminist scholars and activists discussed above who deemphasize gender promote and engage in work that addresses an "indefinite number of issues and cultural analyses" in an effort to understand the intersection of gender, race, sexuality, geography, and nationality. However, as we have illustrated, in this effort to "do it all,"[26] these scholars and activists sometimes intimate that sex/gender is somehow less important or less worthy of attention than other axes of power, while also, often, failing to provide justificatory explanations for the method they use in the practice of intersectional analyses and activism. Indeed, we submit that because these scholars and activists have not explicitly addressed the methodological issues of "which provisions should be attended to, when, and why," they inadvertently reiterate a sexist system wherein traditionally "women's issues" are considered of lesser importance than other social justice causes. Thus our concern goes beyond a lack of clarity regarding what makes such work "feminist"; we maintain that when scholars do not make explicit and reflexive choices regarding the axes of power to which they will attend, they may inadvertently and ironically reinforce some of the power structures they seek to challenge, while also failing to fully explore and describe their use of intersectionality in practice.

We do not accept that sex/gender and issues traditionally linked to women, such as reproductive justice, are distractions or of lesser importance than other issues. To the contrary, we argue that even with the large-scale social and institutional changes to many women's lives brought about by previous social justice movements, but most especially feminisms, much gender work remains. Thus, as we incorporate intersectional thinking into our work, we consistently and strategically choose to focus our attention on sex/gender. Moreover, we maintain that it is this focus that makes our work *feminist*.

When focusing on sex/gender, we try, admittedly with greater and lesser success, to situate our discussions of sex/gender in terms of the multiple axes of power in operation in any given case. As such, we avoid making claims about women as a unified group; to the contrary, we make a concerted effort to acknowledge and interrogate the specificities of, and differences between, women's lives. Yet we object to the notion that our desire to focus on sex/gender is based on what Labaton and Martin describe as "ideological rigidity."[27] Instead, our focus on sex/gender is central to our ongoing commitment to eradicate barriers to women's oppression in all of its complexity, variety, and nuance. Moreover, we do not suggest that all scholars should begin and end with sex/gender. To the contrary, we appreciate that different scholars and activists answer the question "When engaging in intersectional analyses, which provisions should be attended to, when, and why?" differently, and we would hope reflexively and strategically. Yet our commitment to feminism means that our point of departure is always sex/gender, and we make that clear in our work.

WHY SEX/GENDER?

This section will elucidate what placing sex/gender at the forefront of research means in practice and identify key complexities that often emerge when feminist scholars and thinkers engage in feminist research or political praxis. Before we begin this discussion, however, we want to make what perhaps is an obvious point: in each of the examples discussed below—indeed, in *any* discussion related to human beings and human behavior—issues of race, class, gender, sexuality, and national origin, among other things, are part of the scenario.[28] Scholars write from specific subject positions marked by these and other elements that make up our identities, and the people and issues about which we write similarly reflect unique and varied subject positions. We all exist within multiple axes of power, discourse, and materiality. However, as we have argued above, because no one can assume a god's eye view and because no one can possibly address "everything," scholars must make choices about which aspects of the situation we will bring to the forefront and which aspects of the situation will remain in the background.

We discuss three instances of feminist scholarship in which sex/gender is placed in the forefront and we explore the various and diverse reasons for these choices.

Example One: A Matter of Strategy

Loretta Ross is an African American feminist scholar and activist. Well known for her work in the women's health and reproductive rights movement, Ross has been instrumental in efforts to urge mainstream feminist organizations to address their internal racism and classism and to broaden their perspectives so that the concerns of women of color and poor women are taken into account. In a number of interviews and biographical essays, Ross explained that her choice to devote her life to reproductive-rights work stemmed from her personal history. Ross was raped twice as a child, the second time by a family member. The incest led to a pregnancy that

Ross carried to term after she determined that abortion options were too dangerous. As Jennifer Nelson notes:

> Ross represented both of these involuntary sexual encounters, the stranger rape and the coercive relationship with the relative who fathered her child, as well as the contemplation of illegal abortion and the birth of her child, as pivotal events in the development of her awareness of gender oppression. Indeed, opposition to sexual violence and the reproductive rights of women of color became the two most important commitments in Ross's feminist activist history. *Yet, she did not describe these events as overtly linked to racism. . . . Her emphasis* in the *Voices of Feminism* interview and in the *Black Scholar* article *was on the gender injustice she felt as a young woman coming of age in a culture that denied women both sexual and reproductive agency.*[29]

Ross explained her choice to focus on gender oppression rather than racism in a subsequent interview, noting that she "may not have rendered her personal experiences of sexual assault and incest as a teenager as linked to racism because her primary goal as an antirape activist was to convince black communities that rape and incest happen among African Americans."[30] In other words, when recounting her history, Ross's political goals led her to place gender injustice, and not racism, at the forefront of her discussion. As in the discussion of Johnson's work above, Ross was reflexive about her choice to highlight one axis of power over another. Ross wanted members of her community to come to terms with the gender dynamics that marked it. As Ross explained: "The conversation in the black community was that it was a denial that it was a problem at all. That it was a problem at all was finally being acknowledged; this was significant in itself."[31]

Moreover, as Nelson points out, Ross's choice to foreground sex/gender in her personal account does not mean that racism was not a factor in Ross's or other black women's experiences of intrarace rape and incest. Nelson writes: "Of course, racism did have an effect on black women who experienced rape by black men. Most significantly black women were often afraid to speak out about rape for fear that it would increase racist ideas about predatory black male sexuality. *But this was not Ross's point of emphasis.*"[32] Thus, because Ross's goal was to draw attention to the gender injustice that existed within African American communities, in the interviews and articles mentioned above, she chose to place sex/gender injustice, and not racism, at the forefront of her biography. In Ross's case, the foregrounding of sex/gender served a strategic purpose, a purpose that was consciously made and justified.

Example Two: The Limitations and Possibilities Presented by the Research Process

Unlike our discussion of Ross, our second example reveals the challenging and complex limitations and possibilities presented during the research process that sometimes shape the boundaries of analysis for the researcher, while raising the very difficult ethical and political questions that spurred the development of much intersectional thinking. Rather than retreat from the difficult ethical and political questions that our commitment to focus on sex/gender raises, we turn to them next, understanding that we risk criticism. We are willing to do so, however, because we are persuaded by Linda Alcoff when she argues, "it is both morally and politically objectionable to structure one's actions around the desire to avoid criticism, especially if this outweighs other questions of effectivity."[33] Thus, we now turn to a complex example of the ethical limitations and possibilities presented by the research process in order to explore a difficult set of issues in regard to the effectiveness of intersectional ideas in practice.

Negotiating motherhood and a career can be challenging. Both endeavors require a significant commitment of time and energy, and in the contemporary United States, very little support exists for women who seek to be both mothers and professionals. White scholar Lori West Peterson has written about one woman's experiences as she sought to negotiate these roles. Part of a larger project about maternity leave, Peterson engaged in an in-depth interview with "Patricia Newman," an African American single mother.[34] What follows is part of the story Peterson told based on her extensive interview with Newman.

In 1993 Newman became pregnant and took three months' maternity leave. Prior to her leave, Newman was a senior budget analyst for a city government agency in a large metropolitan area. Her job came with significant responsibility, including the supervision of approximately twenty people. Her immediate boss, another woman, was planning to leave the agency and twice asked Newman if she would consider taking over her position. Given her impending maternity, Newman chose not to pursue this promotion. Newman's boss resigned while Newman was on maternity leave and a male coworker was promoted as Newman's supervisor. Upon returning to work, Newman discovered that her new boss had demoted her, taking away her office and her parking space. Peterson asked New-man if she believed gender played a role in these events; Newman answered in the affirmative:

> I think that, I think that there's major significance, because even beyond that. All seniors are now male, well, they were. . . . So, it just seems very strange that an organization that did have a lot of female participation at all levels now was adjusted such that women were not in important or critical roles.[35]

Moreover, Newman indicated that her new boss was specifically critical of her choice to become a single mother:

> PN: I know that he made comments about my being preg-nant and having a child "out of wedlock."
> LP: What kind of comments?
> PN: Something derogatory . . . basically, it was not appropri-ate for me to have done such, especially in my role.[36]

Thus, as Newman described these events, a point around which dis-crimination turned was sex/gender. She maintained that her new boss was threatened by the fact that she was "a very strong, ag-gressive, intelligent woman"[37] who chose to have a child outside of marriage. In short, Newman explained that her boss engaged in punitive behaviors because he did not think she was acting like a "good woman" should act.

As a feminist standpoint scholar, Peterson was aware of inter-sectional ideas and so she asked Newman whether she thought rac-ism was a factor in any of these events. Newman quickly dismissed this suggestion, asserting "No, there are Black Americans, so I don't think it was race."[38] Of course, there is a long and ugly history of racism surrounding African American single mothers in the United States, and it is improbable that Newman was able to enact ma-ternity as a single, African American woman without encountering racism. And so as Peterson acknowledges, Newman's unwilling-ness to consider whether racial discrimination was in play in the instance described may have reflected the fact that Peterson is white and Newman is black. Peterson writes:

> The abruptness of Patricia's response indicates her unwill-ingness to discuss potential racial discrimination. However, Patricia's unwillingness may have more to do with the fact

that I was a young, white, university professor than with her inability to integrate discourse about racial discrimination into her maternity leave account. Obviously, this discrepancy did not exist in terms of sex—we were both female and had experienced maternity and maternity leave—thus a certain bond of trust and similarity was present when discussing gender inequality that was absent within the discursive context of race.[39]

Marsha Houston has documented the history of distrust and suspicion that marks black women's dialogues with white women, thus legitimizing Peterson's insight that Newman may have chosen not to broach the sensitive topic of race with her.[40] Peterson is clearly aware of that distrust and suspicion as well as the potential implications for her research, noting that Newman's response to her query may have reflected the racial difference between the two women and therefore may not reflect the whole of Newman's experiences.

Yet Peterson follows this passage with a caveat, noting, "feminist standpoint theory suggests that members of oppressed groups may have a clearer vision about their oppression. So, Newman may simply be right: racial discrimination was not occurring, or she may have chosen not to address this issue with me."[41] Thus although Peterson recognizes that racism may have been in play in the situation Newman described, she does not dismiss the possibility that Newman's account of the event is valid. Indeed, had she done so, Peterson would have positioned herself as having superior knowledge, which we believe is an intellectually elitist and racist move. Of course, Peterson does not suggest that Newman's experience of the event is a direct mirror of what actually occurred. As standpoint theorists argue, *all* perspectives are limited.[42] Rather, Peterson follows the lead of standpoint theorists who maintain that while we all have limited perspectives, some perspectives are more limited than others. As a white researcher, Peterson recognized that her perspective was more limited than Newman's, and she accepted that the situation *may* have unfolded as Newman described it: the nub around which power turned may have been sexism and not racism, or, Newman may have chosen not to discuss racism with her.[43] In other words, even though, theoretically, Peterson understood the intersection that might be at work between racism and gender oppression in Newman's experience, as a researcher, Peterson acknowledged the possible implications of race without making a definitive claim about how it affected the encounter. As a result, she ended up echoing Newman's own focus on sex/gender injustice to explain what happened.

Certainly, another strategy open to Peterson would have been not to write this case study. After all, by echoing Newman's focus on gender without making a definitive claim about race, Peterson risks that her analysis will be read as a naïve form of feminism,[44] given that a primary goal of feminist scholarship is to interrogate systems of oppression whether or not any particular individual understands that more than one system of oppression is likely operating in her experience. We would challenge this critique. Indeed, the notion that we must always read a core set of power axes at their intersection, regardless of what an actual interviewee says about her own experiences, suggests intersectional ideas must, rigidly, adhere to a certain set of ideologies in every situation and separate from research in practice. In contrast, that Peterson chose to write the case study and risk being criticized for foregrounding sex/gender while also not making definitive claims about race seems like the best Peterson could do in light of the research context in which she found herself. Again, we draw on Alcoff's understanding that taking risks as scholars is sometimes the better choice than not writing at all. As Alcoff argues, and it is worth repeating part of it from above,

> surely it is both morally and politically objectionable to structure one's actions around the desire to avoid criticism, especially if this outweighs other questions of effectivity. In some cases perhaps the motivation is not so much to avoid criticism as to avoid errors, and the person believes that the only way to avoid errors is to avoid all speaking for others. However, errors are unavoidable in theoretical inquiry as well as political struggle, and moreover they often make contributions.[45]

Unlike those scholars who "retreat" from attempting to discuss politically and emotionally charged issues, Peterson took a risk. She believed that Newman's story was important and worthy of scholarly discussion. However, the specific parameters of the research encounter shaped where her focus laid and what she could and could not say, leading her to concentrate on gender oppression while also acknowledging that she could not make a definitive statement about the workings of race. Consequently, as in this case, the *actual practice* of research often shapes—both limits and creates possibilities—how analysis can and should proceed.

Example Three: The Material Weight of Sex/Gender

Our third example is different in kind from the first two; here we discuss not a specific piece of scholarship but instead an instance in which the material weight of sex/gender is such that we believe an analysis would productively place sex/gender at the forefront.

Second-wave white women's liberation grew out of other movements for social justice: the civil rights movement, the anti-war movement, and the new left movement. Not surprisingly, the women working in these movements drew connections between the systems of power the movements were fighting and the sexism that permeated the movements themselves. Yet, when movement women attempted to bring the issue of sexism in the movements to the attention of movement men, they were consistently dismissed or ridiculed.[46] For one veteran white activist, Marilyn Salzman Webb, the straw that broke the camel's back came as a result of a speech she gave at a Students for a Democratic Society (SDS) rally in 1969. In her speech, Webb sought to denounce a system that treats women as objects. In response, the men in the audience heckled her off the stage, yelling things like "'Fuck her!' 'Take her off the stage! Rape her in a back alley!'"[47] Later that night, Webb received threatening phone calls from SDS members, leading her and several other white movement women to leave the male left and form a white women's liberation group.[48]

In this case, a central axis of power upon which the oppressive and potentially dangerous encounter turned was sex/gender oppression. The issue Webb was addressing was sexism in the movement; movement men responded with sexual threats. This is not to say that the power invoked in this case was *only* marked by sex/gender. That Webb was a white woman was significant to the meaning of the men's taunts and Webb's response. Indeed, if Webb had been a black woman addressing sexism within the movement and men[49] had responded with similar taunts, the meaning of those taunts would have been different.

As the instance actually unfolded, men invoked sexual violence to thwart an effort to address sexism. Implicated in this interaction were the sexual politics that marked relationships between men and white women, politics shaped by 1950s' assumptions of middle-class, white women's sexual purity, the sexual revolution of the 1960s, the illegality of abortion, the development of the birth control pill, and attitudes about white women's roles, among other issues. In contrast, implicated in the *imagined* instance are the history of slavery, including the frequency with which black women were the victims of sexual violence perpetrated by white men, the racism that continued to mark U.S. culture in the 1960s, the sexual revolution of the 1960s, the illegality of abortion, the development of the birth control pill, and attitudes about black women's roles, among other issues. Nonetheless, in both the actual and the imagined instances, the men responded to a critique of sexism with threats of sexual violence. So while an understanding of what the sexual threat meant necessarily requires investigating issues beyond sex/gender, the power being invoked involved sex/gender as a highly salient component. As such, again, were we to offer a more sustained scholarly analysis of this event, as feminist scholars we would place sex/gender in the forefront of our discussion, in the context of other axes of power.

IMPLICATIONS

In the three examples discussed above, a (but not *the*) point around which discrimination turned was sex/gender. In all three instances, men asserted power over women. In all three instances, questions of sexuality, sexual violence, and reproduction were in play. Thus some (but not all) of the questions these examples raise include: What happens when relationships of power revolve around sexuality and sexual violence, reproduction, maternity, and the like? What does it mean for relationships between women and men, fathers and mothers, parents and children? How does sex/gender-based discrimination affect individuals' identities as sexual and reproductive beings in both the public and the private spheres? How do sex/gender messages in the larger culture shape how women understand themselves as women and the way we communicate about women and men, fathers and mothers, daughters and sons? Of course, the people involved in the three examples differ in terms of their class status and racial identities, and the examples took place in different parts of the United States and in different historical periods. As such, discussions of each example necessarily reflect the racial, geographic, and historical specificity of each situation. Yet, in each of the examples discussed above, sex/gender has been placed in the forefront for a variety of important political, ethical, or context-specific reasons.

Moreover, as also discussed, the reasons for placing sex/gender at the forefront of the conversation differed. In the first example, Ross's decision reflected a strategic goal: She wanted the reality of gender-based injustice in African American communities to be acknowledged and addressed by members of her community. Thus, while racism may have played a role in her personal history of sexual abuse, she chose to highlight sex/gender injustice when discussing it. In the second example, interviewee Patricia Newman denied that racism played a role in her experiences in the workplace. As author Lori Peterson suggests, Newman's denial may have reflected an aversion to discussing racism with a white researcher, or, it may have been that racism was not salient in the specific instance recounted. Reflecting the limitations and possibilities presented by the data and research process itself, and respecting Newman's right to tell her story as she chose, Peterson chose not to make a definitive claim about racism, instead placing sex/gender at the forefront of her analysis. And, by doing so, Peterson's work illuminates some of the most daunting ethical and political questions about the limits and possibilities presented to feminist thinkers as they engage in research. The third example reflects an instance in which sex/gender injustice is a foregrounded nub that marked the events under discussion. In this example we recounted Marilyn Salzman Webb's experiences in attempting to address sexism in the student movement, an effort that was responded to with sexual threats. As we argued, although of course the incident was infused with issues of race, class, and nationality, among others, a key point around which power was being invoked was sex/gender. As such, as feminist scholars, we maintain that an analysis of the event productively places sex/gender at the forefront. Such an analysis helps us to understand the ways in which power that revolves around sexuality and sexual violence, and is shaped by other axes of power, is invoked. To frame a study with sex/gender in the forefront reflexively and strategically produces a very different kind of feminist work than many white second-wave feminists produced in their essentialist focus on sex/gender, while also being compatible with intersectional thinking.

Indeed, our work consistently has explored questions in which sex/gender are particularly salient. Sara Hayden has engaged in explorations of how specific groups of women have sought to take control of and claim the power to name or define their sexuality and reproduction, how mothers have used maternal metaphors to claim political power, how advocates for reproductive rights have sought to retool choice to reflect a reproductive justice perspective, and how nonmothers have sought to claim the mantle of "good woman" in light of their nonmaternity. Her goal in all of this work has been to understand how the materiality of reproduction and sexuality function specifically. In other words, she has explored how various women have been oppressed around reproduction and sexuality and how women have employed these same issues to challenge oppressive systems and forge new ground.[50] Similarly, Lynn O'Brien Hallstein's previous work on feminist standpoint theory focused on how women's social location in sex/gender oppression provides ways of seeing that can transform how to engage in moral reasoning, while her more recent work as a feminist maternal scholar focuses on how relationships of power are embedded in contemporary motherhood and mothering in ways that both oppress women as mothers and provide women agency within diverse mothering practices.[51]

In all of our work, then, a key issue has been related specifically to operations of power as they are articulated through the lens of sex/gender. Of course, race, class, sexual orientation, and other axes of power also were operative in the material we studied, and we acknowledge that in the past, like many feminist scholars, we may have been less reflexive about the operations of these other power axes than we now would be, given our understanding of intersectionality. Nonetheless, as we incorporate intersectional ideas into our current and future work, the issues we foreground are or likely will be rooted in reproduction, sexuality, or motherhood; therefore, a (but not *the*) key form of oppression or resistance we explore involves gender and sex. It is this focus that makes our work both feminist and distinct from other works. We also believe that the way we ask these questions and proceed is crucially different from the essentialist approaches from the past. In short, focusing on sex/gender today is not always, already the same kind of "monolithic centering" or "ideological rigidity" as it may have once been. Instead, as we move forward, we foreground sex/gender while simultaneously recognizing other axes of power; moreover, because our choice to foreground sex/gender is made reflexively and thoughtfully, we acknowledge the limitations of our work. As we continue our work as feminist scholars, then, we hope to avoid both the pitfalls found in early feminist work that focused *only* on sex/gender as well as the problems found in some third-wave intersectional work in which sex/gender is short shrifted.

In the end, our argument is deceptively simple. Going forward, we will choose to focus our research on issues where sex and gender are significant. It is our hope that our research will help illuminate some of the specific concerns related to issues of sex/gender as they circulate within various modes of power. At the same time, we recognize that our perspective is limited. As such we appreciate that other scholars assume other approaches to similar and different material. We would suggest, however, that as we all do more intersectional work, we make a conscious and concerted effort to be reflexive about where and when our work begins and ends and that we are forthright about providing the justificatory grounds for what makes our work feminist.

Sloop ends his review of books with the following reflection:

> While in the past I was swayed by the argument that individual analyses could focus on particular aspects of identity work as a part of a larger mosaic of criticism within the academic community, each of these efforts by default illustrates the poverty of this position. The richness of these analyses, then, highlights and underlines the ways in which a gender/sexuality project that avoids questions of, say, class and race, not only reinforces the larger material and economic ways in which class and racial borders are reinforced and delimited, but also provides a critique of gender/sexuality issues that has limited explanatory powers. While "cultural criticism as mosaic" may still be an apt metaphor, the connections within each section of that mosaic, and the connections— methodological, theoretical, critical, topical—between elements of that mosaic must be drawn more vividly by each individual critic.[52]

We mostly agree with this claim. We also maintain that analyses of sex/gender must take other axes of power, often including race and class, into account. Where we differ, perhaps, from Sloop is in our emphasis on the fact that all scholarship reflects a perspective. As such, we maintain that both scholars and activists must reflexively and strategically consider which provisions or "connections" they will attend to, when, and why. Recognizing that sex/gender is vulnerable to being downplayed or dismissed, as in fact, are all nodes of power, we choose to keep sex/gender at the forefront of our work, while considering the multiple axes of power within which sex/gender circulates. Moreover, we appreciate that other scholars make different choices, keeping other nodes of power in their sites. As intersectionality becomes more prevalent in communication scholarship, it is with different approaches to scholarship in dialogue that we see the best potential for understanding and challenging the many forms of oppression that continue to exist in our world.

NOTES

1. The authors contributed equally to this chapter.

2. Carissa Showden, "What's Political about the New Feminisms?" *Frontiers* 30 (2009): 190.

3. Cisgender is a neologism that refers to people whose assigned gender is congruent with their gender identity, or, people who are not transgender; see www.wordiq.com/definition/cisgender.

4. We are not embracing a naïve understanding of choice when we make this claim. We recognize that choices are always constrained by a combination of ideological and material factors, and that some people have less ability to "choose" than others. Nonetheless, we believe that even within constraints, scholars and activists necessarily make choices about the issues to which they attend. See Sara Hayden and D. Lynn O'Brien Hallstein, eds., *Contemplating Maternity in an Era of Choice: Explorations into Discourses of Reproduction* (Lanham, MD: Lexington Books, 2010).

5. We purposefully use the term *standpoint* instead of *perspective* because we are drawing on the feminist standpoint difference between the two. As O'Brien Hallstein argues, standpoints are "not something that all women have simply because they have certain experiences of oppression" (11). Indeed, achieving a standpoint requires work: mediation, dialogue, and struggle. It is something that marginalized people must actively, consciously seek. Thus, we are suggesting that our work is not simply our perspective, but rather a location of critique that has been actively developed via the kind of mediation, dialogue, and intellectual struggle addressed in this volume. D. Lynn O'Brien Hallstein, "Where Standpoint Stands Now: An Introduction and Commentary," *Women's Studies in Communication* 23 (2000): 1–15; also see Sandra Harding, *Whose Science? Whose Knowledge? Thinking from Women's Lives* (Ithaca, NY: Cornell University Press, 1991); Nancy Hartsock, *Money, Sex, and Power: Toward a Feminist Historical Materialism* (Boston: Northeastern University Press, 1985); Hilary Rose, "Hand, Brain, and Heart: A Feminist Epistemology for the Natural Sciences," *Signs* 9 (1983): 73–90; and Anne Helene Litwin and D. Lynn O'Brien Hallstein, "Shadows and Silences: How Women's Standpoint and Unspoken Friendship Rules Cause Difficulties Among Many Women at Work," *Women's Studies in Communication* 30 (2007): 111–142.

6. While it is true that key second-wave thinkers—Audre Lorde, the Combahee River Collective, Kimberlé Crenshaw, bell hooks, Marsha Houston, and Iris Marion Young, among others—began to describe intersectional analyses as early as the 1970s, the term *intersectionality* was not used until Crenshaw coined the term in 1991 in her landmark essay, "Mapping the Margins: Intersectionality, Identity Politics, and Violence Against Women of Color." Thus, our interest in this chapter is the contemporary third-wave rendering of intersectionality rather than the early work that may or may not be included in the third-wave understanding of intersectionality. For clarity, we acknowledge that some of the critiques we level against third-wave intersectionality may not be relevant to the work that began in the second wave. We thank Karma Chávez for pointing out potential lineage issues and the inapplicability of some of our critiques in relation to the earlier work on intersectionality.

7. Vivien Labaton and Dawn Lundy Martin, eds., *The Fire This Time: Young Activists and the New Feminism* (New York: Anchor Books, 2004); Showden, "What's Political."

8. Leslie L. Heywood, ed., *The Women's Movement Today: An Encyclopedia of Third Wave Feminism* (Westport, CT: Greenwood, 2006); Leslie L. Heywood and Jennifer Drake, eds., *Third Wave Agenda: Being Feminist, Doing Feminism* (Minneapolis: University of Minnesota Press, 1997); Showden, "What's Political."

9. Showden, "What's Political," 181.

10. Showden, "What's Political," 167.

11. Labaton and Martin, *This Fire*, xxxiv.

12. Labaton and Martin, *This Fire*, xxvii, emphasis ours.

13. Quoted in Kristine Rowe-Finkbeiner, *The F Word: Feminism in Jeopardy: Women, Politics, and the Future* (Emeryville, CA: Seal Press, 2004). Clearly, some third-wave intersectional thinkers might not drop women's issues and instead approach those issues differently i.e., insisting, (rightfully), that poor women of color in the United States have different needs surrounding reproductive rights than white, middle-class women in the United States. Our concern here is with the third-wave intersectional thinking that downplays focusing on women's issues while also deemphasizing gender. Again, we thank Karma Chávez for pointing out this important distinction in her review of another essay Lynn is developing.

14. Labaton and Martin, *This Fire*, xxxi.

15. Showden, "What's Political," 184.

16. Showden, "What's Political," 186.

17. Labaton and Martin, *This Fire*, xxxi.

18. John Sloop, "Review Essay: 'In a Queer Time and Place and Race: Intersectionality Comes of Age,'" *Quarterly Journal of Speech* 91 (2005): 313.

19. Sloop, "Review Essay," 320. Judith Halberstam, *In a Queer Time and Place: Transgender Bodies, Subcultural Lives* (New York: New York University Press, 2005).

20. Sloop, "Review Essay," 323.

21. E. Patrick Johnson, *Appropriating Blackness: Performance and the Politics of Authenticity* (Durham, NC: Duke University Press, 2003), 119, emphasis ours.

22. Judith Rollins, *Between Women: Domestics and Their Employers* (Philadelphia: Temple University Press, 1985), 187, emphasis in the original.

23. Johnson, *Appropriating Blackness*, 129.

24. Johnson, *Appropriating Blackness*, 19.

25. Harding, *Whose Science*; Hartsock, *Money, Sex*; Litwin and O'Brien Hallstein, "Shadows"; O'Brien Hallstein, "Where Standpoint"; Rose, "Hand, Brain."

26. As feminists, we cannot help but notice the parallel between "having it all" that seems to exist within third-wave intersectional thinking and contemporary women's lives, particularly within the context of maternity. It is not an accident that this post–second-wave notion of "having it all" is also deeply embedded in contemporary third-wave intersectional thinking; this notion is also acutely entrenched in the zeitgeist of contemporary understandings of women's lives. This notion is deeply problematic because,

as contemporary feminist work in maternity studies is starting to reveal, the idea of "having/doing it all" and the actual practice of having it all is not only practically impossible, it also, often inadvertently, penalizes women. This often results in specific sex/gender oppression being reiterated or inadvertently reinforced rather than challenged in the context of motherhood, which is parallel to the argument we address next. The parallel between the idea of having it all in both cases, then, is significant and, equally important, may be a specifically post–second-wave issue that feminist scholars might explore further in intersectional thinking and scholarship.

27. Labaton and Martin, *This Fire*, xxvii.

28. We realize that the "among other things" comment might seem unartful. Nonetheless, we use such comments purposefully to reinforce one of our key points—that discussions of situations are always partial; we can never discuss something in its entirety. As such, even when we list elements that make up a scenario, we are necessarily making choices about which elements we list and which elements we leave out. So the statement "among other things" keeps this insight at the forefront.

29. Jennifer Nelson, "'All This that Has Happened to Me Shouldn't Happen to Nobody Else': Loretta Ross and the Women of Color Reproductive Freedom Movement in the 1980s," *Journal of Women's History* 22 (2010): 142, emphasis ours.

30. Nelson, "All This," 142.

31. Nelson, "All This," 142.

32. Nelson, "All This," 142, emphasis ours.

33. Linda Alcoff, "The Problem of Speaking for Others," *Cultural Critique* 20 (1991–1992): 22.

34. Patricia Newman is the pseudonym Peterson gave this interviewee.

35. Lori West Peterson, "Cutting the Meeting Short: Conflicting Narrative Choices in One Woman's Maternity Leave," in *Contemplating Maternity*, 239.

36. Peterson, "Cutting," 240.

37. Peterson, "Cutting," 237.

38. Peterson, "Cutting," 239.

39. Peterson, "Cutting," 239–240.

40. Marsha Houston, "When Black Women Talk with White Women: Why the Dialogues Are Difficult," in *Our Voices: Essays in Culture, Ethnicity, and Communication*, 4th ed., ed. Alberto González, Marsha Houston, and Victoria Chen (New York: Oxford University Press, 2007), 98–104.

41. Peterson, "Cutting," 240.

42. Harding, *Whose Science*; Hartsock, *Money, Sex*; O'Brien Hallstein, "Where Standpoint"; also see Joan W. Scott, "The Evidence of Experience," *Critical Inquiry* 17 (1991): 773–797.

43. Newman's assertion that sexism, not racism, was in play in the event she recounts raises a significant and difficult question: If a woman of color is a victim of sexism, is she always, already, simultaneously a victim of racism? Or, is it possible to understand a situation as marked by race but not racism? In other words, of course, the races of the actors involved

affected the situation Newman described. Patricia Newman experienced discrimination not as a generic woman (there is no such thing) but as a *black* woman. Her race and the race of her boss (which is not specified) clearly affected the meaning of the discriminatory act. Yet the possibility Newman raises is that the nub of power around which the discrimination turned was sexism (shaped by the race of the players) and not racism. We are intrigued by this question, but an effort to explore it in detail is beyond the scope of this chapter.

44. We are deeply indebted to the editors of this volume for pushing us to address whether or not Peterson was employing a naïve form of feminist thinking. Clearly, we do not think that Peterson was; however, insisting that we consider this important point helped us develop our ideas and thinking. Thus, we especially appreciate this push from the editors, a push that was difficult but necessary.

45. Alcoff, "The Problem of Speaking," 22.

46. Sara Evans, *Tidal Wave: How Women Changed America at Century's End* (New York: Free Press, 2003); Astrid Henry, *Not My Mother's Sister: Generational Conflict and Third-Wave Feminism* (Bloomington: Indiana University Press, 2004); Benita Roth, *Separate Roads to Feminism: Black, Chicana, and White Feminist Movements in America's Second Wave* (Cambridge: Cambridge University Press, 2004); Lauri Umansky, *Motherhood Reconceived: Feminism and the Legacies of the Sixties* (New York: New York University Press, 1996).

47. Ruth Rosen, *The World Split Open: How the Modern Women's Movement Changed America* (New York: Penguin, 2004), 134.

48. Rosen, *The World*.

49. Over 20,000 people attended the rally; as such, Webb does not know the race of the men who heckled her (private communication with Marilyn Salzman Webb, August 25, 2011).

50. For example, see Sara Hayden's "Constituting Savvy Aunties: From Childless Women to Child-Focused Consumers," *Women's Studies in Communication* 34 (2011): 1–19; "Lessons from *The Baby Boon*: Family-Friendly Policies and the Ethics of Justice and Care," *Women's Studies in Communication* 33 (2010): 119–137 ; "Purposefully Childless Good Women," in *Contemplating Maternity*, 269–290; "Revitalizing the Debate between <Life> and <Choice>: The 2004 March for Women's Lives," *Communication and Critical/Cultural Studies* 6 (2009): 111–131; "Maternal Metaphors and the Nation: Promoting a Politics of Care through the Million Mom March," *Quarterly Journal of Speech* 89 (2003): 196–215; "Teenage Bodies, Teenage Selves: Tracing the Implications of Bio-power in Contemporary Sexuality Education Texts," *Women's Studies in Communication* 24 (2001): 30–61; "Reversing the Discourse of Sexology: Margaret Higgins Sanger's *What Every Girl Should Know*," *Southern Communication Journal* 64 (1999): 288–306; "Re-claiming Bodies of Knowledge: An Exploration of the Relationship between Feminist Theorizing and Feminine Style in the Rhetoric of the Boston Women's Health Book Collective," *Western Journal of Communication* 61 (1997): 127–163.

51. D. Lynn O'Brien Hallstein's "The Intriguing History and Curious Silences of *Of Woman Born:* Rereading Rich Rhetorically to Better Understand the Contemporary Context," *National Women's Studies Journal* 22, no. 1 (2010): 18–41; *White Feminists and Contemporary Maternity: Purging Matrophobia* (New York: Palgrave Macmillan, 2010); "Public Choices, Private Control: How Mediated Mom Labels Work Rhetorically to Dismantle the Policies of Choice and White Second Wave Feminist Successes," in *Contemplating Maternity*, 5–26; "Second Wave Successes and Third Wave Struggles," *Women's Studies in Communication* 31 (2008): 143–150; "Matrophobic Sisters and Daughters: The Rhetorical Consequences of Matrophobia in Contemporary White Feminist Analyses of Maternity," *Women's Studies* 36 (2007): 269–296. Also Anne H. Litwin and D. Lynn O'Brien Hallstein, "Shadows and Silences: How Women's Standpoint and Unspoken Friendship Rules Cause Difficulties Among Many Women at Work," *Women's Studies in Communication* 30 (2007): 111–142; D. Lynn O'Brien Hallstein, "Where Standpoint Stands Now: An Introduction and Commentary," *Women's Studies in Communication* 23 (2000): 1–15; O'Brien Hallstein, "Postmodern Caring: Feminist Standpoint Theory, Revisioned Caring and Communication Ethics," *Western Journal of Communication* 63 (1998): 32–56.

52. Sloop, "Review Essay," 326.

Part II

Audiences and Audiencing

Chapter 5

Intersecting Audiences: Public Commentary Concerning Audre Lorde's Speech, "Uses of the Erotic: The Erotic as Power"

Lester C. Olson

We have chosen each other and the edge of each other's battles.

—Audre Lorde[1]

In Audre Lorde's numerous public speeches from the mid-1970s until her death at St. Croix in 1992, she usually described herself as a Black, lesbian, feminist, socialist, poet, and mother. For decades, Lorde lived in New York in an interracial family—initially, during the early 1960s, with Edwin A. Rollins, a white gay man who became the father of her two children, Elizabeth and Jonathan; later, for almost two decades, with a white professional woman, Francis Clayton, who helped her to raise her children on Staten Island. An internationally acclaimed poet and political activist, Lorde addressed the topics of race, sexuality, age, sex, and economic class in a wide range of fora and publication outlets: on occasion, single broadside poems and, more typically, pamphlets and books released by small presses. Lorde's entire body of public advocacy was complex, insightful, and instructive in commenting on racism, sexism, ageism, heterosexism, and other varieties of often overlapping biases in U.S. culture during the later half of the twentieth century.

In general, overlapping lesbian feminist and Black feminist social movements for justice constituted the heart of Lorde's extensive network of allies, colleagues, and younger admirers. Their exchanges, dialogues, and disputes enriched Lorde's understanding of "inter-locking oppressions," as interacting systems of power were called years before "multiple jeopardy, multiple consciousness," "matrices of domination," "compounding differences," and "intersectional-ity" emerged as resources to guide critical analysis of political and social conditions.[2] A panoramic view of the primary audiences for Lorde's scholar-activism can be inferred from magazines, journals, and books for feminist, lesbian, and Black readerships to which she contributed during the 1970s and 1980s.[3] As a cofounder in 1980 of Kitchen Table/Women of Color Press, Lorde endeavored with allies Barbara Smith and Chicana-lesbian-feminists Cherríe Moraga and Gloria Anzaldúa to make it possible for diverse "women of Color" to publish their poetry, essays, and other artistic works without constantly adapting their consciousness to publication outlets that were predominantly male, white, or heterosexual. Their strategy of ownership of a press was informed by the Black arts movement,[4] and, more fundamentally, by their recognition of what it meant to own the means of production within capitalism, which these radi-cal feminists usually challenged in their literary and artistic works.[5]

During the mid- to late 1970s, some of Lorde's closest allies were members of the Combahee River Collective, who, in the clas-sic 1978 manifesto, affirmed: "The most general statement of our politics at the present time would be that we are actively committed to struggling against racial, sexual, heterosexual, and class oppres-sion and see as our particular task the development of integrated analysis and practice based upon the fact that the major systems of oppression are interlocking. The synthesis of these oppressions creates the conditions of our lives."[6] The metaphor of "systems of oppression" as "interlocking" recurred during the late 1970s and 1980s, and this sensibility suffused Lorde's public advocacy in that she held that "racism, sexism and homophobia are inseparable."[7] Like Barbara Smith and other Black feminist scholars during the late 1970s and 1980s, Lorde saw that, as Smith generalized, "Black femi-nism, if it is to provide sound analysis of Black women's situation, must incorporate an understanding of economic oppression and rac-ism as well as of sexism and heterosexism."[8] Consequently, Lorde was both an advocate and a model for explorations of interacting systems of power more than a decade before Kimberlé Crenshaw's proposal for intersectionality for analyzing public advocacy in legal systems.

This chapter concentrates on Crenshaw's concept of "intersec-tionality" to scrutinize how diverse audiences have actively inter-acted with Lorde's views by their public commentary on published

versions of her 1980 speech "Uses of the Erotic: The Erotic as Power."
This speech concerning "the erotic" is the most often reprinted of
Lorde's orations.[9] Because of its popularity, it is possible to ascertain
patterns in public commentaries on her speech that evidence intersectionality as a relational factor between a speaker and her audience.[10] This chapter centers primarily on Lorde's self-identifications
as woman, Black, lesbian, and socialist, as these multiple components of her identity intersected with her audiences in her radical
advocacy concerning "the erotic." I argue that public commentaries
usually evoked Lorde's speech as illustration, amplification, or support for the other authors' claims about the erotic, women, pornography, spirituality, or power in ways that usually deflected attention
from Lorde's socialism, lesbian sexuality, and race. One major factor
that contributed to these patterns of commentary was the authoriz-
ing publication outlets' power to deliver readerships that, however
diverse, consisted primarily of white, heterosexual women. Moreover, Lorde's speech had supplemental meanings for women who
recognized pervasive problems posed by patriarchy in the United
States, even as the surface text allowed for varied identifications
among a range of diverse auditors interested in reclaiming "the
erotic" for women. While recognizing the value of Crenshaw's concept to scrutinize how multiple components of an individual's embodied identity can interact with systems of power, this chapter also
evokes an earlier concept of "interlocking oppressions" to silhouette some contours and concerns attending "intersectionality" for
criticism of radical advocacy in general. Although each metaphor for
interacting systems of power has value for communication scholars
attending to the dynamic relationships between an advocate and her
audiences, the early work on interlocking oppressions offers communication scholars something with regard to Lorde's advocacy that
intersectionality does not precisely capture.

 "Uses of the Erotic" has been described as "a feminist classic,"
"virtually canonical," and "groundbreaking."[11] "Uses of the Erotic"
is significant to intersectional scholars for another reason. Its key
terms, "the erotic," "pornography," and "power," are emotionally
charged, ambiguous, and politically and ideologically loaded.[12] To
reclaim "the erotic," Lorde significantly redefined its meanings and,
in the process, she redefined "the pornographic." Lorde's speech
illuminated a patriarchal culture's ramifications for "the erotic"
and spotlighted capitalism's implications for erotic satisfaction as
experienced from artistic labor. Lorde located pornography at the
intersections of patriarchy and capitalism, which she viewed as interlocked, systemic obstacles to women's erotic satisfaction. Yet

"the pornographic," to her, was not simply the graphic, sexually explicit, commercial product produced for profit, typically by men, to the detriment of women. Lorde's expansive sense of pornography encompassed specific modes or styles of human relationships characterized by "plasticized sensation" and "abuse." The pornographic, as the opposite of "the erotic," was likewise complex in its reclaimed meanings.

Lorde defined the erotic to encompass sexual pleasure, as in her description of "moving into sunlight against the body of a woman I love" (58). Her sense of "the erotic," then, allowed for graphic imagery, but not of varieties that dehumanized women. Yet Lorde defined the erotic as much more comprehensive than sexual pleasure in several passages—for example, when she asserted, "The erotic is a measure between the beginnings of our sense of self and the chaos of our strongest feelings. It is an internal sense of satisfaction to which, once we have experienced it, we know we can aspire" (54). When Lorde identified specific examples of "erotically satisfying experience," she mentioned as specific instances "dancing, building a bookcase, writing a poem, examining an idea" (57). To Lorde, reclaiming "the erotic" in its capacious sense was a means for women to recover human agency, despite systemic obstacles posed primarily, in her analysis, by patriarchy and capitalism: "For as we begin to recognize our deepest feelings, we begin to give up, of necessity, being satisfied with suffering and self-negation, and with the numbness which so often seems like their only alternative in our society. Our acts against oppression become integral with self, motivated and empowered from within" (58).[13]

To begin my analysis, I identify the two major fora in which Lorde delivered her speech, a radio broadcast, and the various publication outlets that, by reprinting her speech, made her ideas available to others. This initial step furthers the twin objectives of identifying precisely Lorde's diverse, overlapping audiences and the numerous reprints they have actively interpreted. Moreover, Crenshaw's concept of intersectionality entails attention to specific organizations (such as publication outlets) as systems of power within which multiple components of an embodied identity interact in intricate, at times unanticipated, ways, by foregrounding certain components of an identity while effacing others that may be as germane to a message, if not more so. I then turn to examples of commentary to illustrate broader patterns among those interactions, beginning with economic systems and then considering sexuality and race before contemplating how women's alienation under patriarchy surfaced in a recurring pattern of reception to Lorde's speech. One result of this sequence will be documentation for how intersectionality was a noteworthy factor in how audiences interacted with Lorde's ideas. Another outcome is a better sense of certain risks and limitations of using intersectionality for critical studies of radical advocacy, which, by its very definition, actively sought changes more fundamental and extensive than reform of existing systems.

INSTITUTIONS AUTHORIZING AND CIRCULATING LORDE'S SPEECH

Several organizations featured Audre Lorde's public speech as well as its subsequent radio broadcast and numerous published reprints, making her remarks available to a range of listening and reading audiences interested in feminism and the women's liberation movement. It is necessary to consider these occasions and publication outlets, because Crenshaw's concept of intersectionality does not consist simply in an insight that each person's identity has multiple, social components at the level of language, or representation. More precisely, as a consequence, this language or representation situates multiple components of each person's identity within inherited systems of power in ways that, in combination, can have unanticipated or unrecognized consequences that can harm individuals who are oppressed within more than one system. For example, while women as a group are oppressed within a patriarchal system, additional factors in the system pertaining to sexuality, race, and class, for instance, can interact with patriarchy to further subordinate or elevate them within a culture's hierarchies. From this standpoint, each specific speaking forum and publication outlet can be recognized as an institution that enabled some audiences to hear or read Lorde's ideas, while, at the same time, circumscribing recognition of other, overlapping components of her multiple identities such as her socialism, sexuality, and race.

Lorde delivered her remarks concerning "Uses of the Erotic" for public speeches twice—initially on August 25, 1978, to participants at the Fourth Berkshire Conference on the History of Women, an academic conference held at a prestigious women's college, Mount Holyoke College.[14] The immediate audience for Lorde's speech consisted primarily of white, academic women with an intellectual and political interest in women's history. Significantly, the panel's organizer "wanted to ensure that this Berks would include a lesbian session."[15] Because this was the first time in the organization's history that an entire session centered on lesbians, Lorde's treatment of "the erotic" implicated some heterosexual women's discomfort and hostility for inhibiting erotic satisfaction among women. A caucus on lesbian concerns was formed immediately after the session and, subsequently, extended correspondence pressed issues of explicitly recognizing lesbian sexuality in the organization's intellectual labor.[16]

Three months later, Lorde delivered her speech again during November 17–19, 1978, in San Francisco to the Feminist Perspectives on Pornography conference, sponsored by Women Against Violence in Pornography and Media.[17] This organization was devoted to establishing linkages between pornography and the dehumanization of women's bodies by promoting public discussions, conducting tours of pornography theaters, confronting those responsible for the production of pornography, distributing monthly newsletters, and sponsoring Take Back the Night Marches—in an endeavor "to put an end to all portrayals of women being bound, raped, tortured, killed, or degraded for sexual stimulation or pleasure. We believe that the constant linking of sexuality and violence is dangerous."[18] Lorde's second delivery of her speech occurred within a rhetorical and political campaign to expose dangers posed to women by pornography.

Lorde's speech is remarkable among the conference contributions in that she articulated a vision that women could move forward by reclaiming "the erotic." Her speech did not center on merely rejecting or negating pornography. Nor did Lorde's speech promote any legal mechanisms to limit or prohibit pornography, probably because such strategies would have deferred primary responsibility to others who may not have women's concerns at heart, and because she believed, as she affirmed on various occasions, that "the master's tools will never dismantle the master's house." Indeed, her earlier 1979 speech with that title had challenged reformist feminists to embrace radical feminism. Her poem "Power" (1976) testified to her outrage concerning law enforcement's misuses of power, as did later poems as "Equal Opportunity" (1986) and "For the Record" (1986) as well as her pamphlet *Apartheid U.S.A.* (1986).[19] In regard to radical change, Lorde's sensibility in "Uses of the Erotic" does not mesh ideally with Crenshaw's primary focus on revision of legal systems, because, however worthwhile, to Lorde that sort of primary focus is strategically reformist and seldom radical.

Lorde's speech continued to be disseminated throughout 1979. Pacifica Radio broadcast highlights from the Feminist Perspectives on Pornography conference, under the title "Fair Sex, Fair Game: Women Say No to the Sexual Safari," as well as speeches and panel discussions, among them Lorde's entire speech under the title "Eroticism and Pornography."[20] Pacifica Radio's broadcasts significantly widened the range of audiences that could hear the views expressed at the conference. Men and women alike, regardless of their sexuality or race, could hear highlights from the conference, though most radio listeners for Pacifica would have been progressive and left leaning in their politics.

The trajectory of the print distribution of Lorde's speech is equally important. Shortly after Lorde's initial presentation in 1978, Out & Out Books printed the speech text in a pamphlet titled *Uses of the Erotic: The Erotic as Power*.[21] A typeset note inside the front cover of a second printing of this pamphlet mentioned that this speech text "was first published in a private edition of 250 copies for distribution at the Conference on Feminist Perspectives on Pornography, San Francisco, November 1978." A small, low-budget press located in Brooklyn, New York, Out & Out Books was founded by Joan Larkin to publish short pamphlets and anthologies by lesbian feminist authors, among them Elly Bulkin, Jan Clausen, Jane Creighton, Bernice Goodman, Marilyn Hacker, Joan Larkin, Adrienne Rich, Joanna Russ, and Barbara Smith. Another undated typeset copy of Lorde's speech was distributed by the Lesbian Feminist Clearinghouse at Pittsburgh presumably about that time.[22] Because both of these publishing houses primarily addressed white lesbian feminists, Lorde's statement on the erotic would presumably have reiterated similar dynamics of the Berkshire conference in that their readerships centered on lesbian concerns in dealing with a predominantly heterosexual culture.

The following year, in 1979, the text of Lorde's speech was published again in *Chrysalis: A Magazine of Women's Culture*, for which Lorde was its poetry editor.[23] *Chrysalis* presented itself as "a magazine of women's culture" and, from its founding, sought to represent the women's movement as diverse: "Feminism is not a monolithic movement, but rather includes the experiences, values, priorities, agendas of women of all lifestyles, ages, and cultural and economic backgrounds," the magazine affirmed in the initial issue's front matter.[24] Again, during 1979, *Big Mama Rag*, "a women's journal" in a newspaper format, published Lorde's speech with a head note mentioning that it was from the conference in San Francisco.[25]

In 1980, the anthology *Take Back the Night: Women on Pornography* published conference contributions by Lorde, and others, as well as additional essays on pornography.[26] In the introduction, the anthology's editor commented on the 1978 Feminist Perspectives on Pornography conference that stimulated the anthology: "Over 5,000 women from thirty states participate and return to their own communities to continue the work." She characterized the conference: "For the first time in history, women from across the country gather to discuss the destructive consequences of pornography, to

exchange information and analysis, and to plan strategies for elimi-
nating pornography."[27] In this anthology, the opposition between
the pornographic and the erotic was even more emphatic because
of the anthology's title and because of Lorde's speech's placement
among numerous essays concentrating on pornography and rape.
This anthology, and the Pacifica broadcast, focused on the erotic and
pornography in ways that focused attention primarily on white heterosexuality under patriarchy, while, to a degree, eliding Lorde's criticisms of capitalism and her affirmation of Black lesbian sexuality.

In December 1982, *Ms.* magazine published an excerpted, un-
authorized, and disorganized version, which Lorde protested in a
January 15 letter to an editor as "a three-paragraph non-sequitur
patchwork shred from it, distorting the whole impact of the original
essay."[28] Later, in 1984, the speech was included in Lorde's book titled *Sister Outsider: Essays and Speeches by Audre Lorde.*[29] In 1989,
"Uses of the Erotic" was reprinted in the *Whole Earth Review.*[30] By
the early 1990s, Lorde's complete speech had been reprinted at least
six times, reaching additional audiences with a range of interests
within the women's movement. And, in 1991, the *Utne Reader* published a lengthy excerpt.[31]

Although these publication outlets varied in their readerships in
noteworthy ways, all of them except the *Whole Earth Review* and
Utne Reader consisted primarily of white women interested in the
overlapping concerns of liberation and feminism. Only two of the
outlets concentrated primarily on white lesbian feminists with progressive or left-of-center politics. To my knowledge at this writing,
Lorde's speech concerning "the erotic" has not been published in
print outlets primarily for Black readerships. Her speech was omit-
ted from *I Am Your Sister: Collected and Unpublished Writings of
Audre Lorde* (2009), edited by an accomplished team of Black scholars, who did reprint other works by Lorde from *Sister Outsider, A
Burst of Light,* and elsewhere. Why this is the case is a matter of
speculation.

INTERSECTING AUDIENCES:
PUBLIC INTERACTIONS WITH LORDE'S SPEECH

The publication outlets for Lorde's speeches made audiences of predominantly white and heterosexual women available to Lorde in
consequential ways for interpretations of her speech. Her intersectionality with these audiences both highlighted commonalities and
deflected attention from certain differences between them. At the
time, it may have been risky or unusual for some of these outlets to

circulate her words, but also relatively conventional and even possibly delightful for others to do so. Among the extensive public responses and interactions with Lorde's speech, race and racism were regularly downplayed in that they usually went unmentioned, presumably because most of her audiences were predominantly white and because Lorde did not allude to race explicitly until well into her speech. Yet, her mention of racism was emphatic. Notably few readers seem to have noticed Lorde's criticisms of capitalism as pornographic in its ramifications for artistic labor, even though Lorde devoted an entire section to this systemic concern.

With regard to intersectionality, Lorde refrained from turning to differences among women until well into her speech. This may have allowed her to build identifications among women, creating allies, before considering factors that might be viewed as divisive or adversarial inasmuch as racism and heterosexism complicated dependable alliances among women. Because Lorde's speech depended heavily on a stark opposition between men and women, it may not be immediately evident that other intersections mattered in audiences' patterns of interaction with her speech. Yet intersectionality accounts for several patterns of public engagement with Lorde's speech. In this next section, I organize the patterns of interaction in public commentaries on Lorde's speech through an intersectional lens, by beginning with economic systems, sexuality, and race before turning to commentary concerning patriarchy's implications for women, because Lorde dealt with these subjects in her speech, and because audiences' responses evinced noteworthy elisions, amplifications, and revisions with regard to capitalism, lesbian sexuality, and racial differences. Consequently, these topics illustrate how intersectionality impacted audiences' interpretations of Lorde's speech.

Economic Systems

Lorde's commitment to socialism was one noteworthy factor evident in her speech. Yet few commentaries have discussed Lorde's criticism of capitalism as antierotic, possibly because few were prepared to question the prevailing economic system's ramifications for artistic labor, and because she did not specifically name the system in which profits took priority over human needs. I am referring here to an entire section on capitalism in which Lorde affirmed: "The principal horror of any system which defines the good in terms of profit rather than in terms of human need, or which defines human need to the exclusion of the psychic and emotional components of that need—the principal horror of such a system is that it robs our work of its erotic value, its erotic power and life appeal and fulfillment" (55, see 58). To Lorde, capitalism was an economic system inhibiting the erotic satisfaction from work insofar as it contributed to production for profit, not pleasure in the producing. However, almost all commentaries on Lorde's speech have ignored her analysis of an economic system's impact on "the erotic," as Lorde defined it, usually concentrating instead on sexism under patriarchy. On the one hand, it may have been too risky, daunting, or simply bewildering for Lorde's audiences to experience capitalism in general or labor in particular as pornographic. On the other hand, envisioning labor as erotically satisfying in Lorde's sense might have seemed utopian or metaphoric. In the opposition between capitalism and socialism, the dichotomizing qualities of Lorde's radical advocacy might, moreover, have seemed too reductive for her audiences, because some profitable work may be pleasurable and primarily satisfy fundamental human needs.

One commentary that did focus on economic factors was by Kathlyn Breazeale, who generalized, "Poet Audre Lorde suggests the connection between suppressed energy and oppression." Breazeale continued, "Our passion, both spiritual and physical, draws us into acknowledging that we are connected to others. This is important because corporate structures cannot be dismantled by individuals. We must acknowledge that communities have created structures of exploitation, and therefore communities must work together to dismantle these structures, and to create new ones of mutually enhancing relationships."[32] Other writers might have an economic analysis in view; however, they offer only vague references to "genuine selfhood and power," "visionary social change," or "genuine change."[33] From the deafening silence otherwise concerning capitalism, one could infer reasonably that patterns of intersectionality and differences between the speaker and her audiences' convictions concerning capitalism impacted most commentaries on Lorde's speech about the erotic as power.

Even so, some insightful commentaries concentrated on interconnections between the symbolic and material or corporeal, as exemplified by embodied experiences of the erotic and the pornographic. Anne Balsamo wrote:

Feminist theorists have traditionally asserted that female bodies are not one-dimensional surfaces which bear easy-to-read meanings. Indeed, feminist writers honor the body as the site of the production and reproduction of fragmented

identities and affinities—in short, the site of material practice. They identify the place and meanings of the female
body in mass culture, sometimes to reassert the importance of female sexuality (for example, Audre Lorde [1978]);
sometimes to propose a radically new form of cultural production—writing the body, or the body as instrument; and
sometimes to articulate "the site for the coming together of
feminist theory and politics."[34]

Because these corporeal and symbolic bodies have a sexuality, race, age, and class—among other factors—reading the bodily
basis of Lorde's meanings is more complex than an emphasis on sex
alone might be understood to imply. In connection with pornography as a commercial product, moreover, economic exchanges cannot be neatly separated from corporeal bodies so integral to such
transactions nor can these combined material components be distinguished altogether from specifically symbolic aspects of bodies.
Further interpretive difficulties may have arisen from the bodily
basis for Lorde's claims, because, as she put it, "the erotic cannot
be felt second hand" (59). Referring to Lorde's speech, Elizabeth Alexander observed, "Lorde is preoccupied with things bodily: that
which is performed upon the body versus what the body performs
and asserts."[35] Because each body has a sexuality and a race, as Lorde
mentioned, the next section turns to these potential intersections
among Lorde's audiences of diverse women in relationship to her
speech. Recall that Lorde's speech was spoken and distributed to audiences consisting primarily of women who, though diverse in some
measure, were predominantly white and heterosexual, while only
two reprinted texts circulated primarily among lesbian feminists.

Sexuality

Lesbianism represented another aspect of intersectionality in widely
varying patterns of commentary on Lorde's speech concerning "the
erotic." Certain commentaries probably deflected attention from
Lorde's centering on lesbianism, while others have sharpened her
point about lesbian sexuality. An illustration of the former was Barbara Sellers-Young, who commented, "The diversity of performing
environments and styles reflects the consistent search by women
to understand their sensuality. Either consciously or unconsciously,
they attempt to discover what Lorde identifies as the female power
associated with the erotic."[36] Sellers-Young continued, "The power
women have found varies from 'turning on' males in a physically

safe situation (restaurants and bellygrams), to the discovery of the power of the movement styles of specific ethnic groups, and finally the connection with the power of ancient women's rites and participation in the creation of new ones."[37] Sellers-Young ignored that it was unlikely that Lorde was referring to the erotic as the power of "turning on" males. Had Sellers-Young mentioned Lorde's sexuality, or her views that the erotic could be understood to extend beyond sexual pleasures to labor and working conditions, Sellers-Young would have been less vulnerable to criticism for her appropriation and erasure of lesbian concerns or misgivings about capitalism.

Among those who sharpened and amplified Lorde's point about erotic, lesbian sexuality was Evelyn Torton Beck. To frame her statement, Beck remarked, "In 'The Erotic as Power,' Audre Lorde expresses the interrelationship of the many kinds of powers accessible to us as women, powers that we have been afraid of, because we have been taught that they are inappropriate to us as women." After quoting Lorde's comment that "The erotic is a resource within each of us that lies in a deeply female and spiritual plane, firmly rooted in the power of our unexpressed or unrecognized feeling," Beck asserted, "Lesbian sexuality is not separable from female sexuality. Therefore, if feminists who define themselves as heterosexual live with a fear of lesbianism, they live with a fear of their own possibilities."[38] Additional examples of authors amplifying Lorde's views on lesbianism included Barbara DiBernard, Marilyn R. Farwell, and Janice Gould.[39] In commentaries featuring sexuality, the race of the writers usually went without mention, a signal of presumptive whiteness. In this regard, racial differences, discussed below, are another noteworthy factor in intersecting and overlapping audience members' commentary on Lorde's speech.

Race

Lorde faced rhetorical challenges in discussing "the erotic" because of inherited stereotypes about Black women and lesbians as overlapping social groups, especially the risks of reproducing stereotypes and distorting insights about the erotic, as Lorde defined it. Elizabeth Alexander noted, "Images of black people's bodies in American culture have been either hypersexualized or desexualized to serve the imaginings and purposes of white American men and women." A pattern of oversexualizing and desexualizing lesbians is likewise commonplace in U.S. culture. In other words, overlapping stereotypes portraying both Black women and lesbians may have had an impact on interpreting Lorde's remarks as various audiences endeavored to understand her. Alexander stressed, however, that "Eroticism as she defines it has nothing at all to do with how African-American women are conventionally sexualized."[40]

Women's Alienation under Patriarchal Aggression

In contrast with omissions, elisions, and amplifications with regard to economic systems, sexuality, and race, intersectionality resulting from understanding women's alienation under patriarchy appears to have influenced many commentaries on Lorde's speech, suggesting a broad-based identification between Lorde and her audiences. This pattern of interaction usually concentrated on a binary between the erotic and the pornographic, as well as another binary between living on what Lorde labeled "internal" or "external" directives. Lorde commented on disconnections between mind and body, as well as between self and other, when she remarked, "When we live outside ourselves, and by that I mean on external directives only rather than from our internal knowledge and needs, when we live away from those erotic guides from within ourselves, then our lives are limited by external and alien forms, and we conform to the needs of a structure that is not based on human need, let alone an individual's" (58). In an essay titled "Numbering the Hairs of Our Heads: Male Social Control and the All-Seeing Male God," Anne Marie Hunter emphasized exaggerated surveillance by men in abusive relationships with women. Hunter wrote, "In this disconnection, women's voices and knowledges are lost. Reality becomes shaky and unpredictable. Women experience a profound alienation, confusion and self-doubt."[41] Concentrating primarily on sexism as a system of power, AnnLouise Keating likewise mentioned Lorde's speech in "Making 'Our Shattered Faces Whole,'" as she commented with nuance on racial differences among women.[42] Additional poignant commentaries by Maureen E. Shea and Mary D. Pellauer concentrated on women's alienation as a consequence of patriarchal aggression against women, while interpreting Lorde's speech concerning "Uses of the Erotic."[43]

Yet, to Lorde, the challenges in "reclaiming" the erotic appear to have resulted, in part, from sexism in relations between men and women, but also, in part, from further alienation in dealing with heterosexism, racism, and certain economic systems like capitalism. As a lucrative business that profited economically from women's sexualized dehumanization and objectification, pornography concisely exemplified Lorde's concerns about the systemic roots of antierotic, external impositions on women resulting from capitalism, heterosexism, racism, and patriarchy. In this connection, in an essay titled "Afterword: Voices and Violence—A Dialogue," Ellen Wright Clayton and Jay Clayton quoted from Lorde's speech, but relocated her remarks to present them as "OTHER VOICES: 'In order to perpetuate itself, every oppression must corrupt or distort those various sources of power within the culture of the oppressed that can provide energy for change' (Audre Lorde)."[44] Accordingly, reclaiming the erotic entailed endeavoring to transform systems of capitalism, heterosexism, racism, and sexism, all of which, in Lorde's analysis, contributed to women's alienation and dehumanization. Brenda Carr generalized, "Erotic knowledge thus becomes a tool for critical interrogation of all the forms of 'anti-life' or oppression that Lorde speaks out against." Carr emphasized that, "While Lorde reformulates our cultural understanding of the erotic as purely sexual, she does not de-sexualize it."[45]

In Lorde's analysis, to transform these systems, women individually and collectively needed to heed internal directives instead of the externally imposed, intermeshed demands of patriarchy and capitalism. This general pattern of interpretation may have been heightened by Lorde's emphasis on women reclaiming agency as desiring actors by giving priority to internal directives rather than by relinquishing agency to externally imposed directives. To Lorde, the process of reclaiming the erotic entailed representing lesbians and other women as erotic agents, not only, or merely, the victims of patriarchy.[46] To Judith Mitchell, for instance, "Only when the hierarchical relation of idealized subject/degraded object is dispensed with, when women come to own their own desire as opposed to being objects of male desire, will it be possible to attain the wider sense of the erotic put forward by Audre Lorde, as encompassing the true source of power and pleasure in human life."[47]

CONCLUSION

The bodily basis for experiencing Lorde's topic along with inherited stereotypes about her embodied experience of "the erotic" makes her speech an especially appropriate text for exploring the ramifications of intersectionality because the specific qualities of Lorde's sexuality and race were elided in most public commentaries on her speech. In other words, her audiences' apparent inattention to Lorde's lesbianism, Blackness, and socialism, taken together, tended to recur in many public commentaries. On the whole with remarkably few exceptions, such patterns of commentary transformed her radical advocacy from her embodied standpoint of "interlocking" or "inseparable" oppressions into perspectives that, in fact, did separate them: Most public commentaries refrained from criticizing capitalism or explicitly embracing either lesbians or Black people. A juxtaposition of interlocking oppressions with intersectionality enables us to notice this fundamental transformation in the dynamic relationship between an advocate and her auditors or readerships.

While Kimberlé Crenshaw has emphasized the intersectionality of multiple, demographic components of identities within systems of power, focusing primarily on reform within legal systems, and while Patricia Hill Collins has emphasized how matrices of social variables provide another useful means to complicate what Collins referred to as a "Black feminist" analysis,[48] perhaps an earlier concept of "interlocking oppressions" likewise deserves communication scholars' reconsideration for its depth, vitality, and thoroughness in examining how multiple components of identity can interact with systems of power, and how those interlocking systems can be ignored. Each metaphor for interacting systems of power has value for communication scholars, contingent in some measure on whether the advocacy is predominantly radical or reformist and on each advocate's life situation. At the outset, this chapter evoked an earlier concept of "interlocking oppressions" to silhouette contours and concerns with using the later concept of "intersectionality" for radical advocacy. In general, Lorde's sensibility in "Uses of the Erotic" does not mesh ideally with Crenshaw's primary focus on legal systems within which multiple identities are systemically situated, because, however worthwhile, to Lorde that primary focus was strategically reformist in its politics. For that basic reason, in her speech concerning the erotic, Lorde never turned to law to envision an inhabitable future for women, as did many other public advocates dealing with pornography during the 1970s and 1980s. Yet, consideration of intersectionality as a metaphor helps to chart how Lorde's radical advocacy was transformed with few exceptions into reformist interpretations of her now famous speech. Of course, there is a complex interplay between radical and reformist advocacy that is more intricate than this chapter has time to explore.

Still, "interlocking oppressions" might be more appropriate than "intersectionality" for understanding Lorde's standpoint in her radical public advocacy. This is because, as developed by Black radical feminists in the 1970s and 1980s, "interlocking oppressions" captured the experiences of being "locked into" narrow and limiting views of both sexuality and economic systems. These are the systems of power most featured in Lorde's speech on the erotic. In addition, the language available to Lorde at the historical moment featured "interlocking" or "inseparable" oppressions. Like Smith and certain other Black feminists in the Combahee River Collective during the late 1970s and 1980s, Lorde proposed and enacted her explorations of inseparable, interacting systems of power that impinged on their embodied presence and experiences a decade before Crenshaw's proposal of intersectionality.

Has "interlocking oppressions," as presented in the discourse of the 1970s and 1980s by the Combahee River Collective, Barbara Smith, Audre Lorde, Cherríe Moraga, Gloria Anzaldúa, and other radical "women of Color," become relatively domesticated with regard to sexuality and economic systems in Crenshaw's original essays on "intersectionality" within legal systems? Crenshaw's original essays structured her central analysis on intersections of the demographic categories of race and sex (using "gender" as synonym for sex), while she placed both sexuality and economic systems in the rear ground of her essays. To her credit, Crenshaw mentioned this emphasis explicitly in 1991 in "Mapping the Margins":

> [I]ntersectionality is not being offered here as some new, totalizing theory of identity. Nor do I mean to suggest that violence against women of color can be explained only through the specific frameworks of race and gender considered here. Indeed, factors I address only in part or not at all, such as class or sexuality, are often as critical in shaping the experiences of women of color. My focus on the intersections of race and gender only highlights the need to account for multiple grounds of identity when considering how the social world is constructed.[49]

Despite Crenshaw's caveat in these observations, why has Crenshaw's concept of intersectionality received extensive scholarly attention in comparison with earlier work on "inseparable" and "interlocking" oppressions by Audre Lorde, Barbara Smith, Cheryl Clarke, and others? Is there a reformist appeal to intersectionality for scholars situated within colleges and universities? Smith's book, *The Truth that Never Hurts*, offers as reminders her early essays breaking this ground in a textured way, as does Audre Lorde's *Sister Outsider*. In general, does featuring "intersectionality" rather than "interlocking oppressions" appeal to some precisely because of the downplaying of sexuality and economic systems to be found in the work of the Combahee River Collective and Lorde's extensive intellectual labor throughout the 1970s and 1980s? There are major stakes here in how the past is (mis)represented in the present, in general, as well as communication scholars' recognition of fundamental differences between predominantly reformist and radical advocacy.

On the other hand, reformist and radical activists alike have, in fact, routinely separated out the "inseparable" oppressions, because of expediency and their diverse, symbolic, and corporeal life situations within inherited systems of power. What Black lesbian radical feminists genuinely experienced in their embodied, situated lives as "inseparable" oppressions did not and does not have precisely the same ramifications for white, heterosexual, and/or financially comfortable women and men, however oppressed by systems of power impinging on other components of their identities. Intersectionality, as proposed by Crenshaw, provides a powerful concept for charting these kinds of patterns within inherited, interacting systems of power.

In addition, for reformist advocacy concerning substantive matters wherein multiple components of identities might be separated, de facto, by law in specific systemic respects, communication scholars could reconsider Crenshaw's concept collaboratively in combination with Mari Matsuda's practice that she calls "asking other questions," because this practice provides a means to recognize intricacies of political coalition and academic scholarship across multiple differences of race, sexuality, class, religion, ability, and the like. Matsuda explained, "When I see something that looks racist, I ask, 'Where is the patriarchy in this?' When I see something that looks sexist, I ask, 'Where is the heterosexism in this?' When I see something that looks homophobic, I ask, 'Where are the class interests in this?'" She observed, "[N]o form of subordination ever stands alone."[50] Systems of power intersect in embodied identities in ways that often have cross-cutting valences of consequence among overlapping social groups that a metaphor of "interlocking oppressions" would ignore and "intersections," at least in its earliest formulation, would obfuscate in the absence of "asking other questions," as Matsuda proposed. This crucial factor of cross-cutting valences among political activists and reformers within systems of power is precisely why coalition politics have proven to be fragile, fleeting, and undependable with rare exceptions.

Communication scholars could extend intersectionality, furthermore, to locate differences consciously within social relationships so as to complete the implied, typically unstated comparisons, by making whiteness, heterosexuality, and the like explicit, as I have tried to model in this chapter. What Martha Minow has identified accurately as a "dilemma of difference" complicates any easy resolution to questions about whether to represent situations demographically and/or relationally with complete comparisons.[51] In this regard, communication scholars could continue to study intersectionality with attention to structural, political, and representational components, as Crenshaw suggested.

Finally, communication scholars might acknowledge complexity in multiple and overlapping components of identities by organizing historical, theoretical, and critical analyses to center on recurring, parallel communication practices. These parallel communication practices might be as, or more, fundamental than the demographic, social variables.[52] To be sure, Crenshaw does have sustained discussions of certain types of symbolic and physical experiences (e.g., rape, battering, and violence against women), primarily as a means to foreground specific, systemic ramifications of presumptions concerning demographic categories in relationship to one another within legal systems with race and "gender" in the foreground. However, it can be illuminating to reverse the foreground/rear ground in historical, theoretical, and critical analyses of systems of power and to center parallel communication practices that can help communication scholars understand human differences, human interpretations, and the ways individuals might (mis)understand one another based on their often interlocking and intersecting identities.

NOTES

I am grateful to Jack Daniel and Carol Stabile for comments and suggestions on an earlier version of this essay, which I presented at the National Communication Association in Seattle in 2000.

1. Audre Lorde, "Outlines," from a version of the poem in "Age, Race, Class, and Sex: Women Redefining Difference," *Sister Outsider: Essays and Speeches by Audre Lorde* (Freedom, CA: Crossing Press, 1984), 123.

2. Deborah K. King, "Multiple Jeopardy, Multiple Consciousness: The Context of a Black Feminist Ideology," *Signs* 14 (1988): 42–72; Patricia Hill Collins, "Learning from the Outsider Within: The Sociological Significance of Black Feminist Thought," *Social Problems* 33, no. 6 (1986): 514–532; Collins, *Black Feminist Thought: Knowledge, Consciousness, and the Politics of Empowerment* (New York: Routledge, 1990); Nancy A. Hewitt, "Compounding Differences," *Feminist Studies* 18, no. 2 (1992): 313–326; Kimberlé Williams Crenshaw, "Demarginalizing the Intersection of Race and Sex: A Black Feminist Critique of Antidiscrimination Doctrine, Feminist Theory, and Antiracist Politics," *University of Chicago Legal Forum* 147 (1989): 139–167; Crenshaw, "Mapping the Margins: Intersectionality, Identity Politics, and Violence Against Women of Color," *Stanford Law Review*

43 (1991): 1241–1299; Crenshaw, "The Marginalization of Sexual Violence Against Black Women," *National Coalition Against Sexual Assault Journal* 2, no. 1 (1994): 1–3, 5–6, and 15. As I mentioned in 1998, such metaphors are not altogether intellectually satisfying, though they provide useful partial bases for critical analysis. See Lester C. Olson, "Liabilities of Language: Audre Lorde Reclaiming Difference," *Quarterly Journal of Speech* 84 (1998): 448–470, esp. n 16.

3. For a list of Audre Lorde's publications through 1987, see Ronda Glikin, *Black American Women in Literature: A Bibliography 1976–1987* (Jefferson, NC: McFarland, 1989), 104–109.

4. Cheryl Clarke, *After Mecca: Women Poets and the Black Arts Movement* (New Brunswick, NJ: Rutgers University Press, 2005), esp. 2, 46, 125, 161 ff. See Cheryl Clarke, *"But Some of Us Are Brave* and the Transformation of the Academy: Transformation?" *Signs* 35 (2010): 779–787.

5. On small feminist presses, Jan Clausen, *A Movement of Poets: Thoughts on Poetry and Feminism* (Brooklyn, NY: Long Hall Press, 1982), esp. 17.

6. Combahee River Collective, "A Black Feminist Statement," in Cherríe Moraga and Gloria Anzaldúa, eds., *This Bridge Called My Back: Writing by Radical Women of Color* (Watertown, MA: Persephone Press, 1981; reprinted, New York: Kitchen Table, 1983), 210. The earliest publication of this statement, to my knowledge, is in *Capitalist Patriarchy and the Case for Socialist Feminism*, ed. Zillah Eisenstein (New York: Monthly Review Press, [1978]).

7. Audre Lorde, "The Master's Tools Will Never Dismantle the Master's House," in *This Bridge*, 98.

8. Barbara Smith, "Notes for Yet Another Paper on Black Feminism, or Will the Real Enemy Please Stand Up?" *Conditions: Five: The Black Women's Issue* 5 (1979): 127. See also Barbara Smith, "Racism and Women's Studies," in *But Some of Us Are Brave*, 49; reprinted in *The Truth that Never Hurts: Writings on Race, Gender, and Freedom* (New Brunswick, NJ: Rutgers University Press, 1998), 96.

9. Audre Lorde, "Uses of the Erotic: The Erotic as Power," in *Sister Outsider*, 53–59. Subsequent excerpts will use this version with pagination within parenthesis in the main text, because it is accessible.

10. This claim is based on an arts and humanities citation search of all references to Audre Lorde's prose and poetry.

11. *Whole Earth Review* no. 63 (Summer 1989): 66; Kathleen M. Sands, "Uses of the Thea(o)logian: Sex and Theodicy in Religious Feminism," *Journal of Feminist Studies in Religion* 8 (1992): 11; Catharine R. Stimpson, "Marguerite Duras: A 'W/Ringer' 's Remarks" *L'Esprit Createur* 30, no. 1 (1990): 17; Elizabeth Alexander, "'Coming Out Blackened and Whole': Fragmentation and Reintegration in Audre Lorde's *Zami* and *The Cancer Journals*," *American Literary History* 6 (1994): 700.

12. Barbara Christian, "Dynamics of Difference," *Women's Review of Books* 1 (August 1984): 6.

13. For commentary on this line, see Kathleen Weiler, "Freire and a Feminist Pedagogy of Difference," *Harvard Educational Review* 61, no. 4 (1991): 464–465.

14. An audiotape recording titled "Power and Oppression" of the entire panel has been preserved at the Lesbian Herstory Archives (henceforth LHA), Brooklyn, New York. Several papers from the conference are held at the Schlesinger Library at Radcliffe, but not the texts from the specific panel featuring Audre Lorde. Sara Hutcheon, Reference Assistant, Schlesinger Library, Radcliffe Institute, letter to the author, June 20, 2000.

15. Pamella Farley, letter to the author, October 2, 2000. Heidi Marshall, Archives Technician, letter to the author, June 14, 2000.

16. "Berkshire Conference file," LHA.

17. An audio recording of this speech is held at the GLBT Historical Society, San Francisco. Extensive evidence among this historical society's records of the conference document that videotapes were made of the entire proceedings to broaden its impact. But it has not been possible for me to locate them.

18. Diana E. H. Russell with Laura Lederer, "Questions We Get Asked Most Often," *Take Back the Night: Women on Pornography*, ed. Laura Lederer (New York: Morrow, 1980), 24. At the GLBT History Society, three boxes of records are held in a general collection: "Women Against Violence in Pornography and the Media Records." Several files are devoted to the "National Feminist Conference on Pornography."

19. Poems in Audre Lorde, *The Collected Poems of Audre Lorde* (New York: Norton, 1997), "Power," 215–216, 319–320; "Equal Opportunity," 369–371; "For the Record," 411; Lorde *Apartheid U.S.A.* (Latham, NY: Kitchen Table/Women of Color, 1986).

20. "Fair Sex, Fair Game: Women Say No to the Sexual Safari," recorded at San Francisco during November 1978, produced by Helene Rosenbluth, and broadcast in 1979. Pacifica Radio Archives number KKZ0556. "Eroticism and Pornography/Audre Lorde," Pacifica Radio archives number E2KZ 0884.

21. Audre Lorde, *Uses of the Erotic: The Erotic as Power* (Freedom, CA: Out & Out Books, 1978). About that time, copies of a forty-four-page book titled *Power, Oppression and the Politics of Culture: A Lesbian/Feminist Perspective* were printed. Despite a title implying that the texts were from the conference's panel and despite an identification of the conference as "author," Audre Lorde's only entry in it was a reprint of her earlier essay, "Poetry Is Not Luxury." Berkshire Conference on the History of Women (4th, 1978, Mount Holyoke), *Power, Oppression, and the Politics of Culture: A Lesbian/Feminist Perspective* (s.l.: s.n., [1978]). My claims are based on a copy held at the University of Wisconsin–Madison.

22. A copy is held in the Audre Lorde papers, Box 3, f. 8, LHA.

23. Audre Lorde, "The Erotic as Power," *Chrysalis* 9 (Fall 1979): 29–31.

24. *Chrysalis*, no. 1 (1977): n.p. [3].

25. Audre Lorde, "Erotic as Power," *Big Mama Rag* 7, no. 8 (September 1979): 11, 16.

26. Audre Lorde, "Uses of the Erotic: The Erotic as Power," *Take Back the Night*, 295–300.

27. Laura Lederer, "Introduction," *Take Back the Night*, 15.

28. *Ms.*, December 1982, 78. Lorde to Suzanne Levine, *Ms.*, Jan. 15, 1982 [*sic*: 1983?], held in Audre Lorde's papers at Spelman College Archives.

29. Lorde, "Uses of the Erotic: The Erotic as Power," in *Sister Outsider*, 53-59.

30. Lorde, "Uses of the Erotic: The Erotic as Power," *Whole Earth Review* no. 63 (Summer 1989): 66–69.

31. Lorde, "What Erotic Really Means," *Utne Reader* 24 (May/June 1991): 113–114.

32. Kathlyn A. Breazeale, "Don't Blame It on the Seeds: Toward a Feminist Process Understanding of Anthropology, Sin, and Sexuality," *Process Studies* 22, no. 2 (Summer 1993): 80.

33. AnnLouise Keating "Making 'Our Shattered Faces Whole': The Black Goddess and Audre Lorde's Revision of Patriarchal Myth," *Frontiers* 13, no. 1 (1992): 23; Nina Rapi, "Hide and Seek: The Search for a Lesbian Theatre Aesthetic," *New Theatre Quarterly* 9, no. 34 (1993): 154; Weiler, "Freire," 464–465.

34. Anne Balsamo, "Reading Cyborgs Writing Feminism," *Communication* 10, nos. 3–4 (1988): 339.

35. Alexander, "Coming Out," 697.

36. Barbara Sellers-Young, "Raks El Sharki: Transculturation of a Folk Form," *Journal of Popular Culture* 26 (1992): 148.

37. Sellers-Young, "Raks El Sharki," 149.

38. Evelyn Torton Beck, "Roundtable Discussion: Lesbianism and Feminist Theology," *Journal of Feminist Studies in Religion* 2 (1986): 105.

39. Barbara DiBernard, "*Zami*: A Portrait of an Artist as a Black Lesbian," *Kenyon Review* 13 (1991): 198; Marilyn R. Farwell, "Toward a Definition of the Lesbian Literary Imagination," *Signs: Journal of Women in Culture and Society* 14 (1988): 111–112; Janice Gould, "Disobedience (in Language) in Texts by Lesbian Native Americans," *Ariel: A Review of International English Literature* 25, no. 1 (1994): 37 and 41.

40. Alexander, "Coming Out," 699, 701. There is also discussion of race in Anne Borden, "Heroic 'Hussies' and 'Brilliant Queers': Genderracial Resistance in the Works of Langston Hughes," *African American Review* 28 (1994): 340; Brenda Carr, "'A Woman Speaks . . . I am Woman and Not White': Politics of Voice, Tactical Essentialism, and Cultural Intervention in Audre Lorde's Activist Poetics and Practice," *College Literature* 20 (1993): 145; Keating, "Making," 23.

41. Anne Marie Hunter, "Numbering the Hairs of Our Heads: Male Social Control and the All-Seeing Male God," *Journal of Feminist Studies in Religion* 8 (1992): 22.

42. Keating, "Making," 23.

43. Maureen E. Shea, "Love, Eroticism, and Pornography in the Works of Isabel Allende," *Women's Studies* 18 (1990): 223, 227, 230; Mary D. Pellauer, "The Moral Significance of Female Orgasm: Toward Sexual Ethics

that Celebrates Women's Sexuality," *Journal of Feminist Studies in Religion* 9, no. 1 (1993): 161 and 161, n. 1.

44. Ellen Wright Clayton and Jay Clayton, "Afterword: Voices and Violence—A Dialogue," *Vanderbilt Law Review* 43 (1990): 1811.

45. Carr, "A Woman Speaks," 145.

46. For commentaries to this effect, Martha A. Ackelsberg, "Spirituality, Community, and Politics: B'not Esh and the Feminist Reconstruction of Judaism," *Journal of Feminist Studies in Religion* 2 (1986): 115, n. 8; Joanna Frueh, "The Erotic as Social Security," *Art Journal* 53, no. 1 (1994): 67; L. J. 'Tess' Tessier, "Feminist Separatism—the Dynamics of Self-Creation," *Process Studies* 18, no. 2 (1989): 128; Pamela Annas, "A Poetry of Survival: Unnaming and Renaming in the Poetry of Audre Lorde, Pat Parker, Sylvia Plath, and Adrienne Rich," *Colby Library Quarterly* 18 (1982): 12; Somer Brodribb, "Discarnate Desires: Thoughts on Sexuality and Post-Structuralist Discourse," *Women's Studies International Forum* 14, no. 3 (1991): 141, n. 3.

47. Judith Mitchell, "George Elliot and the Problematic of Female Beauty," *Modern Language Studies* 20 (1990): 16.

48. Collins, *Black Feminist*, 225–230.

49. Crenshaw, "Mapping," 1244–1245. In Crenshaw, "Demarginalizing," she again centers on race and gender with only one passage (151) dealing with what she terms "sexual preference" and "class." There ensues no depth of engagement with either systemic factor. Nor is there any mention of economic systems in general, which is key to Lorde's analysis of the erotic. In Crenshaw's "The Marginalization," recommendation eight mentions poverty and class and recommendations six and nine on multiple vulnerabilities include sexuality. She does do more with class here. Yet again, economic systems go unexamined in an explicit way.

50. Mari J. Matsuda, "Beside My Sister, Facing the Enemy: Legal Theory Out of Coalition," *Stanford Law Review* 43 (July 1991): 1183–1192, quote on 1189.

51. Martha Minow, "Dilemmas of Difference," in *Making All the Difference: Inclusion, Exclusion, and American Law* (Ithaca, NY: Cornell University Press, 1990), 19–97.

52. For sustained illustrations, see Lester C. Olson, "Traumatic Styles in Public Address: Audre Lorde's Discourse as Exemplar," in *Queering Public Address: Sexualities in American Historical Discourse*, ed. Charles E. Morris III (Columbia: University of South Carolina Press, 2007), 249–282.

Chapter 6

Constitutive Intersectionality and the Affect of Rhetorical Form

Leslie A. Hahner

Over the past few decades, the incorporation of intersectional approaches into feminist scholarly practice expressed important challenges against orthodox views on power and identity formation. Intersectionality and similar theorizations reconfigured predominant assumptions on this complex relationship, and, in so doing, prompted scholars in a variety of disciplines to ask provocative questions: How does power influence identity formation? How might we theorize the variability of oppression? Is identity singular, a multiplicity, and/or mobile? In communication, the influence of these models encouraged similar questions inflected with our own disciplinary tendencies: How does communication impact identity construction? How do subjects narrate their identities? Does rhetoric offer recourse to resistance? Our current disciplinary conversations on communication, power, identity, and subjectivity suggest that these questions still motivate much of our research, even if the key terms of intersectionality rarely appear in the pages of our journals. Moreover, as the contributions of this collection demonstrate, feminist communication scholars continue to invigorate scholarly inquiry on intersectionality by couching communication methods as engines for discovering the cartography of identity's travels.

This chapter will continue that project by situating intersectionality as a distinctly rhetorical machination. I read intersectionality not simply as the term used to describe interlocking conditions of identity, but rather as that which also designates the symbolic, material, and affective connections through which a subject engages a particular discourse. Put in the language of rhetorical studies,

intersectionality shapes how an audience reads an address. Ultimately, I argue that intersectionality may be productively reconsid-
ered as the juncture between the constitutive power of discourse
and the audience's affective, embodied acts of identification.[1] By understanding how the constitutive form of discourse interacts with
the subject's investments, feminist communication scholars might
better comprehend how—despite the mobile, multifaceted layers
sedimented in our identifications—particular assertions of identity
become more significant than others. In order to pursue this thesis,
I first offer a brief overview of the potentially problematic tensions
manifest in intersectionality scholarship. I then detail my own theorization of *constitutive intersectionality* and the aspects of affect
that underpin this model.[2] To concretize this theorization, I will frequently reference a brief contemporary example: Feminist Coming
Out Day. Finally, I conclude by discussing the advantages of this
theory and the possibilities for future research.

INTERSECTIONALITY AND IDENTITY

For feminist scholars, intersectionality is an oppositional method
that interrogates the ways in which focusing on singular categories
of identity (e.g., woman) narrows the complex identities of subjects. These authors dissect machinations of power that might limit
identity to an isolated category (e.g., the subject is raced or classed,
not raced and classed) as well as paradigms of identity construction
that view it as additive (e.g., the subject is raced, then sexed, then
classed).[3] Typically, intersectionality is employed as a methodology that explores how modes of identification intermingle as they
travel across the social. In this way, intersectionality is a resistant
approach deploying the multiplicity of identities to reconfigure the
oppressive social norms that govern everyday performances of self.[4]
These critics contend that by reading the intersections, we might
profitably express richer formulas for identity formation. In nearly
all of this scholarship, the individual's identity is the most significant theoretical concept.[5] That is, intersectionality research typically attends to those disciplinary norms that restrict the way in
which individual human subjects fashion their own identities. Although identity remains an important term for critical scholarship,
focusing on identity as it emerges in the individual human subject
orchestrates some key tensions within intersectional analyses that
bear consideration. As I will suggest later in this chapter, a reconfigured understanding of intersectionality as a constitutive juncture
could productively negotiate these tensions.

First, intersectional analyses tend toward a stable view of identity that may replicate some of the problematic assumptions this method purported to critique. Commonly, academic investment in the stability of identity emerges in those scholarly efforts to highlight the duplicity of singular identity categories. That is, when feminist critics lament the social construction of identity as particularly oppressive for certain peoples, they situate this effect as created by the subject *continually* living within multiple categories of limited social mobility. Kimberlé Crenshaw's work on intersectionality is illuminative of this tension. Crenshaw astutely identifies the ways in which systematic mechanisms ideologically fashion the terms through which certain subjects are more violently governed than others. The relationship Crenshaw posits between discourse and identity is quite complex, claiming that our categories of identity are socially constructed, yet still possess value, and from this value become the sites around which power clusters and exercises.[6] Crenshaw's work adroitly negotiates the way in which intersectional identities become cemented. Yet in her efforts to illuminate systematic mechanisms of oppression, Crenshaw too easily disavows the mobility of identification to recuperate identity as an ongoing experience that produces multiplicative oppressions.[7] For example, while discussing the problems associated with the domestic violence shelter Crenshaw is analyzing, Crenshaw writes, "The fact that minority women suffer from the effects of multiple subordination, coupled with institutional expectations based on inappropriate nonintersectional contexts, shapes and ultimately limits the opportunities for meaningful intervention on their behalf."[8] Crenshaw denotes "minority women" as distinct from "minority women victims" of domestic violence.[9] Her language posits minority women as subjects who suffer within an existence of continual subordination. These women live through increasing oppression, an intensity magnified by domestic violence and the poor practices of the shelter. Yet, if, as Crenshaw insists, there are significant "intragroup" differences, then "minority women" cannot be distinguished as always already multiply subordinated. Instead, scholars must carefully attend to the moving contextual contours of identification—much like Crenshaw herself does in her analysis of legal discourse. Importantly for our purposes, Crenshaw's work highlights one tension in intersectionality scholarship: in our efforts to understand the variability of oppression, we too quickly rely on the same stable models of identity we sought to critique.

Second, intersectionality scholars regularly manufacture a tension between social categories of identity and individual experience that often circumvent the complexity of everyday life. Specifically, scholars fail to acknowledge that those socially intelligible categories of identity (e.g., race, class, gender) are not necessarily the categories through which individuals experience the multifaceted layers of contemporary culture. Complexity may beget fluid, changing identifications as well as differences within broad categories. This tension illuminates one conflict in intersectionality's political project: on the one hand, these critics astutely analyze the way in which power congeals oppression, while on the other hand these critics forget that although these sites are plentiful, they do not fully determine the intricacies of experience. Instead, while power may collect around certain sites, these sites cannot be understood as either inexorable or even a fitting moniker for the fluidity of difference. If we situate identity as stable—even as a socially constructed stability—we are still unable to understand the way in which identification travels and only provisionally names the terms of experience. Further, we must remember this theoretical tension not only obscures the possibility of changing identifications but also fails to consider the itinerant nature of oppression that makes it so difficult to combat. Both identification and oppression are continually moving, which not only allows oppressive practices to beguile their impacts, but also creates the possibility that "oppressed" subjects might find pockets of resistance. In either instance, the stakes of identification cannot be determined outside the context in which they emerge, given the very complexities at stake in intersectional analysis.

Additionally, this tension may push theorists to imagine resistance as synonymous with those distinctive experiences that appear to be at odds with social norms. Such an interpretation may elide how performances of identity might both adhere to and diverge from disciplinary codes. For example, Jasbir Puar argues that queer theorists who posit queerness as an intersectional identity that always resists heteronormativity may overlook how this identity is mobile and therefore may sometimes align with or against heterosexual cultural norms.[10] Puar's point is not to discard the import of understanding the effects of power, but to insist that the continual articulation and rearticulation of bodies within and against disciplinary mechanisms is the very receding horizon that entrenches power. As such, even the subjects we assume are more oppressively governed than others may still contribute to upholding the normative. Without recognizing that both subjugation and resistance are temporary points of assemblage, scholars invested in the concept of intersectionality could fashion an antagonism between experiential complexity and social categorization that could neglect the mobility of identification.

Third, scholarship that focuses on documenting the way in which individuals narrate the experiences of living complicated identities organizes a problematic tension between presence and absence that could circumvent a primary tenet of intersectional analysis. If intersectionality scholars are correct that certain experiences become rendered unintelligible by the operations of power, then concentrating on the narration of intersectional identities may suppress those experiences that are not readily told. Specifically, some intersectional scholars contend that in order to render marginal identities intelligible, we must labor to understand how these subjects narrate their identities through an intersectional axis.[11] Although this work is absolutely valuable in terms of unearthing the dimensions of margin and center, the assumptions of this work may weight analyses toward the articulation of identity as presence, covering over the ways in which unintelligible aspects of identification may not be accessible through the language of experience. As Joan Scott argued in her groundbreaking work on the politics of experience, the notion that the subject is able to access an authentic and accurate account of their own identity presumes that the subject holds an unmediated vision of their selfhood.[12] If, as Judith Butler argues, the narration of identity is a retrospective ordering in which the narrator attempts to make sense of their "selfhood" by chronicling the self through convenient terms, then relying on these narratives to articulate complex identities cannot necessarily access what remains unintelligible or those modes of identification disarticulated from the telling subject.[13] Further, even if we presume that the subject is able to negotiate these narrative fault lines, the more problematic tension privileges intelligibility over unintelligibility. This type of criticism ultimately aims to enlarge the domain of intelligibility rather than critique the fundamental problem of bestowing recognition based on intelligibility. As such, those with unintelligible experiences have only one recourse for change: attempting to fashion those experiences into a coherent identity palatable to the status quo.

Given the tensions manifest in intersectionality research, some scholars have chosen to discard this method as simply part of a limited model of identity politics.[14] These scholars assert many of the claims above as the reason why intersectional analysis can never fully articulate the intricacies of human experience. Such a dismissal neglects the advantages of an intersectional methodology. Recognizing the mobility of identifications as enabled and constrained by the effects of power still proves a valuable heuristic for considering the complexity of identity, connected or disconnected from the individual human subject. Further, while there are problematic assumptions in positing identities as durable locations, the importance of understanding the form of intelligible identities as valuable "places" for mobilizing political action cannot simply be dismissed as naïve theorization, but rather may be productively deployed through intersectionality as modes of strategic essentialism. Finally, the way in which intersectionality scholarship attends to the form of identity articulates the significance of style to discerning the contours of both intelligibility and unintelligibility. In short, if feminist scholars seek to theorize the travels of identification, we must carefully adopt this crucial methodology.

CONSTITUTIVE INTERSECTIONALITY

In order to earnestly engage the substantial contributions intersectionality models hold for considering identity, I propose that we might profitably rethink intersectionality not as the durable location through which a multiplicity of identities are manifest, but rather as the assemblage of motivated connections between discourse and subjectivity. In other words, engaging the intersection as the name for the multiple layers of identity misplaces the object of inquiry. Instead, we must study the intersection as the juncture structuring the constitutive relationship between discourse and subjectivity— that point of articulation organizing the variety of identities that might be taken up in the process of subjectification. If we follow the constitutive logic suggesting that discourses invite the adoption of a particular mode of subjectivity, then the intersection should primarily be considered the name for the relationship between an address and an audience. As such, we might accurately rename intersectionality as constitutive intersectionality. A constitutive intersection is the meeting place between discourse and subjectivity that generates affective conditions of subjective comfort and solicits discursively constructed enunciations of desire. The former might be expressed as the notion that certain subjects are privileged by the social order, a license that points to the comfort and discomfort generated and sustained by advantaged or disadvantaged bodies. For example, I easily identify with the names "white," "woman," and "rhetorical critic" at the conferences of my discipline because those names demarcate the opportunities and constraints I encounter and perform in a community of communication scholars. The latter expresses the idea that subjects craft identities by negotiating their desires within the norms of our culture. To further explain this complicated relationship, I continue by sketching the contours of constitutive intersectionality as the motivated tension between discursive form and the uptake of subjectivity.

To more fully evidence my claims about constitutive intersectionality, I will regularly offer examples related to a contemporary case study: Feminist Coming Out Day (FCOD), an event created by two student groups at Harvard University. To provide fair warning, this illustration will only serve as a brief reference point, as I cannot afford the space to engage in a full analysis. In 2010, the Radcliffe Union of Students and the Harvard Queer Students and Allies orchestrated FCOD. Portions of this event corresponded with Women's Week at Harvard and the actual "coming out" occurred on International Women's Day, March 8. The coming out process included feminists on campus wearing T-shirts emblazoned with "this is what a feminist looks like" and an art exhibit featuring students' and professors' portraits accompanied by paragraphs explaining why the portrayed was a feminist. One of the primary planners of FCOD, Lena Chen, argued that the event served to "do some bridge building, since the feminist community hasn't always been the most welcoming toward lesbians and transwomen," but that ultimately the event invited *women* to adopt the unpopular title feminist.[15] In 2011, the event expanded to other universities beyond Harvard. They created a website (www.feministcomingoutday. com) and forums on Facebook and Twitter wherein feminists might post their pictures and proclaim their feminism. With this example, I am drawing attention to the constitutive force of this event as articulated by its planners. They invite their audience to take up a particular assemblage of identity: feminist women. Further, I analyze the rhetorical form employed for this event—outing—and the way in which this style symbolically and affectively privileges and discourages certain performances. As I continue to describe constitutive intersectionality, I will reference this case study to describe the rhetorical relationship between FCOD planners and audiences.

Constitutive Intersectionality and Style

Constitutive intersectionality identifies a meeting place between discourse and subjectivity. This meeting place is articulated through the recognizability and mobility of style. That is, the form of rhetoric invites audiences to respond in a particular fashion. In recent years, rhetorical scholars have developed a renewed consideration of style as the marker identifying the intersection between discourse and audience. This new attention to rhetorical form moves intersectionality away from theorizing hybrid subjectivity to the intersections between the style of discourse and the audience. For example, Karma Chávez suggests that subjects rely on cultural schemes to interpret the bodies of others.[16] Reading the body as text, Chávez points out that within our contemporary culture some Americans in the United States will translate the brown body as an "illegal" immigrant, relying on the metaphorical and stylistic conventions of migration discourse to reach this conclusion. Similarly, in her analysis of female asylum seekers, Sara McKinnon articulates the ways in which the style of narrating the request for asylum delimits how the judge will see these women.[17] If we follow both Chávez and McKinnon, we see style as articulating the norms governing performances of subjectivity.

Still other scholars highlight subjectivity as an intersectional, figural relationship. Darrel Enck-Wanzer's analysis of the Young Lords deploys intersectionality not as the layers of identity, but as a rhetorical form that refuses to be disciplined by a particular communication medium. Intersectional rhetorics use "verbal, visual, or embodied" modes of persuasion to reject the "form of the oppressor's rhetoric and reforms."[18] He highlights this mobile rhetorical form as generating new modes of collective agency. Erin Rand theorizes polemics as a queer ("queer" here is that which cannot be contained or predicted) rhetorical form central to considering rhetorical agency. Reading Larry Kramer's discourse, Rand argues that Kramer's words travel across "a range of different sites."[19] The extent to which Kramer's discourse might be exercised across these different venues articulates the notion that polemics have "unpredictable effects."[20] This unpredictability creates the conditions of possibility for rhetorical agency, given that the rhetorical performance of a norm could result in repeating the convention or radically altering it. The riskiness of language, the idea that it can operate as expected or in unexpected ways, allows for rhetoric to carry the potential for effects in the world. All of these scholars suggest that the form of discourse renders visible key insights about subjectivity. Borrowing the idea that intersectionality is a rhetorical form that names the constitutive relationship between discourse and subject, I contend that the fundamental feature of intersectionality is its mobility, a flow constrained by the formal or stylistic nature of this relationship.

At stake in all these arguments is the relationship between rhetorical form and the capacity for invention. Taking their cue from rhetoricians such as John Lucaites, these authors implicitly or explicitly rely on the notion that the form of discourse "contains a theory of its own agency."[21] Agency hinges on the concept of intersectionality—specifically, that subjective invention is predicated on our relational ties with the form and style of discourse. In this sense, intersectionality is not simply the hybrid nature of identity, but is itself the name for the constitutive capacity of discourse to "enact and structure" the relationship between "speaker and audience, self and other, action and structure."[22] As a relational term, the constitutive intersection best identifies how the form of address organizes the performance of subjectivity. Specifically, the interaction between rhetor and audience fashions the terms through which each becomes intelligible. By identifying the conventions of an address, the audience recognizes the license and restraint governing their relationship to the address and the modes of identification they might adopt. In FCOD, the planners rely on a familiar rhetorical style—the acts associated with National Coming Out Day—to specify the kinds of performances feminists might assume during this event. The point is to use the style of coming out or a public revelation of oneself for the purposes of feminism. Even if the audience disagrees with the planners and their intentions, they nevertheless recognize the style of outing as governing the event. Style constitutes what kinds of performances *should* be adopted. Thinking of intersectionality this way couples a traditional notion of intersectionality as the experience of living a multiplicity of identities with the rhetorical prowess of discourse to constitute a subject. Within the discourses of our example, the planners emphasize the value of some identifications over others. Chen notes FCOD as addressing women, lesbians, and transwomen. This framing pronounces *women* as the subjects of FCOD, while joining other names to that label. Simultaneously, this discourse discourages a whole host of other identifications from emerging. In this way, intersectionality is the juncture through which rhetorical forms value particular identifications and performances.

One of the merits of considering intersectionality as this union is the focus on the mobility of form. In the rhetorical tradition, form refers to the stylistic features of rhetorical address, a set of conventions that may be deployed across disparate contexts and result in unpredictable effects. For my purposes, mobility is the central feature of intersectional analysis. The virtue of intersectional work is the aspiration to theorize the complexity of identity construction, a process predicated on an ever-changing relationship between context, discourse, and subject. As such, the complexity of identity is predicated on mobility. Mobility, here, is not simply how the subject changes aspects of identification based on different contexts. Rather, mobility becomes the basis for theorizing the travels of both discourse and identity. In other words, neither discourse nor the articulation of identity are stable locations, but each is a mobile point of articulation working to contain the complexity of discursive effects and identifications. This unpredictability is the necessary condition for persuasion, or in the terms of intersectional analyses, adopting intelligible or unintelligible identities precisely because mobility creates the possibility for iteration or change.

The notion of a feminist coming out relies on the mobility of rhetorical form. Mobility allows the form of coming out to travel to new places. Whereas planners note that outing is a rhetorical act associated with the LGBT community, they now situate that performance as a feminist project. This effect comes about from the travels of outing as a rhetorical form. Yet this mobility is simultaneously constrained by the way FCOD planners describe their purpose. For example, Chen rejects the notion that this event coopts the practice of outing from the LGBT community and affirms her desire to bridge the feminist and LGBT communities by publicly inviting women to out themselves as feminists.[23] In these statements, Chen posits coming out as a point of articulation between two distinct identifications. Chen distinguishes the feminist community and the LGBT community as oppositional. She suggests that they may find common ground through a feminist coming out. Throughout her discourse, Chen deploys some assumptions: feminists are women; the LGBT community is averse to feminism given long-standing exclusions; coming out is a rhetorical act that can effectively produce solidarity between these groups. In effect, these discursive articulations rhetorically constitute the preferred subjects of FCOD and in so doing limit the mobility of identifications at play. The audience may not respond in the manner requested, or even agree with Chen, but nevertheless this discourse arranges the terms of response. Audiences will adopt, reject, or modify the constitutive force of this event by considering their own position in relationship to the rhetorical situation. Even if an audience member disagrees with the event's framework, they nevertheless stylize their conduct within or against the requested proclamation. While Chen's own assertion of identity, her discourse, and her audience remain in the process of exchange, there is little recognition of this mobility. Most responses, even if they vary from Chen's framework, still respond to or through the process of outing. Yet, in order for rhetoric to hold force in the world, all these players must remain movable. Both her address and the performance of subjectivity correspondent to that address engage in a kind of flow that may result in radical changes to both.

Significantly, the radical potential in the mobility of form is managed by affective investments. In other words, while mobility is the structure that allows for the travels of identity, scholars must still grasp how modes of identification intensify in certain sites. In my view, to understand how certain identities become privileged, scholars must incorporate a theorization for how both discourses and the uptake of subjectivity are underwritten by affective invest-ments. Specifically, feminist scholars must comprehend the ways in which desire attempts to secure stability in the midst of ever-changing identifications, as well as how the unnamable compo-nents of affective comfort encourage the audience to adopt certain identities. Through reading the conditions of affect and how those relate to desire, scholars might better understand how particular as-sertions of identity become more or less significant. Mobility may be the necessary condition for understanding change, but in order to theorize the ways in which identities become sticking points, we must unearth the politics of affect.

Constitutive Intersectionality and Identification

First, to understand the ways in which certain identities become privileged, we cannot simply view the discursive machinations of the social as fashioning norms, but must view this interaction as articulating and disarticulating advantageous positions through the comfort of style. Half of this idea is already taken as gospel by those in the field of communication. Scholars such as Kenneth Burke and Maurice Charland clearly distinguish the ways in which rhetoric constitutes the location through which the audience comes to adopt the identities of certain subject positions.[24] Charland's constitutive rhetoric relies on Althusser to make the case that the hail of dis-course structures the relationship between discourse and audience. But, as much as Charland deploys Althusser, he also uses Burke's theorization of identification to understand how rhetoric shapes the relationship between address and audience. Discourse is not simply a mode of address: It also accounts for the location of the audience as subjects. The style of address manages how audiences come to read it and their appropriate response. With our example, FCOD planners employ outing to engender a certain response. Those who identify as feminist women are invited to proclaim their feminism in an effort to rehabilitate the title. This framing encourages the adoption of a particular performance of subjectivity.

However, Burke did not theorize identification as a simple as-sociation. Identification is not merely how the rhetor invites the audience to identify with her, but for Burke, the fundamental division within and between human being(s) generates the desire for identification via the symbolic.[25] As Charland briefly notes at the end of his essay, both discourse and embodied experiences highlight this fundamental division and produce the need for the affective comfort of feeling connected with others and with the self as a whole.[26] Desire undergirds both the creation of discourse and the audience's response to such discourse. By symbolically privileging certain identifications, these attachments mark such desire by delimiting the terms of similarity and difference. With FCOD, planners exhibit the desire to re-create the terms of similarity and difference through coming out. They hope this rhetorical form will allow for the comfort of connection among reportedly disparate peoples. As a rhetorical act, then, FCOD fashions a place and name that invites its audience to find similarities under the title feminist. Yet both the rhetor and the audience must desire to traverse the lines of division within the self and across the social in order to adopt, reject, or modify the provisional name attempting to join this division. In this way, the symbolism of address constitutes this relationship and enacts a condensation that favors certain identifications. As with FCOD, its constitutive force encourages identifying as woman.

If we read symbol making as conveyed through rhetorical forms, then we see style as a set of generic conventions that renders intelligible the constituted relationship between audience and address. Style names the supposed intent and impact of a text and the preferred response of the audience. For instance, we read the event of coming out as requesting a narrative that discloses a personal identity, not necessarily as a process of disclosing the identities of others. Although outing others sometimes occurs for political or ethical purposes, the considerable debate about this practice demarcates the conventions of outing: The subject discloses some personal truth and expresses membership in a community. Yet outing also has no specific mandate that determines exactly what the audience will do with it. The audience could just as easily out another, engage in a critique of the process of outing, or publicly reject the idea that outing actually does anything to transform the self or the community. But notice that the opportunities for figuring subjectivity in relationship to this event are orchestrated through the privileged subjectivity enunciated by its style (e.g., personal, public disclosure) and the ways in which the audience as a subject negotiates its own desires in relationship to that truth telling. Style is negotiated between the invitation to come out and the response of the audience. This negotiation hinges on the deployment and uptake of style as a set of identifiable conventions articulating the norms of rhetorical address and subjective performance. Style is shorthand for the way in which subjects recognize the conventions of address and figure their own identity in relationship to that form. In terms of this chapter on constitutive intersectionality, the style of rhetorical address privileges certain identities through how it invites subjects to respond.

Further, style fashions the comfort and discomfort generated from identifying with or against cultural norms. We are comfortable when we know the rules of response that govern us as audience members, and we know that rejecting that norm may result in some discomfort for ourselves and/or our audience. For example, we know that outing asks us to identify ourselves with names that make sense to others (e.g., feminist, lesbian, queer), and that if our identifications do not align with publicly recognizable categories, we must explain or sophisticate our message. Without that, not only might our outing seem less than comprehensible, but we may engender a discomfort for ourselves or our audience by upending that norm. While that discomfort may be productive, it nevertheless demonstrates the privilege of custom. Style is a slippery quality that simultaneously identifies a convention and carries with that convention the possibility that it could be performed otherwise. In our illustration, the style of coming out demands a naming, and yet the subject may perform that naming in ways that adapt the terms of response. One poster on the FCOD website, Remy Corso, tries to adapt this convention by performing his outing as a transmasculine "feminist, but . . . ," and reframing feminism as "co-creating a world in which gender liberation is a reality for all people, all bodies, everyone."[27] This individual attempts to negotiate the norms governing response by outing himself as a "feminist, but . . . ." He reconfigures his outing as not simply about feminism, or the divisions between the LGBT community and feminism, but as an act that seeks gender liberation beyond the transwomen and lesbians Chen notes. In effect, his performance attempts to undermine the sex/gender Chen's feminism presumes to address: women. Yet his address still comfortably operates within the style of outing and the publicly recognizable naming it requests. With this response, we see how the invitation to subjectivity marks the boundaries and comforts of convention.

Constitutive Intersectionality and Affect

The comfort of convention, however, is not simply a discursive effect focused on the intelligible identifications of the subject, but also generates preferential modes of bodily performance. If we follow scholars theorizing affect, we understand that affect directs the intensity of attachments.[28] In other words, the "feel" of stylistic conventions produces unintelligible conditions that privilege certain modes of identification. For Brian Massumi, the body senses these conditions, deposits preconscious memories, and recalls the force of those attachments in similar circumstances.[29] Still other scholars, Lauren Berlant and Sara Ahmed, among others, suggest that the force of these affective intensities arranges the stickiness of particular identifications.[30] For these scholars, conventional rhetorical form relies on a familiar space and feel, a style that the body recognizes and responds to as a kind of "gut" reaction. For example, outing is an act that is more often extended as an invitation to bodies that are presumed to be uncomfortable passing, or trying to misfit themselves within the normative. These bodies are asked to use outing as a mechanism that promotes visible solidarity. Outing induces these bodies to respond through a publicly recognizable corporeal and symbolic style. Chen relies on this figural relationship in her planning for FCOD. She projects a desire onto the convention of outing that hopes to situate feminist bodies as a publicly marked community. Rhetorical style, then, is not only a discursive domain for subjective comfort, but it also orchestrates the affective, embodied economies that guide the adoption of particular identifications.

Ahmed references affective intensities as a kind of "comfort" wherein the institutional arrangements of place urge an ease or disease for particular bodies.[31] For instance, the discourses and practices of FCOD attempt to situate the woman's body as a figure that should publicly declare, or out, itself as feminist. For some, this type of marked body does not fit the convention of outing. Indeed, some bloggers noted that feminists should not appropriate the form of outing given that in the United States, feminists do not encounter the same violence as the queer community for publicly identifying themselves.[32] This response is not simply focused on outing as a political act, but notes the comfort and discomfort articulated to certain bodies that exhibit an orientation. Read more generally, the "feel" of convention is an affective attachment that arranges the limits and licenses of some bodies and motivates the subject to adopt and reject particular modes of identification. As a group, then, these scholars point us to see the intersections between discourse and subjectivity as affectively managed through invitations to adopt certain modes of subjectivity.

Taken together, symbolic and affective components of rhetorical address constitute preferred identities. Further, these machinations render socially intelligible subjectivities and the modes of identifi-cation that become attached to these positions as objects of desire in two ways. First, the confines of preferred subjectivity and its atten-dant identifications are demarcated and indicate the means through which certain bodies may or may not traffic in certain spaces. Affec-tive and symbolic connections between discourse and subject high-light modes of identification that are privileged in certain locales and disavow a whole series of other identifications that are not. The privileged subject comes to understand themselves as the name that finds comfort and agency in the space of advantaged identifica-tions. Indeed, this is precisely the reason FCOD planners adopted the form of coming out—it is a publicly recognizable rhetorical act seen as effecting a transformation of social and political valences. Here the intersection names the invitation to take up particular per-formances of subjectivity and highlights the privilege and comfort of that name.

Second, by articulating preferred modes of identification, rhe-torical discourse distinguishes points of access and refusal, allowing subjects to see something beyond the object, or name, of identifica-tion. Specifically, by privileging certain modes of subjectivity, rhe-torical discourse establishes these recognizable places as objects of desire that could allow the ambiguous complexities of experience to bask in the glow of comprehension. Privileged identifications il-luminate the space of comfort for those who can and do take up these named identities. Those bodies that perform less recognizable identifications long for the space in which their experiences have an advantaged name and locale. Harvard's student groups situate FCOD as that which attempts to bridge two communities and recu-perate the title feminist. This framing enunciates a longing: that a feminist outing might both resignify "feminist" and dissolve those political differences that divide those fighting for gender equality. In effect, FCOD privileges particular identities—women and LGBT— and yet simultaneously obscures the very complicated experiences and identifications that do not find either a home or the resolu-tion of political difference within this event. The "out feminist" becomes an object of longing that covers over the differences this figure excludes. For instance, as Remy Corso points out, the out feminist covers over the exclusion of those who do not identify as woman. Ultimately, the constitutive intersection does not simply favor certain identities but simultaneously structures the subject as an object of desire that effaces difference. The intersection is the connection between discourse and identification managed by af-fective investments. Thus, intersectional scholarship in this vein would illuminate the rhetorical mechanisms that obscure the very complexities of experiences that remain unnamed.

CONSTITUTING THE INTERSECTION

Where, then, is the intersection? The intersection is not found in the multiple identities of the human subject. Nor is the intersection an effect simply given to subjects by structures of power. The intersection is the motivated juncture between discourse and subject. It is a term that names the formal set of conventions that engender the adoption of particular identities. Despite the fact that all subjects experience aspects of identity as a multiplicity that may never be properly named, rhetorical forms generate those modes of identification that come to hold power within a given situation. These intersections are managed by several components of affect. First, the constitutive power of rhetorical address structures the bond between audience and address. Next, the desire for symbolic union, the need to bridge the divide within and between us, undergirds this relationship. Much like Crenshaw's claim that certain experiences resist telling, desire, here, is an aspiration to render intelligible the complexity of experience.[33] The process of subjectification encourages subjects to find comfort and similarity within the symbolic, ill-fitting labels attempting to join rhetorical discourse with audience. This constitutive effect is enunciated through the convention of style that renders intelligible the licenses and constraints of discourses and subjects. Conventions of address provide cues to both rhetor and audience as to what sort of performances and identifications are preferred. Further, the repetition of convention becomes the mechanism through which privileged bodies find comfort in familiar locales, and disadvantaged bodies discover the moving monotony of discomfort. Put simply, the repetition of convention ensures its status as a "home" for those bodies who are attracted to that familiar style, while simultaneously the repetition of that convention iterates discomfort for those bodies who rarely align with the normative. Thus, if all subjects are crisscrossed by categories of identity, constitutive intersectionality explains the theoretical mechanisms that limit the identities that might be adopted in a given situation. As we see with FCOD, the rhetorical practices surrounding this event privilege identifications traveling with the name "woman" and discourage identifications connected with the name "men."

I would argue that theorizing intersectionality as an assemblage of motivated relationships between discourse and subjectivity more fully accounts for the mobility of identity. When we reframe our scholarship in intersectionality as a relational perspective rather than a nominal term, such a shift emphasizes the notion that the categories of social identity as expressed by the individual subject are valuable not simply for the layers of identity they illuminate, but also for the ways in which certain categorizations come to bear the capacity of articulating lived complexity. Desire may push us to adopt certain names, but as Elsbeth Probyn argues, we may want to unpack this name to determine the work that term does to cover over and illuminate the intricacies of experience. For Probyn, it is "through and with desire that we figure relations of proximity to others and other forms of sociality."[34] As with FCOD, outing rhetorically projects the desire to resignify feminism as a name with social prominence. Further, it situates this act as transformational for the feminist and LGBT community. Planners hope to install new possibilities for identification against alienating differences. As such, this name indicates the stakes of the social relationships at play. Given the privilege attached to the name, the markers we use to figure relations of belonging and difference may be the very terms we must dislodge from the status of objects if we are to determine how these relational terms do not simply articulate what we are, but also assert what we desire to be. As Aimee Carrillo Rowe provocatively writes, "the power of our belongings—our longings to be with others, to belong—hold [sic] tremendous sway over the subjects we are becoming."[35] This longing for belonging is a relational and communicative activity in which the identities we affirm may operate "through the suppression and subordination of other social identities."[36] As is clear in the FCOD example, the outing of the feminist community may come at the cost of disavowing some identities (e.g., men, transmasculine) from the feminist project. Our assertions of identity, then, are not necessarily what we are, but rather they articulate our relational desires.

In order to understand the rhetorical work at play between identification and desire, feminist communication scholars should redirect our pursuit of narrating the complexity of identity into a vigorous exploration of the constitutive power manifest in discursive form. Certainly, reading the form of address in a given context highlights the ways in which convention privileges certain identifications, but reading style might also provide scholars clues for reading the way in which modes of identification become disarticulated from the telling subject. For Carrillo Rowe, feminist scholars' investment in the individualized subject of rights precludes us from thinking of politics and power relationally.[37] The human subject may be the location in which we typically find assertions for recognition, but these assertions cannot help us negotiate the terrain of the unintelligible, given that to take up subjectivity requires that complexities of experience become condensed into intelligible names and categories. Rather, we must adopt an investigation of form as the mode through which norms become visible and the means through which the unintelligible resists formalization. The benefit of such an approach is that by unearthing the ways in which particular rhetorical forms move across the social, scholars might be better able to read not simply how particular privileges become attached to human subjects, but how these privileges become connected to other kinds of subjects. For example, while rhetorical address often constitutes an audience as human actors, this discourse might also translate the rights and responsibilities of supposed human agents to institutional and imagined subjects. As with the example of FCOD, the process of coming out operates through a peculiar subjective logic that vacillates between the individual human subject and the overarching community. This metonymic logic suggests that the human actor's rhetorical address simultaneously speaks for the community.

Further, a constitutive logic presumes that while there are forms that symbolically privilege particular names (for FCOD, these include woman, lesbian, and transwoman), these names are fashioned relationally to differences that resist telling (for FCOD, these differences might translate as man, transmasculine, and queer). In other words, privileging certain identities operates by distancing other identities as different. This harkens back to Burke's theorization of identification. For Burke, symbols of identification are fraught with division, a coupling that suggests subjects are dependently constructed through imagined relations of similarity and difference. Given that identification operates on privileging selected similarities, it generates these connections by occluding difference—including differences within the self and those who do not share in the stakes of identification. Put simply, when rhetoric generates a "we," it also generates and obscures a "they." Those imagined locations of difference are created through the formal conventions of rhetoric, yet they resist intelligibility because they travel in the negative space within the symbolic. The form of address makes apparent the terms of identification. Yet simultaneously that address operates on differences that are only relationally "present." This negative space is part of the stylistic convention of address; it is the relation of difference scholars must explore to understand more clearly the intersection between rhetorical form and the constitution of subjective identities. Thus, by reading the dialectical work of rhetorical address, scholars are better able to understand the complexity of identifications at play, articulated through imagined relations of similarity and difference.

Viewing intersectionality as the study of the constitutive relationship between rhetorical address and subjective identification allows for a nuanced theorization for understanding the "places" needed for mobilizing political action. In other words, intersectional scholars encourage us to see the locations in which modes of oppression intersect and to unearth in those locales the standpoint through which activists might mobilize effective political actions.[38] In my view, these locations are not durable sites provided by the structural conditions of power, but they are created and re-created through the constitutive power of style. As such, the place for mobilizing political action is not only within an identity category, but might also be understood productively as the deployment and redeployment of rhetorical forms. Given that rhetorical forms generate preferred modes of identification, to study the form itself allows scholars to unpack the ways in which identification as a mode of subjectivity might become constrained but is also enabled. If we understand the rhetorical form as a mobile convention, we may be better able to theorize both iteration and change. This view allows for the possibility of radicalizing the norm (the possibility that the norm could be otherwise) and suggests that this radicalizing possibility must inhere in the norm itself if the audience is to recognize the convention. If both the radical and the normative operate within the style of rhetorical address, then the "place" for activism and intersectional scholarship might just be to appraise the political potential in radicalizing conventional form.

My goal has been to argue that intersectionality names the assemblage of motivated relationships between rhetorical discourse and the uptake of subjectivity. This juncture is productively named *constitutive intersectionality* and invites feminist communication scholars to see the intersection as a rhetorical arrangement. Drawing on the affective and discursive components of the rhetorical situation, I suggest that rhetorical forms structure the constraints and freedoms of subjectivity. The texture, feel, and symbolism of address may limit the mobility of identifications. The relationship between rhetorical address and the constitution of the audience rests on a dialectical relationship between imagined relations of similarity and difference. Our longings to belong can drive us to adopt privileged identities. Yet engendered within this symbolism are negative spaces that resist telling—locations of difference created through and against those identifications privileged by the constitutive power of rhetoric. To study the constitutive composition of rhetorical forms does not simply illuminate the relationships through which subjects might adopt intelligible identities, but could also allow scholars to unpack the mechanisms that obscure the unintelligible. The form of address articulates the comfort of convention. Further, the performance of this convention becomes a means through, or against, which the normative might be adopted or radicalized. As such, the mobility of form is a crossroads feminist scholars might productively travel to answer the crucial questions intersectionality poses. Engaging the intersection as a rhetorical juncture between audience and address may assist feminist critics in taking seriously the revolutionary potential that resides in the interstices between discourse and identification.

NOTES

1. This chapter will focus on the affective components of identification as those symbolic and corporeal connections through which desire is generated.

2. While each of these terms identifies a longer scholarly tradition, in this chapter I am combining them to theorize a new model of intersectional scholarship.

3. See, for example, Kimberlé Crenshaw, "Mapping the Margins: Intersectionality, Identity Politics, and Violence against Women of Color," *Stanford Law Review* 43 (1991): 1241–1299; Adrien K. Wing, "Brief Reflections toward a Multiplicative Theory and Praxis of Being," in *Critical Race Feminism: A Reader*, ed. Adrien K. Wing (New York: New York University Press, 1997), 44–50; Iris Marion Young, *Intersecting Voices: Dilemmas of Gender, Political Philosophy and Policy* (Princeton, NJ: Princeton University Press, 1997).

4. See, for example, Patricia Hill Collins, *Black Feminist Thought: Knowledge, Consciousness, and the Politics of Empowerment* (Boston: Unwin Hyman, 1990); Kimberlé Crenshaw, "Demarginalizing the Intersection of Race and Sex: A Black Feminist Critique of Antidiscrimination Doctrine, Feminist Theory and Antiracist Politics," *University of Chicago Legal Forum* (1989): 139–168.

5. See, for example, Crenshaw, "Mapping"; Wing, "Brief Reflections"; Emily Grabham, Davina Cooper, Jane Krishnadas, and Didi Herman, *Intersectionality and Beyond: Law, Power and the Politics of Location* (New York: Taylor and Francis, 2008); Diana T. Meyers, *Being Yourself: Essays on Identity, Action, and Social Life* (Lanham, MD: Rowman & Littlefield, 2004); Young, *Intersecting Voices*.

6. Crenshaw, "Mapping," 1297.

7. Crenshaw's most trenchant critiques of exclusion emerge in her close reading of legal communication. While these moments in the "Mapping"

essay more closely align with my advocacy in this chapter, Crenshaw and similar authors posit a stickiness to identity that belies the intragroup differences they forward.

8. Crenshaw, "Mapping," 1251.

9. Crenshaw, "Mapping," 1251.

10. Jasbir K. Puar, *Terrorist Assemblages: Homonationalism in Queer Times* (Durham, NC: Duke University Press, 2007), 23.

11. See, for example, Cerri A. Banks, *Black Women Undergraduates, Cultural Capital, and College Success* (New York: Peter Lang, 2009); Mimi Schippers, "The Social Organization of Sexuality and Gender in Alternative Hard Rock: An Analysis of Intersectionality," *Gender and Society* 14 (2000): 747–764.

12. Joan W. Scott, "The Evidence of Experience," *Critical Inquiry* 17 (1991): 773–797.

13. Judith Butler, *Giving an Account of Oneself* (New York: Fordham University Press, 2005).

14. See, for example, Elizabeth Grosz, "Differences Disturbing Identity: Deleuze and Feminism," in *Working with Affect in Feminist Readings: Disturbing Differences*, ed. Marianne Liljeström and Susanna Paasonen (New York: Routledge, 2010), 101–111; Puar, *Terrorist*, 211–216.

15. Lena Chen, "feminist coming out day: marrying feminism with gay rights," *Gurl.com*, accessed October 12, 2010 http://www2.gurl.com/feminist-coming-out-day-marrying-feminism-with-gay-rights/.

16. Karma R. Chávez, "Embodied Translation: Dominant Discourse and Communication with Migrant Bodies-As-Texts," *Howard Journal of Communications* 20 (2009): 18–36.

17. Sara L. McKinnon, "Citizenship and the Performance of Credibility: Audiencing Gender-based Asylum Seekers in U.S. Immigration Courts," *Text and Performance Quarterly* 29 (2009): 205–221.

18. Darrel Enck-Wanzer, "Trashing the System: Social Movement, Intersectional Rhetoric, and Collective Agency in the Young Lords Organization's Garbage Offensive," *Quarterly Journal of Speech* 92 (2006): 176.

19. Erin J. Rand, "An Inflammatory Fag and a Queer Form: Larry Kramer, Polemics, and Rhetorical Agency," *Quarterly Journal of Speech* 94 (2008): 298.

20. Rand, "Inflammatory," 298.

21. Quoted in Cheryl Geisler, "How Ought We to Understand the Concept of Rhetorical Agency," *Rhetoric Society Quarterly* 34 (2004): 13.

22. Geisler, "How Ought," 13.

23. Chen, "feminist coming out."

24. Kenneth Burke, *A Rhetoric of Motives* (Berkeley: University of California Press, 1969); Maurice Charland, "Constitutive Rhetoric: The Case of the Peuple Québécois," *Quarterly Journal of Speech* 73 (1987): 133–150.

25. For an insightful essay on this, see Bryan Crable, "Distance as Ultimate Motive: A Dialectical Interpretation of *A Rhetoric of Motives*," *RSQ: Rhetoric Society Quarterly* 39 (2009): 213–239.

26. Charland, "Constitutive," 148.

27. Remy Corso, January 14, 2011, post on "This Is What a Feminist Looks Like," FeministComingOutDay.com, http://feministcomingoutday.com/post/2813811189/remy-23-minneapolis-gender-liberation-is-for#notes/.

28. See, for example, Lawrence Grossberg, *We Gotta Get Out of This Place: Popular Conservatism and Postmodern Culture* (New York: Routledge, 1992); Brian Massumi, "The Autonomy of Affect," in *Parables for the Virtual: Movement, Affect, Sensation,* ed. Brian Massumi and Stanley Fish (Durham, NC: Duke University Press, 2002), 23–45.

29. Massumi, "Autonomy," 23–45.

30. Lauren Berlant, *The Female Complaint: The Unfinished Business of Sentimentality in American Culture* (Durham, NC: Duke University Press, 2008); Sara Ahmed, *Queer Phenomenology: Orientations, Objects, Others* (Durham, NC: Duke University Press, 2006).

31. Ahmed, *Queer,* 112.

32. leonineclaire, "Feminist Coming Out Day—March 11th 2011," *Feminist Hub,* November 28, 2010 http://thefeministhub.tumblr.com/post/1712194458/feminist-coming-out-day-march-11th-2011/.

33. Crenshaw, "Mapping," 1242.

34. Elsbeth Probyn, *Outside Belongings* (New York: Routledge, 1996), 13.

35. Aimee Carrillo Rowe, "Subject to Power—Feminism without Victims," *Women's Studies in Communication* 32 (2009): 27.

36. Probyn, *Outside,* 101.

37. Carrillo Rowe, "Subject to Power," 14.

38. Crenshaw, "Mapping," 1297. A similar claim emerges from Stuart Hall, "Ethnicity: Identity and Difference," *Radical America* 23 (1989): 18.

Chapter 7

Spheres of Influence:
The Intersections of Feminism and
Transnationalism in Betty Millard's
Woman Against Myth

Jennifer Keohane

A woman Communist is a member of the Party just as a
man Communist, with equal rights and duties. There can
be no difference of opinion on that score.
—Vladimir Lenin[1]

Stolidly repudiating "special organizations" for communist
women, Vladimir Lenin in a 1919 pamphlet trumpeted the prevailing belief that the ideology of communism was gender neutral.
He emphasized that all workers were subordinated to their capitalist employers. Indeed, Marxism-Leninism, the foundational theory
of communism, understood women's oppression primarily in economic terms that would be immediately and automatically resolved
with a socialist government. Such views were dominant in the Communist Party USA (CPUSA) until 1948 when Betty Millard exposed
communist theory as deeply entangled with gendered ideologies in
her groundbreaking pamphlet *Woman Against Myth*. The twenty-
three-page pamphlet challenged Karl Marx's and Frederick Engel's
arguments that class exploitation and private property were the
causes of women's oppression by pointing out the significant ways
in which religion, language, laws, and popular culture intersected to
subordinate women. "We can see that it is the delimiting of women
to the role of wife and mother that is responsible for the superficial values thrown at us from every page of women's magazines,"

Millard maintained.[2] She argued further that traditional gender ideals portrayed in popular magazines were inextricably linked to dominant representations of the Cold War American home. Millard exposed constructions of this space as infused with gendered understandings of containment more than twenty-five years before Marxist Henri Lefebvre undertook a similar critique of capitalist space in *The Production of Space*. Tremendously influential, Millard's pamphlet formed the foundation of the Party's analysis of women's oppression for the following decade.[3]

The success of Millard's pamphlet was, of course, not a foregone conclusion. Because of the constraints imposed by communist theory and negative media representations of both bourgeois feminists and the Soviet Union, Millard had to open up an oppositional space for the creation of the communist feminist subjectivity she advocated. In her pamphlet, she represented this oppositional space as the culmination of a transnational narrative that rejected the containment of the capitalist, American home and the traditional gendered roles that went along with it. Defying the popular myth that feminists and communists were masculine, she performed femininity channeled through a teacherly ethos. By creatively grounding her brand of feminism in a transnational ethic and severing representations of women from consumption and the home, Millard not only extended traditional communist class analysis to recognize the ways in which forces other than economic oppression intersected to subordinate women, but she also demonstrated the previously denied gendered aspects of communism itself. However, despite Millard's astute analysis of the intersection of gender, space, and economic oppression, she had little to say about how race imbricated the popular and historical discourses she explored and thus ignored unique problems facing women of color. Despite her privileging of a certain conception of whiteness throughout the pamphlet, Millard's insightful attention to gender and class illustrates an early example of intersectional analysis.

Millard was not, of course, the first woman to call attention to the ways in which spatial limitations and other forms of oppression intersected to protect male privilege. Indeed, the themes she took up can be placed in a trajectory that stretches back to some of the earliest writing on patriarchy and oppression originating with Mary Wollstonecraft's 1792 *A Vindication of the Rights of Woman*. Wollstonecraft argued that the lack of educational opportunities afforded women underwrote the prevailing ideology of domestic containment. Moreover, she also suggested that "intellectual confinement" facilitated women's economic dependence on men, which rendered the institution of marriage a sham.[4] Education was the pillar of her answer to oppression, a solution predicated upon the opening up of space to women in the classroom. In this way, Wollstonecraft acknowledged the intersections of space, gender, and economic status as they combined to support male supremacy.

Intersectional analysis of varying degrees of sophistication continued to be a cornerstone on which feminists based their arguments for change, and in 1949, Millard's fellow communist Claudia Jones used an intersectional spatial analysis to illustrate the ways in which Millard privileged whiteness in her pamphlet. Jones considered the racialization of space and paid special attention to the ways that the Cold War suburb imprisoned Black domestic workers in the houses of their white female employers.[5] The socialist feminists of the 1960s and 1970s took up these tools of analysis, and activist Angela Davis famously observed that "racism and sexism frequently converge."[6] Thus, Millard's pamphlet fits into a long trajectory of feminist theorizing of space and what we now call intersectionality, and it helped spur the CPUSA to take up such analysis in a more sophisticated manner. This chapter, then, explicates Millard's pamphlet as an example of early intersectional analysis. By this I mean that Millard recognized and began to theorize the ways that multiple loci of power, such as popular culture and sexism, complexly converged *with* capitalism to keep women in subordinate positions to men. However, by attending to the shortcomings of Millard's arguments, this chapter also highlights intersectional rhetorical analysis as a critical approach that can call attention to the ways in which discourses mask and privilege particular identity components, such as race. Finally, by exploring the spatial dimensions of Millard's rhetoric, primarily represented in the home and the Soviet Union, this chapter contends that space both structured and served as another axis around which systems of oppression interlocked in Cold War America.

To understand how Millard theorized these intersections, in the first part of this chapter I located Millard's rhetoric in a trajectory of intersectional theorizing. I then situate the pamphlet in its historical context by summarizing the specific ideologies of gender and the home circulating during the Cold War. In the third section, I explore the ways in which Millard called attention to the intersections between gender and class that were manifested in the spatial restriction of many women to the Cold War home. But Millard recognized that the limitations of class and gender could also be contested in space and wove a transnational narrative as one means of such resistance. Next, I show that Millard used a teacherly ethos throughout her pamphlet as a means of occupying a socially acceptable space for women. Millard's strategy illustrates that as women argued to challenge existing spatial limitations, they often had to do so from accepted spatial locations. I then consider some of the limitations of Millard's intersectional analysis, chiefly her privileging of whiteness. Ultimately, though, I contend that Millard's negotiation of spatial limitations played a significant role in opening up space for feminism in the radical left. These strategies and the pamphlet were important precursors to the socialist feminism that would emerge in the 1970s.

FEMINISM, SUBJECTIVITY, AND COLD WAR POLITICS

The CPUSA was the largest radical party in the United States in the 1930s and 1940s. Although it only had about 75,000 to 80,000 members after World War II, historians Harvey Klehr and John Earl Haynes write that "in terms of its institutional power through the labor movement, numbers of full-time party functionaries, financial resources, and influence and prestige in liberal and labor circles, Communist strength was never higher than in the immediate postwar period."[7] Indeed, in the pre- and postwar periods, Americans joined the CPUSA to support the Party's work on labor regulations, rent control, women's equality, and minority rights.[8] The Party's role as the vanguard of leftist reformers would not last. By late 1947 and early 1948, the Party's membership began to decline, and leaders were never able to reverse the sharp downward trend. Moreover, the Harry Truman administration began to target communists, arresting eleven high-ranking Party leaders in 1948 for violating the Smith Act, which made it a crime to advocate the overthrow of the U.S. government by force or violence.[9] Millard confronted a Party in the early stages of decline, despite very recent memory of the Party as the leader for progressives across the country. Her rhetoric needed to negotiate prevalent anticommunism as she sought to persuade a large bloc, women, to join the Party.

In addition to anticommunism, another rhetorical barrier Millard faced in recruiting women to the CPUSA was larger discourses circulating in U.S. newspapers about the Soviet Union as a masculinized place with no consumerist comforts. Harry Schwartz reported in an April 1948 issue of the *New York Times Magazine* that, "In Moscow it is almost impossible to buy such common household necessities as chairs, window screens, nails, knives, and drinking glasses. Electric vacuum cleaners and refrigerators aren't even being made!"[10] To most, consumption of household goods was a uniquely

American act that demonstrated the superiority of the capital-ist United States over communist Russia.[11] To reject the capitalist home was to reject a representation of American identity, meaning Millard had to tread carefully as she attempted to open up space for communist feminism in the United States.

Moreover, communism was seen to erase femininity, enslaving men and women equally to the Soviet state. For example, a *New York Times Magazine* headline claiming to answer the question "Why Russian Women Work Like Men" described Russian women as "stolid" and "dowdy," laboring as engineers, construction work-ers, and bus drivers because there were not enough Russian men to do these jobs. The author noted, "In general, the Soviet Union seem-ingly believes that looking prettily feminine is 'bourgeois' and there-fore to be avoided."[12] The implication was clear: Russian women were inferior to the beautiful, feminine, and charming American women who fulfilled their proper roles in the home by raising ener-getic children and buying domestic goods for their happy homes. Of course, CPUSA members did not view the Soviet Union negatively as the broader American culture did. Nonetheless, Millard had to endeavor to overcome these associations because of the importance of recruiting women in 1948.[13]

It was not just broader American culture that argued women belonged in the Cold War, consumerist home. Communist men fre-quently held such attitudes as well. When the communist newspa-per the *Worker* called for opinions on the problems with balancing women's political organization and housework in 1948, Harold B. wrote: "I would be the first to admit that women's position is unen-viable," he affirmed. "But they are not going to solve their problems by hog-tying their husbands. As the bread-winner the man not only has to work during the day, he has to work after hours to protect his job. He's fighting not only for himself, but to feed, clothe, and shelter his wife and family as well. If this means that his wife is confined to the home, it's tough, but she has to recognize that this is not something he is responsible for."[14] Like many communist men, Harold B. blamed capitalism for women's confinement and elevated the class struggle above sex-based oppression. This letter and the many others like it illustrate the primary obstacle Millard faced: the representation of feminism as the false consciousness of bourgeois women and the opposition of many progressive men.

Just as Millard could not turn to the male CPUSA leaders, she also could not turn to the few groups still speaking out for women's equality in the late 1940s and early 1950s to support her case. "Fem-inism" was a term claimed by the upper-class National Woman's

Party (NWP), an organization that the Communist Party thought to be drastically misinformed about the origins of women's oppression. Indeed, the leaders of the NWP were highly educated, upper-class, white women. The NWP never tried to recruit working-class women, and instead strictly focused on passing the Equal Rights Amendment (ERA). Communist women opposed the ERA because they thought it would undercut important labor protections for female workers.[15] Despite their opposing views of how to emancipate women, both organizations were working in a general climate of antifeminism because of the postwar glorification of the domestic ideal.[16]

As a result of the large-scale dismissal of feminism as bourgeois, CPUSA leaders probably thought they were doing enough to placate the women in their Party at the beginning of 1948. Leaders likely never agreed that supporting a fight against women's oppression was a high priority for the CPUSA; however, as soon as the phrase "male chauvinism" appeared in the party presses, communist women embraced it vigorously.[17] One reader wrote on the letters page, "We women would like to see some study of male chauvinism in the United States. And we would like a weekly or bi-weekly column in the Sunday *Worker* which would discuss the concrete examples of male chauvinism and the Marxist solutions to them. And don't put it on the 'Woman's Page,'" she requested. "Print it where men will read it too."[18] Letters to the editor began to appear for the first time in the newspapers asking for help with issues of sexism.

Of course, communist women could never fully stamp out male supremacy, but through their publications, they did make important contributions that sustain activism for women's equality in a time period largely assumed to have no feminist activity. In the next section, I analyze Millard's pamphlet illustrating how she wove a transnational narrative to enact her argument against domestic containment.

SPHERES OF INFLUENCE: DOMESTIC CONTAINMENT AND TRANSNATIONALISM

In 1975, Henri Lefebvre famously called for a critique of space, suggesting that social space is never neutral, but is ideological, implicated in power arrangements, and conditioned by society's modes of production. "Capitalism and neocapitalism," he argued, "have produced abstract space, which includes the 'world of commodities,' its 'logic,' and its worldwide strategies, as well as the power of money and that of the political state."[19] Specifically, Lefebvre saw the space of capitalism as founded on networks of banks, malls, business centers, and airports. These spaces gave rise to discourses that valorized relationships built on exchange.[20] Likewise, places and spaces were structured by power relationships for Millard. Millard appraised the way capitalism also constructed the American home, which was supported by prominent discourses advocating female-driven consumption. She then questioned the stability of the gendered constructs that provided the foundation for the capitalist, Cold War home. Millard anticipated the intersection of capitalism, space, and ideals of gender as they circumscribed appropriate behavior for American women.

Such a critique was, as Lefebvre would later recognize, undeniably a risky undertaking. The American postwar home was the bulwark of stability in uncertain times. To Americans, communism was a global and national contagion to be contained, just as the home, and representations of it, conditioned acceptable behavior for women and men, cultivating a middle-class ethos. "In the domestic version of containment, the 'sphere of influence' was the home," historian Elaine Tyler May argues. "Within its walls, potentially dangerous social forces of the new age might be tamed, where they could contribute to the secure and fulfilling life to which postwar women and men aspired. Domestic containment was bolstered by a powerful political culture that rewarded its adherents and marginalized its detractors."[21] And this was the problem for Millard. Women were chastised for working outside the home, but for the working class, economic necessity drove such arrangements. The Cold War had a multifaceted impact on rhetoric, however. Social and cultural discourses were turning inward, to the home, just as dominant political discourses were turning outward, to a focus on the international and transnational. Millard also turned outward in her pamphlet, performing a spatial critique by rejecting domestic confinement and inserting women into political discourse through the transnational vision of her brand of communist feminism.

Millard opened her spatial critique by illustrating the taboos against women working outside of the home and concluded that popular representations of the space of the factory gendered women workers as masculine.[22] She also explained how understandings of domestic containment were even more problematic for working-class women. "For women there is generally reserved a quieter, more veiled kind of lynching," she wrote. "Many of the thirty-eight million American housewives are doomed to circumscribed, petty lives, to the stultification of whatever abilities and interests, outside of motherhood, they may have had. Especially is this true of women of the working class and farmers' wives, who cannot afford maids and household conveniences."[23] Using language that clearly evoked constricted space and suffocation through the dramatic and racialized image of lynching, Millard critiqued the powerlessness of housewives to grow in roles other than mothers, even as her narrative upheld a vision of the white nuclear family that could be liberated by an imagined Black maid. She also portrayed the class limitations facing working-class women who could not buy appliances to ease their domestic labor. In contrast, she described her end goal of socialism in the language of openness and opportunity for women, free from the containment of the house. "The day will come," she claimed, "when it will no longer be necessary for any woman to refer to herself as merely a 'housewife.' And when that day comes there will open out before women such a future of accomplishment and satisfaction as we can only dream of today."[24]

Millard refused to be contained in the home and broke the walls of domestic confinement by rhetorically moving through international space. This movement was a significant component of Millard's vision of female emancipation, for as social geographer Yi-Fu Tuan writes, "Spaciousness is closely associated with the sense of being free. Freedom implies space; it means having the power and enough room in which to act."[25] Seeking freedom, Millard used her descriptions of the Soviet Union as a way to enact the power to move through international space, far away from the restrictions of the American home. In the first part of the pamphlet, she located herself primarily in the United States. There, Millard described problems facing American housewives and narrated a history of American women's activism for equality that focused on Elizabeth Cady Stanton and Susan B. Anthony. In the next section, Millard wove a transnational narrative based in the Soviet Union to see what women's emancipation could look like, all the while critiquing the way capitalism constructed the U.S. home.

As she moved through the space of the Soviet Union, Millard crafted a transnational narrative through her detailed descriptions of the nurseries, the factories with intercom systems that allowed working mothers to talk to their children in daycare, and the schools where women were increasingly being educated.[26] She also depicted relationships in the Soviet home. Millard grounded her account in illustrations of these specific places, and she rhetorically traveled from one to another, enjoying the freedom allegedly granted to women in the Soviet Union. She began her story in the Soviet home, stating, "No Soviet woman is forced to work if she would rather stay home and live on her husband's wages (and many still do); but it is a basic principle of Soviet thought that woman must assume responsibility outside of the home if she is to realize all her potentialities as citizen, wife, mother and creative individual."[27] Women in the Soviet Union enacted citizenship by moving outside the home. Staying in the domestic space was an option, but it was not the only option. Millard's declarative, matter-of-fact tone and her familiarity with "basic principles of Soviet thought" suggested a transnational awareness that could break through containment.[28]

After she described the Soviet home, Millard located herself in the factory, where she claimed Soviet women enjoyed equality. "The Soviet Union," she wrote, "has established a network of aids to women, and especially mothers, that is without parallel in other countries. Most notable are the factory and neighborhood nurseries that, staffed by trained specialists, care for the children while their mothers work."[29] Again, with attention to detail, Millard continued to illustrate how two-way public address systems and joint holiday celebrations allowed working mothers to see their children, and she even described the children as "happy" and "healthy," suggesting that she had actually been inside the factories and seen the children herself.[30] She then explained how easily accessed such facilities were, unlike the conveniences in the United States, which were too expensive for the working class. These descriptions positioned Millard within the factories as she constructed her transnational narrative.

Next, Millard moved to the schools. "Every factory and farm has become an education center; trade unions offer courses on a variety of subjects right on the spot, and have built up a vast network of factory libraries and study clubs. As a result, women who were 80 per cent illiterate in 1917 already by 1939 formed half the student body in higher institutions of learning."[31] Mirroring the schedule of movement in a workday, Millard then returned to the Soviet home to describe how the changes in work and education promoted a more fulfilling family life. She suggested that Soviet marriages were based on equality and mutual love instead of dependence or economic need. She also noted that prostitution had been eradicated because women were "more intelligent mothers and more interesting companions as wives."[32] With these rhetorical movements and her rich descriptions, Millard performed her argument that women were more emancipated in the Soviet Union and rejected the contained, domestic space of the American home. In addition, by highlighting Soviet women's ability to mother and work at the same time, she undermined the stability of the separate spheres doctrine and instead suggested that the factory and the home, the public and private, could and should be blended. She described a new mode of inhabiting space that recognized the intersection of class and gender.

The equality and cooperation in the Soviet household laid bare the instability of the American home. Countering discourses that the American home was the beacon of stability in a rapidly changing and dangerous world, Millard claimed that, in fact, the competitive stress of the capitalist system strained relationships in the home. "In America today," she stated, "one out of three marriages ends in divorce, a startling fact which has been the subject of innumerable magazine articles and sermons. But no moral preachments can disguise the fact that it is socialist Russia that is establishing new highs in family stability while capitalist America is witnessing an increasing breakdown in family relationships." Millard continued, "The conclusion is unavoidable that the one is a reflection of the cooperative relationships that permeate the whole of socialist society, while the other mirrors the insecurity and corrosive stresses of our competitive system."[33] Millard strategically *displaced* the American, capitalist home as the central locus of stability by linking it with capitalist competition and *replaced* it with the Soviet, socialist home, which she argued was based on equality. Taking advantage of the American focus on stability, she suggested that, contrary to fears, only when equality was achieved for women would the home be truly strong. It is important to underscore, however, that Millard stopped short of altogether rejecting domesticity and childrearing as paths for women, advocacy that may have been too radical for both 1940s America and American communists. Instead, she suggested that happy, stable homes could only be achieved in a socialist system that allowed a blending of work life and home life.

Millard replaced the American capitalist home with a different vision of habitation that focused not on consuming, dominantly represented as the duty of the middle-class housewife, but on producing. She foregrounded Soviet women as satisfied producers, instead of merely consumers:

> We can see, for instance, that it is the delimiting of women to the role of wife and mother that is responsible for the superficial values thrown at us from every page of women's magazines. After a hundred years of the modern struggle for women's equality Soviet women are urged in their magazines to educate themselves and grow, to fulfill their production quotas and thus add to the happiness and well-being of the nation; while judging from the number of square feet given over to the subject in every issue of the *Ladies*

Home Journal, the highest ideal of American womanhood is
smooth, velvety, kissable hands.[34]

In this passage, Millard critiqued the feminine gender ideal presented
to American women in the popular media as trivial. At the same
time, she addressed the equation of consumption with appropriate
femininity and of the common representation of Soviet women as
masculinized workhorses for the state. She drew the line at *degree* of
consumption, suggesting that Soviet women still consumed beauty
products, but just to a lesser extent. In this way, she sought to offset
the prevailing narrative that there were no consumer products or
attractive women in the Soviet Union, which would have rendered
Soviet women a poor model for emulation by American women who
contemplated joining the CPUSA. "It goes without saying," Millard
countered, "that all normal women, including Soviet women want
to be as attractive as possible and also to achieve a happy marriage;
but the tremendous over-emphasis on superficial attractiveness in
our society results in such a reversal of values that a woman's interests and abilities and achievements become the least important
things about her."[35] Even in the CPUSA, then, the critique of wom-
en's roles could only go so far: The space Millard invited women to
inhabit was still predicated upon normative gender expression and
heterosexual marriage.

Millard performed an educated worldliness in her narrative.
Because of her free traversing of international space, Millard cul-
tivated a transnational ethos seen in her attention to the relationship between global forces and the home.[36] A transnational, writes
Eithne Luibhéid, is someone who acts, thinks, feels, and develops
identities within social networks connected to two or more societ-
ies simultaneously.[37] As a result, transnationalism implies a way of
inhabiting space markedly different from the woman confined in
the home, and Millard embraced intersections between the Soviet
Union and the United States based in freedom of movement. To
stress the importance of uninhibited movement, she wrote, "It is
only to the degree that woman has been excluded from the productive process and from the larger activities and problems outside the
home that she finds difficulties in expressing herself as a human,
thinking person."[38] Women grew in sophistication and intelligence
by being active outside the home, Millard claimed, underscoring the
importance of emancipation.

The culmination of her transnational narrative opened an oppositional space for the cultivation of the communist feminist
subjectivity far from bourgeois feminist subjectivity. Millard did

not completely repudiate the home or a vision of domesticity for women. However, her strategy of displacing the home by exposing it as a site of capitalist consumption and replacing it with a vision of the home as a site of equality and production allowed her to reject the gender relations of male breadwinner and female homemaker, granting women more options. She negotiated the disempowered status of women who found themselves outside society's prescribed role and rejected domestic containment by giving herself the authority to speak about the Soviet Union as an eyewitness. By moving through the space of the Soviet Union that she rhetorically created, she performed the emancipation of women that she sought. Moreover, she created distance between herself and the bourgeois NWP by grounding the space for women's emancipation in a transnational sensibility.[39]

Unique in its transnational orientation, Millard's strategy was both necessary and risky. By grounding feminism outside the borders of the United States, she attempted to avoid cooptation by the NWP. By destabilizing the American home, she critiqued capitalism in line with her communist ideology. Despite her trenchant critique of the intersections of capitalist space, gender, and popular culture, Millard's strategy invites consideration of the ways in which she may have reinscribed a white, middle-class ethos through her transnational performance. In the next section, I consider how Millard tempered the elitism of her identity by performing transnational femininity.

"GIRLS WHO WEAR GLASSES": TRANSNATIONAL FEMININITY AND THE MARXIST SUBJECT

While Millard used a transnational narrative to escape the confines of the feminized American home, American political leaders trumpeted tough masculinity to defeat communism. Millard had to negotiate dominant representations of appropriate gender roles both in her home country and in her host country. She confronted portrayals of masculinized Soviet women laboring in male jobs and visions of the spinster feminist in the United States. To compound these difficulties, Millard was arguing for a communist feminism in a Marxist-Leninist tradition that largely failed to recognize femininity, seeing women as just one more group to be used in building the communist state, which idealized a masculine citizen worker. Her arguments had to be amenable to male communist leaders, female communists, and female noncommunists, who were the target of the massive 1948 recruiting drive. Millard sought to counter dominant media portrayals of communists and feminists by performing femininity, but she disassociated femininity from consumerism and, again, grounded it in transnationalism.[40] She adopted a teacherly ethos, which enabled her to model an authoritative femininity not at odds with communism or broader American culture. The intersection of this gendered persona with a transnational sensibility was the oppositional space needed for the creation of a communist feminist subjectivity.

Millard performed transnational femininity by first portraying herself as the sophisticated traveler who had seen the world outside U.S. borders. Millard structured her pamphlet in a problem/cause/solution format and held up the Soviet Union as the solution to women's oppression. Millard's transnational narrative, based in the Soviet Union and described in the previous section of this chapter, also fit into her larger performance of emancipated femininity. The locations in which she placed herself included homes, schools, and nurseries.[41] Thus, Millard focused her account on spaces already inhabited by women. She narrated views of factories and farms as well, but only in the company of Soviet women who had allegedly achieved equality in these arenas. Her transnational travels did not include meetings with any political leaders or tours of spaces of government activity. Millard's primary focus was on the Soviet home, where she read magazines and saw plays, describing one such Russian play where the heroine gave up her medical studies to get married but was soon divorced when her husband found a more interesting woman with a job. "The happy ending came only when the heroine went back to her career," Millard wrote. "The Hollywood thesis in reverse."[42] Thus, although Millard rhetorically placed herself in the Soviet Union in her pamphlet, the sites she occupied were primarily domestic, and she maintained her femininity by locating herself in traditionally female spaces. Moreover, her descriptions of factories were situated within the context of child care and motherhood. Millard complicated the strict separation between public and private by suggesting that the domestic sphere and the workplace could be one.

Millard demonstrated the potential compatibility between femininity and communism by granting herself feminine authority through a teacherly ethos. This performance not only made the educated superiority she enacted legible, it also empowered a performance of femininity grounded in production rather than consumption. Teaching had long been a career path open to women, and educating the sons of the nation to take over as leaders of the next generation had been seen as one of the most important duties of

American mothers. Millard performed her teacherly, feminine ethos by using simple, declarative statements, asking questions to gently guide her reader, and using history and communist theory as lessons for the future she sought to craft. The pamphlet often reads as an informative history lesson about women in the Soviet Union and the radical nature of historical activism for woman's rights. For example, Millard introduced her reader to the importance of the year 1848 by pointing to historical struggles for labor and the first woman's rights convention in Seneca Falls.[43] Indeed, Millard claimed that the woman's suffrage movement was revolutionary and "full of meaning for us today." However, she stated, "we have all but forgotten this struggle and the people who led it."[44] By noting this lapse in historical memory, Millard set herself up to serve as a teacher and inform her audience of these struggles. Moreover, her reliance on statistics, religious doctrine, the dictionary, and myriad magazines and newspapers for evidence lent to the pamphlet a sophisticated, educated, girls-wearing-glasses tone, one that would be crafted by an experienced teacher.

Millard's pamphlet, of course, was not geared to an audience of school-age children seeking information about communism. Nonetheless, the teacherly ethos she adopted likely made her poignant critiques of men in the progressive movement seem culturally appropriate and feminine without being too harsh and feminist. Millard's matter-of-fact tone made her critiques of communist men and women seem like simple corrections to misguided children.[45] For example, she stated, "A man who does half of the household chores after he and wife have come home from work will not feel that he is doing his wife a favor; for equality cannot be given as a favor but only recognized as a fact."[46] Thus, Millard's cultivation of a teacherly ethos allowed her to access femininity without reducing it to consumerism and granted her power over progressive leaders by claiming the historical and theoretical knowledge to correct and teach them like the naughty boys they were. Millard was clear and direct without oversimplifying, and she focused her attention on informing her audience about the idealized community in Russia. As a result, she performed what I have called transnational femininity. Coupled with the teacherly ethos, Millard struggled to create a femininity in communism that could pave the way for women's emancipation.

Implicated in Millard's gender performance were representations of the masculinity of Soviet women, American feminists, and female consumers. She tempered the radical nature of her critique of the progressive movement's failures to address women's concerns with her feminine, teacherly persona that empowered her as a feminine agent without requiring her to be a consumer in the postwar economy. Moreover, the intersectional and transnational identity she performed granted her the authority to speak about the Soviet Union as an imagined community to be emulated. She described scenes of domestic bliss in Russia like a traveler writing in a journal, as someone who had been there. Millard performed and modeled a femininity not completely at odds with communism, an important step in articulating ideas that would challenge many men in the Communist Party.

CONCLUSION

Exploring the gendered and spatial contexts of communism, consumerism, and feminism in postwar America illuminates otherwise ignored dynamics of the struggle to sustain women's activism during a time when the domestic ideal was glorified. It reveals that pamphlets and books debated much more than just who was supposed to do the housework and raise the children. Rather, such discourses imbricated concerns about containing communism, consumption of household goods, class, movement, and femininity. In her 1948 pamphlet, Millard performed her key arguments by weaving a transnational narrative based in the Soviet Union and enacting a teacherly ethos that granted her the authority to speak on behalf of confined women while chastising chauvinistic progressive men. Combining theory and education, she opened up space where she invited progressive women to inhabit a communist feminist identity far from representations of the bourgeois feminists in the NWP. This identity depended on an intersectional understanding of the ways in which multiple facets of postwar life, including capitalism, oppressed women.

Despite the overall positive reception of Millard's pamphlet, Millard's intersectional approach neglected important aspects of the battle for women's equality. "To deepen and extend the role of Negro women in the struggle for peace and for all interests of the working class and the Negro people means primarily to overcome the gross neglect of the special problems of Negro women," Millard's comrade Claudia Jones asserted. "This neglect has too long permeated the ranks of the labor movement generally, of Left-progressives, and also of the Communist Party."[47] Jones's essay appeared in *Political Affairs* in 1949, partly as a response to Millard. Despite Millard's insightful critique of language, religion, popular culture, and their contributions to female oppression, she said little about the unique disempowerment facing Black women. Indeed, she completely neglected questions of how or whether Black women's oppression differed qualitatively and quantitatively from white women's oppression.[48] As Millard sought to break women out of the Cold War, capitalist house, she never considered the question of who would do the domestic labor if women were not there. Jones highlighted the likely answer: Black women employed as domestic servants. In her essay, she considered the implications of domestic containment on Black women and revised Millard's racialized narrative of white housewife containment. Moreover, Jones engaged the unique popular media representations of Black women that, combined with class prejudice, hindered their ability to find employment and provide for their families. Jones took up Millard's call to contribute more theory and understanding of women under communism. As historian and archivist Kate Weigand notes, "in the racist and sexist environment of the United States in the 1950s, the Communist Party became a center of writing and thought about the experiences of African American women and a source of support for some of their efforts."[49] With the publication of Jones's response in *Political Affairs*, the Party slowly moved toward a more sophisticated consideration of the intersections of class, gender, *and* race.

Beyond the omission of race, however, Millard's pamphlet invites scholars to consider some of the ways intersecting oppressions are experienced spatially. The confluence of gendered and classed narratives about women in Cold War America was maintained and profoundly experienced by many women in a very specific vision of the home. As historian Anne Enke writes, "Despite post–World War II gains in women's social and political status, everyday spaces continued to structure and naturalize racist hierarchies and gender and sexual norms."[50] Moreover, Millard's focus on the transnational illustrates the ways in which creative geographies can be a means for contesting oppression based in the usual trifecta of gender, class, and race. But even a transnational rhetorical journey to the Soviet Union was constrained by the need of the traveler to occupy a socially acceptable location for white women in ethos and tone. As a result, even as space provided one means to contest intersecting oppressions, it too came with limitations. Ultimately, though, as scholars have begun to recognize, space both structures and intersects with other interlocking systems of oppression.[51] Millard's intersectional analysis was preceded by Wollstonecraft's early calls for women's education and succeeded by Jones's and Davis's attention to Black women's worlds of labor. The strategy of highlighting and attempting to untangle lived experiences of oppression has a long history in feminist rhetoric, and Millard's creative negotiation of the spaces between transnationalism and the American home introduced the CPUSA to intersectionality in a way that Party leaders took seriously. Indeed, even as the CPUSA crumbled under the weight of McCarthyism in the 1950s, the Party presses churned out more pamphlets and newspaper articles encouraging their membership to contemplate the place of women in society and the class struggle, and the rank and file responded with vigorous debate on these intersections.

NOTES

I thank Susan Zaeske, Robert Glenn Howard, Sarah Meinen Jedd, Karma Chávez, and Cindy Griffin for their insightful comments on this chapter.

1. As cited in Clara Zetkin, *Lenin on the Woman Question* (New York: International Publishers, 1919), 15.

2. Betty Millard, *Woman Against Myth* (New York: International Publishers, 1948), 21.

3. Kate Weigand, *Red Feminism: American Communism and the Making of Women's Liberation* (Baltimore: Johns Hopkins University Press, 2001), 64. Millard's pamphlet was serialized in the Marxist magazine *The New Masses* beginning in December 1948. I use the longer, pamphlet version released later that year for my analysis.

4. Cindy L. Griffin, "Web of Reasons: Mary Wollstonecraft's *A Vindication of the Rights of Woman* and the Re-Weaving of Form," *Communication Studies* 47 (1996): 275.

5. See especially Claudia Jones, "An End to the Neglect of the Problems of the Negro Woman," *Political Affairs* 28, no. 6 (June 1949): 51–67.

6. Angela Y. Davis, *Women, Race, and Class* (New York: Vintage, 1983), 94.

7. Harvey Klehr and John Earl Haynes, *The American Communist Movement: Storming Heaven Itself* (New York: Twayne, 1992). See also David A. Shannon, *The Decline of American Communism: A History of the Communist Party of the United States since 1945* (New York: Harcourt Brace, 1959), 91–95; Joseph R. Starobin, *American Communism in Crisis, 1943–1957* (Berkeley: University of California Press, 1972), 113.

8. For a look at the Party's activism along these lines, see Randi Storch, *Red Chicago: American Communism at its Grassroots, 1928–1935* (Urbana: University of Illinois Press, 2007).

9. See Geoffrey R. Stone, *Perilous Times: Free Speech in Wartime from the Sedition Act of 1798 to the War on Terrorism* (New York: Norton, 2004), 396. As Stone notes, the communist leaders who were arrested in 1948 were not charged with actually attempting to overthrow the government or even

with advocating the overthrow of government, but instead with "conspiring to advocate" government overthrow.

10. Harry Schwartz, "Russia Itself Reveals Russian Weakness," *New York Times Magazine*, April 25, 1948, 12.

11. Richard Nixon and Soviet Premier Nikita Khrushchev's 1959 "Kitchen Debate" is another example of the centrality of the American home and capitalism in Cold War discourse. See K. A. Cuordileone, *Manhood and American Political Culture in the Cold War* (New York: Routledge, 2005), 181–182; Nancy F. Cott, *Public Vows: A History of Marriage and the Nation* (Cambridge, MA: Harvard University Press, 2000), 197.

12. Gertrude Samuels, "Why Russian Women Work Like Men," *New York Times Magazine* November 2, 1958, 22.

13. Weigand, *Red Feminism*, 80.

14. Harold B., "Fight for Women's Rights Impractical," *Worker*, June 13, 1948, 9.

15. Elizabeth Gurley Flynn, "Life of the Party," *Worker*, April 9, 1939. This article is also reproduced in Rosalyn Fraad Baxandall, *Words on Fire: The Life and Writing of Elizabeth Gurley Flynn* (New Brunswick, NJ: Rutgers University Press, 1987), 215–217.

16. Leila J. Rupp and Verta Taylor, *Survival in the Doldrums: The American Women's Rights Movement, 1945 to the 1960s* (Columbus: Ohio State University Press, 1990), 18.

17. Weigand, *Red Feminism*, 80.

18. "Asks Articles on Male Chauvinism," *Daily Worker*, January 28, 1948.

19. Henri Lefebvre, *The Production of Space*, trans. Donald Nicholson-Smith (Cambridge, MA: Blackwell, 1991), 53.

20. Lefebvre, *Production of Space*, 56.

21. Elaine Tyler May, *Homeward Bound: American Families in the Cold War Era* (New York: Basic Books, 1988), 14. See also Cuordileone, *Manhood and American Political Culture*, xx.

22. Millard, *Woman Against Myth*, 12.

23. Millard, *Woman Against Myth*, 5.

24. Millard, *Woman Against Myth*, 12.

25. Yi-Fu Tuan, *Space and Place: The Perspective of Experience* (Minneapolis: University of Minnesota Press, 1977), 52.

26. Millard, *Woman Against Myth*, 18.

27. Millard, *Woman Against Myth*, 18.

28. It is unclear whether Millard had ever been to the Soviet Union or if she just found information about the Soviet Union in newspapers and other reports. Negative reports of life in the Soviet Union abounded in outlets like the *New York Times*. More positive tellings appeared frequently in the *Worker*, *Daily Worker*, and other communist publications. My hunch is that she had not traveled there because she was not a high-ranking member of the Party. This fact, of course, does not prevent her from weaving a travelogue rhetorically.

29. Millard, *Woman Against Myth*, 18.

30. Millard, *Woman Against Myth*, 19.

31. Millard, *Woman Against Myth*, 19.

32. Millard, *Woman Against Myth*, 19–20.

33. Millard, *Woman Against Myth*, 20–21.

34. Millard, *Woman Against Myth*, 21.

35. Millard, *Woman Against Myth*, 21–22.

36. See Jonathan Corpus Ong, "The Cosmopolitan Continuum: Locating Cosmopolitanism in Media and Cultural Studies," *Media Culture Society* 31 (2009): 449–467.

37. See Eithne Luibhéid, *Entry Denied: Controlling Sexuality at the Border* (Minneapolis: University of Minnesota Press, 2002), xxiv.

38. Millard, *Woman Against Myth*, 22.

39. Millard exalted the Soviet Union as a place of equality and emancipation for women, but a note is required about the CPUSA's treatment of the Soviet Union under Joseph Stalin. Despite the Party's reverence for the Soviet Union, conditions in the country and its surrounding regions were quite horrible. Instead, during the late 1930s, Stalin launched the Great Terror to purge the Soviet Communist Party of those accused of terrorism or treachery, who were sent to work camps to die of starvation or executed. More than 680,000 were executed from 1937–1938, and 1.3 million were in work camps in 1939. In addition, there was widespread famine and violence, which Stalin attempted to camouflage by importing grain and barring visitors. Nikita Khrushchev exposed Stalin's crimes in a 1956 speech that shook the CPUSA to its core. Beforehand, they had either not known or not noticed Stalin's dictatorial regime. My intention is certainly not to excuse Stalin's crimes or the CPUSA for its tacit consent to them. Thus, Millard's claims about the Soviet Union should not be taken as the objective reality of life in Russia, but understanding how she constructs the Soviet Union is useful to unpack her transnational feminist project. For more on Stalin's crimes, see Shelia Fitzpatrick, *The Russian Revolution* (New York: Oxford University Press, 2008), 165–166; Glenda Gilmore, *Defying Dixie: The Radical Roots of Civil Rights, 1919–1950* (New York: Norton, 2008), 148–154.

40. I understand gender to be performative, in line with Judith Butler's notion of gender performativity. See "Performative Acts and Gender Constitution: An Essay in Phenomenology and Feminist Theory," in *Performing Feminisms: Feminist Critical Theory and Theatre*, ed. Sue-Ellen Case (Baltimore: Johns Hopkins University Press, 1990), 519–531; Judith Butler, *Undoing Gender* (New York: Routledge, 2004).

41. Millard, *Woman Against Myth*, 19.

42. Millard, *Woman Against Myth*, 20.

43. Millard, *Woman Against Myth*, 4.

44. Millard, *Woman Against Myth*, 4.

45. Millard, *Woman Against Myth*, 13.

46. Millard, *Woman Against Myth*, 23.

47. Claudia Jones, "An End to the Neglect of the Problems of the Negro Woman," *Political Affairs* 28, no. 6 (June 1949): 51.

48. Weigand, *Red Feminism*, 101.

49. Weigand, *Red Feminism*, 107.

50. Anne Enke, *Finding the Movement: Sexuality, Contested Space, and Feminist Activism* (Durham, NC: Duke University Press, 2007), 6.

51. For more on the importance of space, see Enke, *Finding the Movement*; Edward W. Soja, *Thirdspace: Journeys to Los Angeles and Other Real-and-Imagined Places* (Malden, MA: Blackwell, 1996); John Howard, *Men Like That: A Southern Queer History* (Chicago: University of Chicago Press, 1999); George Chauncey, *Gay New York: Gender, Urban Culture, and the Making of the Gay Male World, 1890–1940* (New York: Basic Books, 1994), 23; Nan Alamilla Boyd, *Wide Open Town: A History of Queer San Francisco to 1965* (Berkeley: University of California Press, 2003), 14.

Chapter 8

Essentialism, Intersectionality, and Recognition: A Feminist Rhetorical Approach to the Audience

Sara L. McKinnon

Feminist rhetorical scholars of the past forty years have mobilized around the challenge of women being seen as rightful public subjects with valid political claims.[1] Many feminist rhetoricians argue that this problematic exists because patriarchal social structures, maintained through the deployment of gendered discourses, keep women bound to the private, the personal, the quiet, and to their bodies.[2] Others scholars call for a revisioning of the ways we examine women's rhetoric by questioning differences in style that permit women's speech to be received and heard in the public.[3] This work, while important, continues to center the voices of white, upper and middle-class, professional-status, heterosexual women as the figures evidencing women's potential access, while marginally acknowledging the ways race, class, gender, sexuality, ability, age, and nationality intersect and constitute, in dramatic ways, the recognition that different women receive as public subjects with public voices.

Numerous scholars in the field have been vocal in critiquing such assumptions.[4] Recognizing the ways mainstream rhetorical criticism and white feminist rhetorical critics deploy women of color to prop up projects of normativity, Olga Idriss Davis calls Black women to cultivate a "Black women's standpoint in rhetorical criticism" that will "challenge academic hegemony."[5] To do this she calls Black women scholars to "serve as a keeper of rhetorical culture by revealing the long-standing diversity of ideas, culture, and aesthetics of Black women's intellectual tradition and the way in which Black women have constructed theory and its practice in their daily lives."[6] In addition to calling for the recognition and validation of women-of-color critics' voices, others demonstrate the need to expand the purview of what counts as a rhetorical text worthy of analysis.[7] This chapter contributes to this trajectory of loosening rhetoric's parameters by offering a framework for exploring the power of the third component of rhetoric's triad—the audience—in instituting conditions for access. Specifically, I develop here an intersectional methodology for analyzing an audience's reliance on essentialist discourses when determining whose voices, bodies, and experiences should have access to material and discursive space in the public.

Inspired from the work of feminists of color and critical race scholarship, this methodology provides a way of reading discourses of essentialism intersectionally as they produce how subjects are recognized in the public. This framework offers feminist rhetoricians two resources. First, it provides a way of reading essentialism as it plays out in the audiencing of rhetorical subjects. Second, it draws attentiveness to the intersubjectivity between the speaking subject, the audience, and the historicity that renders these subjectivities significant and meaningful. To develop this framework, I first review feminist scholarship concerning essentialist discourses and then read this work through theories of recognition. I then demonstrate the framework's operation and utility with a short case study drawn from a recent U.S. asylum case. After working through the case study of the transnational space of the U.S. immigration courtroom, I conclude with thoughts about the import of this methodology of understanding audience and essentialism, and I consider how transnational attentiveness may move feminist rhetorical studies in the direction of radical intersectionality.

THE PROBLEM OF ESSENTIALISM

In her metatheoretical analysis of rhetoric's engagement with public sphere theory, Cindy L. Griffin illuminates how essentialist discourses are deployed to maintain boundaries around the public sphere as a site of deliberation intended for white, upper- and middle-class, heterosexual, property-owning men.[8] Essentialist discourses, which Griffin defines as discourses based on "fixed, unchanging characteristics that determine an individual's behaviors or actions," circulate to endow particular subjects with normalized and naturalized public subjectivity, while others struggle to gain access.[9] Griffin's work takes on the barriers imposed when gender is deployed in essentialist ways toward justifying the public as a space properly, or originally, intended for white male elites. She explains that essentialism grounds the historical formation of the public sphere and, consequently, these discourses determine what rhetorical subjects and acts will be recognized as public ones. Not only have scholars theorized the public as separate from the private, where certain subjects and topics are deemed appropriate to exist and to be spoken about, but they assume an "alienated" rhetor, one autonomous from other subjects who can thus deploy the tools of persuasion to affect other autonomous subjects and, ultimately, win.[10] Finally, Griffin explains that essentialist discourses are sedimented in the public through the perpetual reliance on dichotomies and hierarchy as the starting point for conceptualization and theorizing.[11] Read in connection, these strategies function to pigeonhole subjects and speech into boxes and then to render particular boxes as the natural, rightful way to be public and be in the public. While Griffin's critique privileges gender as a primary discursive construct, her point is strengthened when read alongside intersectional theories to understand the ways essentializing discourses of race, class, age, sexuality, nationality, or linguistic ability interlock, binding subjects to singular modalities of recognition that are often situated on the margins of public recognition.

Toward this end, Griffin's work finds support in the robust body of feminist writing that problematizes essentialism. These feminists address the dangers of such discourses as modalities for conceptualizing identities,[12] bodies,[13] and politics.[14] Not surprisingly, much of the concern with essentialism has been white feminists' use of it as a means to advance political and theoretical work in the name of "women" or "feminists." Angela Harris describes this as feminists' penchant for "the second voice," or the dogged inclination to "speak for all."[15] Chandra Talpade Mohanty's work provides a useful example of the "second voice" in practice through the analytical categories that scholars use in describing their research subjects. A label such as "the Third World Woman," she writes, "inadvertently produces Western women as the only legitimate subjects of struggle, while Third World women are heard as fragmented, inarticulate voices in (and from) the dark."[16] While Trina Grillo, Gayatri Spivak, and others explain that there is a time and place for essentialism, specifically when it is deployed strategically and is explicitly "considered temporary, and is contingent," for the most part essentialist discourses are "unconscious, self-protective, self-advancing," and hence dangerous.[17] This literature, in conversation with Griffin's explication of essentialism's boundary-keeping capacities, provides a rich theoretical platform from which to ground the development of this framework for analyzing the production and circulation of essentialist discourses in public spaces. Specifically, I offer recognition as a potential tool to the feminist rhetorician interested in understanding how subjects are audienced (in and through essentialist discourses) in public settings by authority figures endowed with the power to recognize certain subjects as fit for the public.

INTERSECTIONAL RECOGNITION

In a previous essay, I examined the power of the audience by focusing on the way asylum judges in U.S. courtrooms receive and evaluate non-U.S. women as public and political subjects.[18] Specifically, I argued that conventions of narrative rationality, good speech, and embodied affect are the mechanisms that asylum judges use when evaluating women's claims to political and public voice. A guiding, yet unstated, assumption in this work is that such evaluations happen within dynamics of recognition such that the action of audiencing is one not *of* another subject, but of audiencing *alongside, in relation,* or *bound* to that other subject. The nature of audiencing, through this formulation, means that the possibility to be seen as a subject with a public, political voice is contingent upon the audience who receives the subject and her claim, and the acknowledged intersubjectivity between the speaker and audience. Here, subjects are recognized as representatives of others (e.g., who they look like, act like, sound like, appear connected to), but their audience and their audience's positionality in systems of power also constitute them. It is this dynamic of recognition that I develop here toward understanding the ways women's claims are audienced through essentializing discourses to frame how they should (or should not) enter the public.

Audience has an important place in rhetorical studies as kin to rhetor and text in the tripartite of analysis. Yet rhetoricians have tended to pay more attention to the audience's showy sisters— rhetor and text—in developing theory. Michael Calvin McGee offers an important point of departure in theorizing the audience with his critique of rhetoric's uninterrogated use of "the people." Toward developing an alternative to the one-dimensional audience, he asks that we account for the audience's groundedness in "human society"[19] by engaging with the audience "meaningfully, not of one's own, but of *the people's* repertory of convictions, not as they ought to be, but as they are (or have been)."[20] This critique paved the way for scholars to cultivate attentiveness, by examining the rhetor's and text's power over, mindfulness to, or influence on the audience. For example, those aware of rhetoric's constitutive function now understand that the rhetor and text, in combination, have the power to induce a collective sense of identity in the audience.[21] Perelman and Olbrecht-Tyteca are perhaps most clear in the effort to derive a rhetorical theory that centers the audience. They instruct critics to recognize the two audiences, the universal and the particular, which are considered when developing a rhetorical text, and then to analyze the text according to both audiences.[22] Here, the success of the text is contingent on its mindfulness to the audience. Although this theory doesn't explain *how* the audience matters, it does acknowledge the audience's power to "license," in the words of Richard Schechner, rhetoric's legitimacy.[23]

As an intervention in these text- and rhetor-centered theorizings of audience, I begin with the perspective that the audience's ability to "license," to acknowledge, to grant access, should draw feminists back to the foundations of rhetoric's hallowed tripartite. Specifically, if we claim an investment in understanding the conditions of access for marginalized groups, then we should spend concerted effort working to examine the discourses and logics through which these conditions are materially implemented. Moreover, to complexly understand this power to license we must go beyond theorizing the audience and rhetor as autonomous subjects who speak to or hear each other. Instead, we must develop frameworks that illuminate how audiences use their own identities and histories as sieves to categorize, interpret, and acknowledge those who stand and speak in their presence.[24] Recognition necessitates that we do this work of decentering the singular subject in our thinking about subjectivity, insisting that we see the recognition of subjects as always, already multiple and intersecting.

Jointly with decentering the singular subject, recognition provides a means to understand the involvement of an audience's positionality in the rhetor's chances for recognition. When marginalized rhetors stand and speak before deciding audiences, they are read not just as themselves (and who they represent) but are recognized within a reflection of the audience. As Jessica Benjamin writes, when we stand before another subject we do not merely see an Other, but recognize an Other in relation to ourselves and the relationship between the two selves.[25] Recognition happens when the intersubjectivity of subjects is understood in so much as both subjects are recognized as full speaking subjects, and it is this ethical moment that so concerned Hegel, Lévinas, Buber, and others who theorize the moment of intersubjective awareness.[26]

Rather than idealizing this moment of recognition, though, I focus on what theories of recognition tell us about the *process* of recognizing subjects. For example, when recognition does not happen, one result is assimilation where the differences between the subjects are ignored toward privileging similarities. In this reduction of "difference to sameness"[27] the Other is only recognized for her or his sameness to the other subject. Importantly, it is this version of intersubjectivity that Mohanty and others critique when white Western feminists claim intersubjectivity by using rhetorical gestures of "like me" and "just like us" as support for their claims of unity in "global sisterhood."[28] In these moments, essentialist discourses that privilege the similarities between the subjects serve as the primary mechanisms that the audience uses in witnessing and evaluating the rhetor. Here, recognition does not happen because the audience is incapable of seeing past their own subjectivity enough to understand the differences between the subjects.

There are also moments when an audience discursively recognizes an Other as interminably and radically different from the subject him- or herself. In these moments there is a refusal to recognize the similarities that exist between the two subjects and the ways the subjects constitute each other. Essentialist discourses here serve to create distance between the audience and a speaker, subsequently justifying the audience's refusal to grant access. This use of difference is not new to women-of-color feminists who first insisted upon theory and politics that accounted for interlocking oppressions. As Audre Lorde writes:

> [I]t is not those differences between us that are separating us. It is rather our refusal to recognize those differences. . . . Too often, we pour the energy needed for recognizing and exploring difference into pretending those differences are insurmountable barriers, or that they do not exist at all. This results in a voluntary isolation, or false and treacherous connection.[29]

Lorde calls us to understand the relationality involved when we interact with people across lines of difference, for it is not that the differences between subjects cannot be recognized, but we often cannot get over ourselves enough to see them. Feminists who theorize difference demonstrate in their work numerous ways that difference is negotiated through an intersubjective encounter. Marsha Houston, for example, illuminates that white women in friendship with Black women often highlight the racial difference that exists between them by ignoring or minimizing the effect of race in their friendship.[30] The "boomerang perception" described by Elizabeth

Spelman is yet another strategy where a process of recognition is being deployed toward privileging difference. The subject highlights the difference of the Other in order to refigure the self at the center of the relationship.[31] Other strategies involve white people *center staging*, *deflecting*, *refusing*, and *analogizing* when conversations about difference happen.[32] These strategies, which all might fit under the umbrella of what María Lugones labels the "arrogant perception,"[33] focus on regaining a perceived loss of power, attracting attention back to white people, or calming white people's anxieties. Importantly, these strategies are deployed as white people see the Other through themselves, recognize the differences that exist between the subjects (and the ways they are complicit in the maintenance of those differences), and rather than engaging with the differences, some white people deploy essentialist discourses of the Other to deny the validity and legitimacy of the subject.

A final component that recognition offers to analyses of audience is a way of reading history in the rhetorical encounter between audience and subject. Historical mindfulness means paying attention to significant and formative events of the past, and more importantly, paying attention to the historicity between audience and subject. As Judith Butler advocates, recognition is always historically contingent:

> When we consider that the relations by which we are defined are not dyadic, but always refer to a historical legacy and futural horizon that is not contained by the Other, but which constitutes something like the Other of the Other, then it seems to follow that who we "are" fundamentally is a subject in a temporal chain of desire that only occasionally and provisionally assumes the form of the dyad.[34]

Butler explains that our interactions involve not only engagements with other subjects, but also engagements with who they were before and who we imagine them to be after us. Recognition is approached when subjects comprehend the ways that they, not only in the present, but also historically, and further, in the future, are intersubjectively bound. Although full recognition is only ever approached, subjects must move toward it with the understanding that when they recognize an Other through this frame, they approach recognition of self.

Deep historical groundedness is not a new approach for feminists who theorize difference within the context of relationships and relationality. Mab Segrest, for example, offers an analysis of white people's perpetual failure to have meaningful conversations about race and racism as constituted by the history of U.S. slavery that produced in whites "amnesia" and ultimately an inability to feel across racial differences.[35] As seen in Segrest's analysis, historicity becomes the third actor of influence in the framework that intermediates between the audience and Other. Put into play, this framework should call us to be attentive to that which lies outside of the rhetorical context proper but nonetheless intervenes; specifically the historical, geopolitical, and economic "legacies" and "horizons" that constitute one's subject position.[36] From this perspective, recognition means mindfulness to what is always (un)recognizable, never quite knowable, but always constituting the "Other of the Other."[37]

With this sense of what recognition offers as a theoretical foundation for analyzing processes of audiencing with intersectional attentiveness, in the next section, I develop this framework as a rhetorical method for reading processes of audiencing. I then use the analytic to understand the dynamics of audiencing in one woman's case for political asylum in the United States.

AUDIENCING IN U.S. ASYLUM CASES

Women's gender-based claims to U.S. asylum entail calls for rights and recognition. Asylum applicants ask for the right to remain in a country based on protections offered them through the United Nations Declaration of Human Rights. Importantly, the success of an asylum seeker hinges on the state's recognition of the applicant's subjectivity and the state's boundedness to the applicant. An asylum seeker claims a right when she enters a state and attests to her need for refuge. It happens when she states before an officer—"I have a right not to be removed from this country." The right is perhaps even more pronounced when the claimant proclaims the right after being placed in removal proceedings. In these instances the claimant is, in effect, saying, "I know that I have a right to stay in this country because my rights as a human were violated, so I give you permission to try and remove me."

The call to recognition manifests when the asylee stands before the court and testifies to her fear of persecution. Here, she asks the federal judge before her to confirm her experiences and subjectivity. In this moment, her claim of right rests with the audience. While some describe this moment of audiencing as a mere fact of interpreting the law, I argue that the process of evaluation is largely made up of the audience interpreting the subject against the audience's own subjectivity and imaginaries. And, as I demonstrate elsewhere, moments of recognition can either result in women claimants being seen as threatening, and thus in need of expungement, or as a discursive gift to the state's project of modernity.[38]

These speech acts are potentially threatening because the subject speaking before the state is a non-U.S. citizen and she is claiming a right to the state, which international human rights protocols grant her the power to do. Such claims serve to remind the state that it is never completely autonomous in its actions as sovereign and that its borders are porous and penetrable. These speech acts can also be threatening because of the particular experiences that gendered applicants call the United States to recognize as political. It is only in recent history that the United States has taken issue with gendered violence within the state. Violence such as intimate partner violence, rape, and forced sterilization were, in recent history, unacknowledged gendered abuses that the United States either sanctioned or ignored. Each claim to asylum on the basis of gender-based persecution calls state actors to reflect on the state's complicity in abuses against women. And with certain claims, the acts of persecution are not in the past, but they are acts of violence that women in the United States routinely negotiate. Thus, the recognition called for in these cases necessitates that the nation-state confront more than just the claim itself; the claimants demand deep interrogation of the state's historical and contemporary relationship to women.

Audiencing Sonia Maribel Juarez-Lopez

Guatemalan citizen Sonia Maribel Juarez-Lopez originally applied for affirmative asylum in 1990 on behalf of herself and her two sons. She was first interviewed in 1991, although the state appears to have lost record of that meeting. She did not hear anything from the United States again until 2002 when the Department of Homeland Security contacted her for yet another asylum interview, again for which the state could not produce records. Shortly thereafter, Juarez-Lopez and her two Guatemalan-born sons were placed in removal proceedings, which allowed her to make her asylum case, yet again, through the defensive asylum process before a judge. During this testimony, Juarez-Lopez claimed asylum on the basis that she was a member of a social group of "poor young women in Guatemala" who are "particularly vulnerable to rape and other forms of sex-based discrimination."[39] Juarez-Lopez also argued that the government of Guatemala had proven unwilling to protect young women from such violence.

To evidence her claim, Juarez-Lopez testified that a man began routinely raping her when she was twelve years old, at one point forcing her to live with him. Despite moving to live with her sister in a different city, the assaults continued, and throughout the course of the abuse, resulted in the two pregnancies of her boys. The man, de la Pena, also physically abused her and threatened her life if she either told her parents or notified the police.

During the asylum hearing, the judge repeatedly interrogated the feasibility of Juarez-Lopez's testimony. As reported in court accounts, "After Juarez-Lopez had given account of being raped for the first time at age 12 or 13, the judge asked, 'Now, how do I know this was not a consensual arrangement?'"[40] This question back to Juarez-Lopez completely ignores what she had revealed through testimony; instead, the question moves to the assumption that Juarez-Lopez's relationship with de la Pena was something all together different from what she had stated. The response serves as a gesture of erasure in that the judge never engages with the question of Juarez-Lopez's eligibility; instead, he moves immediately to the process of recognizing her subjectivity in determining whether she should gain protection.

Specifically, the question about the nature of her relationship with de la Pena begins the chain of recognizing Juarez-Lopez through essentialist discourses of difference that ultimately result in the denial of her case. Juarez-Lopez responded to this loaded question by insisting that she would not lie about such severe experiences, particularly in front of her children. However, the judge retorted, explicitly stating the imagined Other through which he came to recognize Juarez-Lopez as deceitful, opportunistic, and ineligible for asylum. The judge states in response:

> But, nevertheless, unfortunately on occasion people lie. And even in this country young ladies who had arrangements with other boyfriends later charged them with rape. And in some cases innocent boys are sent to jail because the lady changed her mind. How do I know that this is not the incident in your case?[41]

At first glance, the judge's comments here seem to be merely rude and misguided. Upon a secondary read, however, the logic of the judge's audiencing this claim at the intersections of gender, sexuality, race, age, class, and nationality becomes clear. Specifically, the judge deploys a chain of implicit and explicit discourses first relying on essentialist discourses at the axes of sexuality, gender, age, and race, and then later nationality and class, to resolutely recognize Juarez-Lopez as a subject of difference—one that is deceitful, opportunistic, and undeserving.

In his first two probes into the veracity of Juarez-Lopez's testimony, the judge interprets her as a subject of suspicion because of her past sexual involvement and (assumed) association with her persecutor. This happens first through an essentializing evaluation of young, brown, assumedly heterosexual women's reproductivity. In this case, that Juarez-Lopez was twelve years old when the abuse began makes it easy for the judge to audience her testimony through ageist discourses that frame young, brown, heterosexual women and girls as more interested in intimate relationships, having sex, and having children at a younger age than their white heterosexual counterparts.[42] These heterosexist and ageist assumptions about young, brown women's penchant for relationships and babies, when combined with sexist and racist discourses about targets of sexual assault, then serve as easy discursive vehicles for the judge to evaluate Juarez-Lopez as suspicious and hence ineligible. Second, these intersections render Juarez-Lopez as a suspicious subject when speaking about sexual violence. Research demonstrates that regardless of class and color, when asked for their perceptions of female targets of rape, male respondents "attribute heightened responsibility to her," and view women as "unlikable" and "as responsible for her participation."[43] When rape happens between acquaintances, the blame and assumed culpability placed on the target increase.[44] This happens largely because the accepted rape narrative in the United States prefigures a virginal white woman as the target and a man of color who is a stranger to the victim as the assailant.[45] When these narrative elements are not present, the logic of interpreting the sexual encounter takes a different form. As Sarah Gill explains:

> Society perceives certain victims of rape such as women of color, prostitutes, promiscuous women, and women who date Black men as being promiscuous and therefore less truthful because they do not fit the stereotype of the passive and chaste rape victim. As a result, when a woman assumed to be promiscuous is raped, people do not believe her: prosecutors are less likely to prosecute, jurors are less likely to convict, and judges are less likely to impose severe sentences.[46]

In Juarez-Lopez's situation, the judge's repeated questions about the nature of her relationship with de la Pena revolve around the repetition of the assault and the fact that she was forced to live with him for an extended time period. Read through essentializing discourses about nonvirginal, nonwhite young women who claim rape, Juarez-Lopez can only be given recognition as a subject of suspicion.

Importantly, even if de la Pena were a stranger who assaulted her one time, Juarez-Lopez might already be situated as a subject of suspicion because of the essentialist discourses that shape U.S. perceptions of the sexuality of women of color. Specifically, women of color are figured in the United States as naturally more "wild," "freaky," and inviting than white women.[47] Importantly, these constructions of Black and brown women's sexuality have a deep history in antebellum treatment of Black women in the United States as "property," and "flesh,"[48] the long history of women of color working outside the home,[49] and nineteenth-century exhibitions of Black and brown women's bodies as "exotic" and "overtly sexual."[50] Patricia Hill Collins and others make this point specifically about representations of Black heterosexual women's sexuality, but Hill Collins explains that this discourse of sexual abandon applies to brown women as well in the Western imagination: "Black sexuality need not be associated with bodies that have been racially classified as 'Negro,' 'mulatto,' or 'Black.' Western imaginations have long filled in the color, moving women from Black to White and back again depending upon the needs of the situation."[51] Importantly, these essentialist discourses about women of color play out in dramatic ways when women testify in U.S. courtrooms to sexual violence. For example, assailants in the rape cases of women of color not only received less severe sentences, but convictions also resulted less frequently than convictions in white women's cases.[52]

In addition to the abstract Other, the judge's logic of recognition conjures specific women who fit this frame of making up rape, such as the 1985 Crowell-Dotson rape trial in which Gary Dotson was convicted for raping Cathleen Crowell, who, five years after the conviction, confessed that she fabricated the rape as a story to tell her parents because she was worried that she might be pregnant.[53] Kristen Bumiller writes that while we have very few explicit examples of this false accusation narrative, the discourse of the shifty woman who falsely accuses men of rape doggedly remains in the United States as a primary modality through which U.S. Americans make sense of rape narratives. Toward evidencing this point, she recounts a story she overheard between two women after seeing the news that the three assailants in the Madison, Wisconsin, rape trials were acquitted. One woman expressed to the other, "'This is really too bad. When a girl makes a story up like this, it makes it more difficult for the woman who is *really* raped.'"[54] A discourse of deceit is certainly pervasive in constructions of women's sexuality,[55] but Bumiller points us to the process of litigation in rape trials as primarily purposed with rendering the female target's narrative and personhood questionable.[56] Here, the context of the courtroom, where a judge audiences Juarez-Lopez's testimony, then, comes to matter for the space holds the discursive weight of perpetually calling into question women's claims of rape and sexual assault.

As if doubt on account of Juarez-Lopez's gender, age, and racial identities together were not enough, the judge uses racist nationalistic discourses to interpret Juarez-Lopez as ineligible. He persistently probes once more:

> How do I know that you're not making up this story? That you're coming here as an economic refugee and you have no legal right to be here and you're making up a story so you can claim asylum? And there's reasons [sic] for you to misstate the facts, because you want to stay here and there's no other way that you can stay here unless you make up a story. Now, how do I know, do I have anything other than your statement that you claim that you were raped by this young man in Guatemala?[57]

That Juarez-Lopez fled Guatemala becomes yet another narrative element leading the judge to distrust Juarez-Lopez's claim of sexual violence. While thousands of Guatemalans were able to gain asylum in the United States around the time that Juarez-Lopez first applied for asylum, by 2004 the U.S. perception of Guatemalan refugees had changed. Instead of seeing migrants as potentially fleeing political insecurity, U.S. officials saw Guatemala as an impoverished country that sent many of its citizens north to the United States.[58] When Juarez-Lopez confirms her class status in Guatemala as "poor" through her social group membership, it gives the judge the evidence needed to further confirm the veracity of his suspicious reading. In this vein, Juarez-Lopez is not just a woman of color who should be distrusted because of her sexual history and race, but her nationality and class positionality also provide for him a possible motivation for Juarez-Lopez's deceit. In the face of being forcibly removed to an impoverished country or staying in the United States, one might see the necessity to lie. Furthermore, as a mother of two Guatemalan-born children and two U.S.-born children, she may lie to keep her family together. This narrative of immigrants as dishonest is based on an essentializng discourse about citizenship that locates "good" and "proper" citizenship as birthright citizenship (of white people), and it is based in a history of exclusionary U.S. immigration laws that forced immigrants to construct fictitious narratives and identities to gain access to the state.[59] As Daniel Valentine and John Knudsen reveal, "mistrust" is the primary modality through which refugees are received in U.S. publics.[60] The discourse of the deceitful migrant pervasively influences the ways immigration judges go about evaluating asylum cases.[61] Carol Bohmer and Amy Shuman explain that not only do judges believe they have the faculty to accurately distinguish a truthful story from a deceitful one, but that this process is a primary modality through which they audience claimants who stand and speak before them.[62] Juarez-Lopez, because of the intersections of discourses about sexuality, race, gender, age, nationality, and class, then comes to be easily audienced as dishonest about the persecution she experienced as rape.

Inevitably the judge denied Juarez-Lopez's claim to asylum because he did not find her claim credible or plausible. Of central importance in his reasoning is the absence of corroborating evidence to demonstrate that "Juarez-Lopez' relationship with de la Pena was not consensual."[63] Juarez-Lopez appealed the immigration judge's ruling to the Seventh Circuit Court of Appeals. In reviewing the case, the appellate justices were struck by the absence of an actual analysis of the case. Specifically, they acknowledge that in the judge's process of recognizing Juarez-Lopez, he could not move past what he immediately saw before him. The judge based his decision completely on his impression of Juarez-Lopez. The appellate court explains:

> In denying the family's application for asylum, the IJ [immigration judge] did not analyze whether the events Juarez-Lopez described could constitute past persecution or give rise to an objectively reasonable fear of future persecution. Instead, the IJ based his decision entirely on his finding that Juarez-Lopez was not credible.[64]

The judge believed so much in his powers to evaluate accurately that he never examined Juarez-Lopez's eligibility. The mere fact of her intersecting identities and her story rendered her intelligible and certainly unacceptable as a political subject.

CONCLUSION: HOW AUDIENCES ESSENTIALIZE

The purpose of this chapter was to develop a framework for analyzing the significance of essentialist discourses in audiences' recognition of political subjects. To do this I have read feminist theories about essentialism and intersectionality against those who theorize the process of recognition between subjects to generate a framework for evaluating how audiences rely on essentialist discourses to evaluate the subjects (and their speech) who stand before them.

Toward using this framework to analyze political speech and subjectivity, the first step is to look for the claims to right and recognition produced by marginalized subjects in the public sphere before audiences with the power to endow legitimacy to the subject and claim. In analyzing these types of speech and speaking subjects, the framework outlined above then calls us to examine the rhetorical moves that individuals make in seeking rights and recognition for their claims. This is done, specifically, by examining how an audience uses processes of recognition to evaluate the claim and claimant. This involves analyzing the specific responses and reactions that the audience offers, but also the story behind the response, in particular, the interlocking essentialist discourses that serve as the warrants to the audience's recognition. As evidenced in the case study above, marginalized people's calls for recognition and rights are often perceived, in some way, as threatening to the audience. The critic first analyzes the specific responses and reactions of the audience, and then addresses the foundational elements of the audience's interpretation. This means questioning the discourses and histories that intervene and intersect as the audience recognizes the individual who stands and speaks before them.

As the case study reveals, the judge in Juarez-Lopez's case relied primarily on interacting essentialist discourses of gender, race, age, sexuality, nationality, and class in recognizing the subject. The judge's perception of Juarez-Lopez as a threatening figure to U.S. ideals of proper speaking subjects set in motion the process of recognition. Once he perceived Juarez-Lopez as challenging, the judge then fixated on invalidating her claim. Although the judge might have turned to examine her eligibility, he was too concerned with her personhood and thus attended instead to the process of recognition in evaluating her eligibility. First, the judge deployed essentialist discourses to erase the legitimacy of Juarez-Lopez's claim to asylum. He then mobilized these discourses to reject her eligibility for political recognition. We see here that when essentialist discourses stand in as the primary mechanism used to recognize a subject, the only recognition available to that subject is what the audience's imagination affords.

As an analytic framework, this method for analyzing the audience's power to license is certainly constrained in its utility by the speech situation and the authority of the audience within that context. However, it is well suited for engaging the dynamics that play out in courtroom rhetorics where judges and juries are tasked with the power to determine guilt or innocence, freedom or restraint, and, for Juarez-Lopez in the case study above, protection or deportation. It also might be useful as a framework for examining moves of recognition that happen in the rhetorical interactions of *apologia*, truth and reconciliation commissions, and state hearings concerning civil and human rights. Although theories of the audience have come a long way in rhetorical studies, most research within the field still assumes an audience that is relatively passive, rational, and autonomous (unless the audience is a rhetorical critic who actively audiences in order to create a text). The enlightenment legacies of this audience exist, in part, because the field prefigures the rhetor as a heterosexual, middle- or upper-class, white man who is naturally endowed with the legitimacy to speak in public. I posit that a more concerted examination of the audience and the process of audiencing within courtrooms and these other rhetorical contexts may help to loosen the stronghold of these exclusionary assumptions on the ways we theorize rhetoric and rhetorical subjects.

This method also moves us closer to doing radical, rigorous intersectional work. Griffin and Chávez demonstrate in the introduction to this volume that one of the persistent ways feminist communication scholarship continues to elide rigorous intersectionality is by theorizing identities using stabilizing terminology, definitions, and descriptions. To do radical intersectional work we must recognize the fluidity, historicity, and contradictions present in the way subjects recognize themselves and others, but also remain attentive to that which exists outside commonly recognized borders. As this analysis of the immigration courtroom—a necessarily transnational space—suggests, one way we may remain attentive beyond borders is to understand our sites of inquiry as always, already transnational.

A transnational lens draws our attention to the ways people, objects, and discourse move across space and time, but it also highlights the transitory, mutable, in-flux nature of our subjects and objects of study. Transnational highlights "the *trans*versal, the *trans*actional, the *trans*lational, and the *trans*gressive aspects of contemporary behavior,"[65] while insisting that we see what we study as constituted by more than the mere "fiction" of the sovereign, singular nation-state.[66] Instead, transnational illuminates the significance of the "in-between slash (between the international and national),"[67] the interplay between states, and the tensions produced by movements of political, economic, and symbolic power across space and time. It shifts the analytic eye to the ways that states, global governance institutions, corporations, and human rights actors are invested in the work of regulating subjects for political, economic, and cultural projects. A transnational focus also enables scholars to theorize identities and rights as never merely what they appear to be on the surface, and never singularly in one place at any time. Instead, a transnational approach helps us to see that discourses and knowledge about identities and rights are on the move, circulating, popping up differently in localized contexts, reifying, and resisting state, capital, and sociocultural norms and conditions. Transnational attentiveness provides theoretical nuance to intersectionality in that it necessitates we start first with the questions of how intersectionality is produced differently in particular contexts, how it moves, and how it is constantly being renegotiated alongside contestations over global relations of power. While transnationality on its own does not ensure that our work will be radically intersectional, it leads us to ask the right type of questions—about invisibility, investments, structures of power, and movement—so that our work may *stand in the intersection* without reproducing the very essentializing discourses and normative ideals that we strive to denaturalize.

NOTES

1. This list of scholarship is by no means conclusive: A. Cheree Carlson, *The Crimes of Womanhood: Defining Femininity in a Court of Law* (Urbana: University of Illinois Press, 2009); Bonnie J. Dow, "The 'Womanhood' Rationale in the Woman Suffrage Rhetoric of Frances E. Willard," *Southern Communication Journal* 56 (1991): 298–307; Bonnie J. Dow and Mari Boor Tonn, "'Feminine Style' and Political Judgment in the Rhetoric of Ann Richards," *Quarterly Journal of Speech* 79 (1993): 286–302; Carrie Crenshaw, "The 'Protection' of 'Woman': A History of Legal Attitudes towards Women's Workplace Freedoms," *Quarterly Journal of Speech* 81 (1995): 63–82; Crenshaw, "The Normality of Man and Female Otherness: (Re)Producing Patriarchal Lines of Argument in the Law and the News," *Argumentation and Advocacy* 32 (1996): 170–185; Olga Idriss Davis, "A Black Woman as Rhetorical Critic: Validating Self and Violating the Space of Otherness," *Women's Studies in Communication* 21 (1998): 77–89; Davis, "Theorizing African American Women's Discourse: The Public and Private Spheres of Experience," in *Centering Ourselves: African American Feminist and Womanist Studies of Discourse*, ed. Marsha Houston and Olga Idriss Davis (Cresskill, NJ: Hampton Press, 2002), 35–51; Rita Felski, *Beyond Feminist Aesthetics: Feminist Literature and Social Change* (Cambridge: Harvard University Press, 1989); Nancy Fraser, "Rethinking the Public Sphere: A Contribution to the Critique of Actually Existing Democracy," in *Habermas and the Public Sphere*, ed. Craig Calhoun (Cambridge: MIT

Press, 1992), 109–142; Sally Miller Gearhart, "The Womanization of Rhetoric," *Women's Studies International Quarterly* 2 (1979): 195–201; Nilüfer Göle, "Islam in Public: New Visibilities and New Imaginaries," *Public Culture* 14 (2002): 173–190; Cindy L. Griffin, "The Essentialist Roots of the Public Sphere: A Feminist Critique," *Western Journal of Communication* 60 (1996): 21–39; Griffin, "Rhetoricizing Alienation: Mary Wollstonecraft and the Rhetorical Construction of Women's Oppression," in *Readings in Rhetorical Criticism*, ed. Carl R. Burgchardt (State College, PA: Strata Publishing, 2000), 507–526; Susan Zaeske, *Signatures of Citizenship: Petitioning, Antislavery, and Women's Political Identity* (Chapel Hill: University of North Carolina Press, 2003).

2. Mary P. Ryan, "The Public and the Private Good: Across the Great Divide in Women's History," *Journal of Women's History* 15 (2003): 11–27; Hortense J. Spillers, "Mama's Baby, Papa's Maybe: An American Grammar Book," *Diacritics* 17 (1987): 65–80; Jordynn Jack, "Acts of Institution: Embodying Feminist Rhetorical Methodologies in Space and Time," *Rhetoric Review* 28 (2009): 285–303; Carlson, *Crimes of Womanhood*; Nan Johnson, "Reigning in the Court of Silence: Women and Rhetorical Space in Postbellum America," *Philosophy and Rhetoric* 33 (2000): 221–242; Belinda A. Stillion Southard, "Militancy, Power, and Identity: The Silent Sentinels as Women Fighting for Political Voice," *Rhetoric and Public Affairs* 10 (2007): 399–418.

3. Karlyn Kohrs Campbell, "The Rhetoric of Women's Liberation: An Oxymoron," *Quarterly Journal of Speech* 59 (1973): 74–86; Campbell, "Style and Content in the Rhetoric of Early Afro-American Feminists," *Quarterly Journal of Speech* 72 (1986): 434–445; Dow and Tonn, "Feminine Style."

4. Lisa A. Flores, "Creating Discursive Space through a Rhetoric of Difference: Chicana Feminists Craft a Homeland," *Quarterly Journal of Speech* 82 (1996): 142–156; Radha S. Hegde, "A View from Elsewhere: Locating Difference and the Politics of Representation from a Transnational Feminist Perspective," *Communication Theory* 8 (1998): 271–297; Aimee M. Carrillo Rowe, "Locating Feminism's Subject: The Paradox of White Femininity and the Struggle to Forge Feminist Alliances," *Communication Theory* 10 (2000): 64–80; Davis, "Black Woman."; Davis, "In the Kitchen: Transforming the Academy through Safe Spaces of Resistance," *Western Journal of Communication* 63 (1999): 364–381.

5. Davis, "Black Woman," 80.

6. Davis, "Black Woman," 80–81.

7. Campbell, "Women's Liberation."; Campbell, "The Nature of Criticism in Rhetorical and Communicative Studies," *Central States Speech Journal* 30 (1979): 4–13; Campbell, "Style and Content"; Carrie Crenshaw, "Resisting Whiteness' Rhetorical Silence," *Western Journal of Communication* 61 (1997): 253–278.

8. Griffin, "Essentialist Roots."

9. Griffin, "Essentialist Roots," 22.

10. Griffin, "Essentialist Roots," 29–30.

11. Griffin, "Essentialist Roots," 31.

12. Diana Fuss, *Essentially Speaking: Feminism, Nature, and Difference* (New York: Routledge, 1989); Kimberlé Crenshaw, "Mapping the Margins: Intersectionality, Identity Politics and Violence against Women of Color," *Stanford Law Review* 43 (1991): 1241–1299; Linda Garber, *Identity Poetics: Race, Class, and the Lesbian-Feminist Roots of Queer Theory* (New York: Columbia University Press, 2001).

13. Lois McNay, "The Foucauldian Body and the Exclusion of Experience," *Hypatia* 6 (1991): 125–139; Susan Bordo, "Feminism, Foucault and the Politics of the Body," in *Up against Foucault: Explorations of Some Tensions between Foucault and Feminism*, ed. Caroline Ramazanoglu (New York: Routledge, 1993), 179–202; Elspeth Probyn, "This Body which Is Not One: Speaking an Embodied Self," *Hypatia* 6 (1991): 111–124.

14. Elizabeth Spelman, *Inessential Woman: Problems of Exclusion in Feminist Thought* (Boston: Beacon Press, 1988); Aimee Carrillo Rowe, *Power Lines: On the Subject of Feminist Alliances* (Durham, NC: Duke University Press, 2008); Laura Alexandra Harris, "Queer Black Feminism: The Pleasure Principle," *Feminist Review* 54 (1996): 3–30.

15. Angela P. Harris, "Race and Essentialism in Feminist Legal Theory," *Stanford Law Review* 42 (1990): 589.

16. Chandra Talpade Mohanty, "On Race and Voice: Challenges for Liberal Education in the 1990's," *Cultural Critique* 14 (1989): 180.

17. Trina Grillo, "Anti-Essentialism and Intersectionality: Tools to Dismantle the Master's House," *Berkeley Women's Law Journal* 10 (1995): 21.

18. Sara L. McKinnon, "Citizenship and the Performance of Credibility: Audiencing Gender-Based Asylum Seekers in U.S. Immigration Courts," *Text and Performance Quarterly* 29 (2009): 205–221.

19. Michael Calvin McGee, "In Search of 'the People': A Rhetorical Alternative," *Quarterly Journal of Speech* 61 (1975): 238.

20. McGee, "In Search of," 249.

21. Maurice Charland, "Constitutive Rhetoric: The Case of the 'Peuple Quebecois'," *Quarterly Journal of Speech* 73 (1987): 133–150; Michael C. Leff and Ebony A. Utley, "Instrumental and Constitutive Rhetoric in Martin Luther King Jr.'s 'Letter from Birmingham Jail'," *Rhetoric and Public Affairs* 7 (2004): 37–51; Alissa Sklar, "Contested Collectives: The Struggle to Define The 'We' In the 1995 Quebec Referendum," *Southern Communication Journal* 64 (1999): 105–122; Zaeske, *Signatures of Citizenship.*

22. Chaïm Perelman and Lucie Olbrecht-Tyteca, *The New Rhetoric: A Treatise on Argumentation* (South Bend, ID: University of Notre Dame Press, 1991).

23. Richard Schechner, *Peformance Theory* (New York: Routledge, 1988).

24. Robert R. Williams, *Hegel's Ethics of Recognition* (Berkeley: University of California Press, 2000).

25. Jessica Benjamin, *Shadow of the Other: Intersubjectivity and Gender in Psychoanalyis* (New York: Routledge, 1998).

26. Spoma Jovanovic and Roy V. Wood, "Speaking from the Bedrock of Ethics," *Philosophy and Rhetoric* 37 (2004): 317–334; Williams, *Hegel's Ethics of Recognition*.

27. Chandra Talpade Mohanty, *Feminism without Borders: Decolonizing Theory, Practicing Solidarity* (Durham, NC: Duke University Press, 2003).

28. Jessica Benjamin, "The Shadow of the Other (Subject): Intersubjectivity and Feminist Theory," *Constellations: An International Journal of Critical Democratic Theory* 1 (1994): 234.

29. Audre Lorde, ed., *Sister Outsider: Essays and Speeches* (Berkeley, CA: Crossing Press, 1984), 115.

30. Marsha Houston, "When Black Women Talk with White Women: Why the Dialogues Are Difficult," in *Our Voices: Essays in Culture, Ethnicity, and Communication*, ed. Alberto González, Marsha Houston, and Victoria Chen (Los Angeles: Roxbury, 2000), 98–104.

31. Spelman, *Inessential Woman*.

32. Mab Segrest, *Born to Belonging:Writings on Spirit and Justice* (New Brusnwick, NJ: Rutgers University Press, 2002); Raka Shome, "Outing Whiteness," *Critical Studies in Media Communication* 17 (2000): 336–371; Trina Grillo and Stephanie M. Wildman, "Obscuring the Importance of Race: The Implications of Making Comparisons between Racism and Sexism (or Other -Isms)," *Duke Law Journal* 1991 (1991): 397–412.

33. María Lugones, *Pilgrimages/Peregrinajes: Theorizing Coalition against Multiple Oppressions* (Lanham, MD: Rowman & Littlefield, 2003).

34. Judith Butler, *Undoing Gender* (New York: Routledge, 2004), 151.

35. Segrest, *Born to Belonging*.

36. Dawn Rae Davis, "(Love Is) the Ability of Not Knowing: Feminist Experience of the Impossible in Ethical Singularity," *Hypatia* 17 (2002): 148.

37. Butler, *Undoing*.

38. Sara Lynn McKinnon, "The Discursive Formation of Gender in Women's Gendered Claims to U.S. Asylum," doctoral dissertation, Arizona State University, 2008.

39. *Juarez-Lopez v. Gonzales*, No. 06-3143 U.S. App. LEXIS 9881, 3 (2007).

40. *Juarez-Lopez v. Gonzales*, 2.

41. *Juarez-Lopez v. Gonzales*, 2.

42. Leo R. Chavez, "A Glass Half Empty: Latina Reproductivity and Public Discourse," *Human Organization* 63 (2004): 173–188; Lorena García, "'Now Why Do You Want to Know About That?': Heteronormativity, Sexism, and Racism in the Sexual (Mis)Education of Latina Youth," *Gender and Society* 23 (2009): 520–541.

43. Patricia A. Tetreault and Mark A. Barnett, "Reactions to Stranger and Aquaintance Rape," *Psychology of Women Quarterly* 11 (1987): 357.

44. Dominic Abrams, G. T. Viki, B. Masser, and G. Bohner, "Perceptions of Stranger and Acquaintance Rape: The Role of Benevolent and Hostile Sexism in Victim Blame and Rape Proclivity," *Journal of Personality*

and Social Psychology 84 (2003): 111–125; Susan T. Bell, Peter J. Kuriloff, and Ilsa Lottes, "Understanding Attributions of Blame in Stranger and Date Rape Situations: An Examination of Gender, Race, Identification, and Students' Social Perceptions of Rape Victims," *Journal of Applied Social Psychology* 24 (1994): 1719–1734.

45. Sarah Gill, "Dismantling Gender and Race Stereotypes: Using Education to Prevent Date Rape," *UCLA Women's Law Journal* 7 (1996): 27–79; Kristin Bumiller, "Rape as a Legal Symbol: An Essay on Sexual Violence and Racism," *University of Miami Law Review* 42 (1987): 75–91; Crenshaw, "Mapping."

46. Gill, "Dismantling Gender and Race Stereotypes," 44.

47. Patricia Hill Collins, *Black Sexual Politics: African Americans, Gender, and the New Racism* (New York: Routledge, 2004), 27.

48. Spillers, "Mama's Baby, Papa's Maybe."

49. Gill, "Dismantling Gender and Race Stereotypes."

50. Collins, *Black Sexual Politics*; Mary Beltrán, "The Hollywood Latina Body as Site of Social Struggle: Media Constructions of Stardom and Jennifer Lopez's 'Cross-over Butt'," *Quarterly Review of Film and Video* 19 (2002): 71–86; Diane Railton and Paul Watson, "Naughty Girls and Red Blooded Women: Representations of Female Heterosexuality in Music Videos," *Feminist Media Studies* 5 (2005): 51–63; bell hooks, "Selling Hot Pussy: Representations of Black Female Sexuality in the Cultural Marketplace," in *Writing on the Body: Female Embodiment and Feminist Theory*, ed. Katie Conboy, Nadia Medina, and Sarah Stanbury (New York: Columbia University Press, 1997), 113–128.

51. Collins, *Black Sexual Politics*, 29.

52. Crenshaw, "Mapping," 1251.

53. Montgomery Brower and Civia Tamarkin, "Jailed for a Rape that Never Happened, Gary Dotson Has His Name Cleared at Last," *People*, August 28, 1989, 80.

54. Bumiller, "Rape as a Legal Symbol," 80.

55. Jane E. Larson, "'Women Understand So Little, They Call My Good Nature "Deceit"': A Feminist Rethinking of Seduction," *Columbia Law Review* 93 (1993): 372–472.

56. Bumiller, "Rape as a Legal Symbol."

57. *Juarez-Lopez v. Gonzales*, 2.

58. James Smith, "Guatemala: Economic Migrants Replace Political Refugees," *Migration Information Source*, April 2006, accessed January 10, 2011 http://www.migrationinformation.org/feature/display.cfm?ID=392.

59. Denise A. Segura and Patricia Zavella, eds., *Women and Migration: In the U.S.-Mexico Borderlands* (Durham, NC: Duke University Press, 2007); Estelle T. Lau, *Paper Families: Identity, Immigration Administration, and Chinese Exclusion* (Durham, NC: Duke University Press, 2007); Sarah J. Mahler, *American Dreaming: Immigrant Life on the Margins* (Princeton, NJ: Princeton University Press, 1995).

60. E. Daniel Valentine and John C. Knudsen, *Mistrusting Refugees* (Berkeley: University of California Press, 1995), 2.

61. Carol Bohmer and Amy Shuman, *Rejecting Refugees: Political Asylum in the 21st Century* (New York: Taylor and Francis, 2008).

62. Bohmer and Shuman, *Rejecting Refugees*.

63. *Juarez-Lopez v. Gonzales*, 4.

64. *Juarez-Lopez v. Gonzales*, 4. Importantly, this case is not isolated as numerous defensive asylum cases are denied on the basis of "adverse credibility."

65. Aihwa Ong, *Flexible Citizenship: The Cultural Logics of Transnationality* (Durham, NC: Duke University Press, 1999), 4, emphasis in the orginal.

66. Kamala Visweswaran, *Fictions of a Feminist Ethnography* (Minneapolis: University of Minnesota Press, 1994).

67. Raka Shome, "Transnational Feminism and Communication Studies," *Communication Review* 9 (2006): 256.

Contributors

Karma R. Chávez (Ph.D., Arizona State University) is an assistant professor of rhetoric in the Department of Communication Arts at the University of Wisconsin–Madison. Her research emphasizes coalition and alliance building, social movement, and the rhetorical practice of marginalized groups using queer feminist of color theories. Most specifically, her current research examines discourses of queer migration and coalition politics, and along with Eithne Luibhéid, she is the cofounder of the Queer Migration Research Network. Her first solo-authored book, *Queer/Migration Politics*, is under review at a university press.

Cindy L. Griffin (Ph.D., Indiana University) is professor of communication studies at Colorado State University. Her research interests include feminist theories that challenge many of the foundational assumptions of the rhetorical tradition, developing theories and rhetorics of intersectionality, invitational rhetoric, and exploring the relationships between civility, power, and rhetoric. She is the author of *Invitation to Public Speaking* (Cengage, 2012), coauthor of *Feminist Rhetorical Theories* (with Sonja Foss and Karen Foss; Waveland, 2006), and has published articles and book chapters that engage feminism with rhetorical and communication theories. She also served as the editor of *Women's Studies in Communication* from 2006 to 2010.

AUTHOR BIOGRAPHIES

Leslie A. Hahner (Ph.D., University of Iowa) is an assistant professor at Baylor University. Her research interests include visual and spatial rhetoric, critical theory, and rhetorical history. Her work has recently appeared in *Communication and Critical/Cultural Studies* and the *Quarterly Journal of Speech*.

D. Lynn O'Brien Hallstein (Ph.D., Ohio State University) is an associate professor of rhetoric in the College of General Studies at Boston University. Her current research focuses on contemporary maternity, feminist theory, and women's studies in communication. She has been published in *Quarterly Journal of Speech*, the *Western Journal of Communication*, *Women's Studies in Communication*, *Text and Performance Quarterly*, *Communication and Critical/Cultural Studies*, *National Women's Studies Journal*, and *Women's Studies*. She recently published *White Feminists and Contemporary Maternity: Purging Matrophobia* (Palgrave Macmillan, 2010), and she is the coeditor with Sara Hayden of *Contemplating Maternity in an Era of Choice: Explorations into Discourses of Reproduction* (Lexington Books, 2010). She has an additional coedited collection titled, *Academic Motherhood in a Post-Second Wave Context: Challenges, Strategies, and Possibilities*, with Andrea O'Reilly (Demeter Press, 2012).

Sara Hayden (Ph.D., University of Minnesota) is a professor of communication studies at the University of Montana. Her research focuses on the rhetoric of women's health, sexuality, and maternity and has been published in journals including the *Quarterly Journal of Speech*, *Communication and Critical/Cultural Studies*, *Women's Studies in Communication*, and the *Western Journal of Communication*. She served as editor of *Women's Studies in Communication* from 2004 to 2007 and she is coeditor, with D. Lynn O'Brien Hallstein, of *Contemplating Maternity in an Era of Choice: Explorations into Discourses of Reproduction* (Lexington Books, 2010).

Marsha Houston (Ph.D., University of Massachusetts) retired in 2009 from the University of Alabama–Tuscaloosa as professor of communication studies. She also served on the faculties of the University of Southern Mississippi, Spelman College, Georgia State University (where she was chair from 1987 to 1990), and Tulane University (where she held the Dreux chair in women's studies). She is coeditor of the award-winning intercultural communication anthology *Our Voices: Essays in Culture, Ethnicity, and Communication* (Oxford University Press, 2011), now in its fifth edition, and of *Centering Ourselves: African American Feminist and Womanist Studies of Discourse* (Hampton Press, 2002), as well as the author of numerous articles and chapters on African American women's language and communication. A pioneering Black feminist communication scholar, she received the Francine Merritt Award for outstanding service to women in the communication discipline in 1994 and is included in *Black Pioneers in Communication* (Jackson and Givens, 2006). She currently is preparing her papers for donation to the University of Oregon's archive on women and language research at the invitation of the archive, consulting on issues of workplace diversity, and enjoying her grandchildren.

Jennifer Keohane (M.A., University of Wisconsin–Madison) is a doctoral candidate in rhetoric in the Department of Communication Arts at the University of Wisconsin–Madison. Her current research explores labor rhetoric in the United States, feminism, and the Cold War. In 2010, she was awarded the Gerard A. Hauser Prize by the Rhetoric Society of America for the best student essay submitted to the annual conference.

Sara L. McKinnon (Ph.D., Arizona State University) is an assistant professor of rhetoric in the Department of Communication Arts at the University of Wisconsin–Madison. Her research focuses on questions of subjectivity, agency, and legal access within refugee and asylum-seeking communities and she is continually interested in the role of the state and global capital in determining access and subjectivity for marginalized groups and individuals. Her essays have appeared in *Women's Studies in Communication*, *Text and Performance Quarterly*, and the *Quarterly Journal of Speech*.

Lester C. Olson (Ph.D., University of Wisconsin–Madison) is a professor of communication at the University of Pittsburgh, where he specializes in public address, visual rhetoric, and human rights advocacy. His books include *Emblems of American Community in the Revolutionary Era* (Smithsonian Institution Press, 1991), *Benjamin Franklin's Vision of American Community* (University of South Carolina Press, 2004), and, with coeditors Cara A. Finnegan and Diane S. Hope, *Visual Rhetoric* (Sage, 2007). His essays concerning Audre Lorde's public advocacy can be found in the *Quarterly Journal of Speech* (1997, 1998), *Philosophy and Rhetoric* (2000), *American Voices* (2005), *Queering Public Address* (2007), and *The Responsibilities of Rhetoric* (2010).

Shanara Rose Reid-Brinkley (Ph.D., University of Georgia) is an assistant professor of communication and director of debate at the University of Pittsburgh. Reid-Brinkley focuses her scholarly research on African American culture at the intersection of race, gender, class, and sexuality. Her research interests are interdisciplinary, spanning the study of rhetoric and public discourse, black feminist theory, and poststructural theories of discourse with an emphasis on hip-hop culture and politics. She is the author of the 2008 Elaine Brown award-winning essay "The Essence of Res(ex)pectability: Black Women's Negotiation of the Representation of Black Femininity in Rap Music and Music Video," from the Black Women Historians Association.

Kate Zittlow Rogness (Ph.D., University of Denver) is an assistant professor of communication studies at Monmouth College. Her research focuses on the connections between agency and publicity in nontraditional rhetorical texts, particularly as they relate to forms of intersectional subjectivity. Her chapter in this book, "The Intersectional Style of Free Love Rhetoric," was developed from her dissertation titled, "Re-inscribing the Boundaries of Feminist Rhetoric through Free Love: A Feminist Rhetorical Analysis of Victoria Woodhull, Emma Goldman and Voltairine de Cleyre," which was nominated for the 2008 Kramarae Outstanding Dissertation Award. Selected publications include: "Beyond Rights and Virtues as Foundation for Women's Agency: Emma Goldman's Rhetoric of Free Love," in the *Western Journal of Communication*, "Critical Publicity as a Form of Generative Rhetoric," in the *Proceedings of the Seventeenth NCA/AFA Conference on Argumentation* (National Communication Association, 2009), and "Lucy Hayes Recusal from the Women's Rights Movement: Iconic Implications of the First Lady in the Public Sphere," in the *Proceedings of the Fifteenth NCA/AFA Conference on Argumentation*, ed. Patricia Riley. (National Communication Association, 2005).

Carly S. Woods (Ph.D., University of Pittsburgh) is an assistant professor with a joint appointment in the Department of Communication Studies and the Women's and Gender Studies Program at the University of Nebraska–Lincoln. Her primary research interests include rhetorical history and theory, gender and sexuality studies, and argumentation. Her work has been published in *KB Journal*, *Communication and Critical/Cultural Studies*, and *Contemporary Argumentation and Debate*.

Index